GW00359611

AMY LAWRENCE

arrow books

1 3 5 7 9 10 8 6 4 2

Arrow Books
20 Vauxhall Bridge Road
London SW1V 2SA

Arrow Books is part of the Penguin Random House group of companies whose addresses can be found at global.penguinrandomhouse.com.

First published in Great Britain by Century in 2019
Published in paperback by Arrow Books in 2020

www.penguin.co.uk

A CIP catalogue record for this book is available from the British Library.

ISBN 9781787460041

Printed and bound in Great Britain by Clays Ltd, Elcograf S.p.A.

Penguin Random House is committed to a sustainable future for our business, our readers and our planet. This book is made from Forest Stewardship Council® certified paper.

For Luca and Nico

If you just go for a run, as Michael Thomas put it,
you might end up somewhere miraculous.

CONTENTS

PROLOGUE

Feelings

I HAVE BEEN an Arsenal supporter since 1953 when I was eight years old. A season ticket holder from 16. A tiny shareholder since I was 18. In 1971 I never missed a single game. I was at White Hart Lane when we'd last won the league. My support for The Arsenal has survived two marriages.

In 1985 I started to miss games. I was developing an addiction to cocaine and heroin that ruined my life and those around me. By 1988 I was virtually homeless and no longer wanted to live. I somehow ended up in rehab in the West Country. I was lucky and came out of the rehab clean a week or so before the Liverpool game. I went into a tiny flat nearby.

I had lost interest in virtually everything, including my beloved Arsenal. I knew the game was on TV. In fact I had declined a ticket to the game a week or so earlier. I was too ashamed to meet up with my old Arsenal pals. Although I was clean I was not sure I wanted to live. I did not even want to watch the game on TV. Scared of all the feelings and emotions it would bring up. The good news about giving up drugs is that you get your feelings back. The bad news is that you get your feelings back.

I stared at my TV for an hour before kick-off. I imagined all my friends at Anfield, a ground I had been to many times. Eventually I plucked up courage. I watched the game. I cried, laughed and cried and laughed some more. In that moment Michael Thomas scored, I suddenly knew I wanted to live. I wanted to return to

London, see my children and get back to a decent life. I also wanted to be at Highbury again. Watching the game gave me the greatest gift ever. A gift drugs could not give me and money could not buy. HOPE!

I have stayed clean ever since. I have truly had a life beyond my wildest dreams. But that's another story.

Anonymous

FOREWORD

CANNON ON THE SHIRT

by Thierry Henry

The values carried by the Arsenal players from 1989 who I got to know changed something in me massively. I arrived with my socks above my knees. Some of the guys were looking at me. Why are you going with that? Are you a ballet dancer? But that was me. I took everything that was needed to be taken in order to play at Arsenal even though I also wanted to be me.

I always say they kicked me into understanding what Arsenal Football Club was. It's a heavy shirt. Once you know your shoulders are OK to wear it then you can go on to do some amazing stuff. Tony Adams, Lee Dixon, Martin Keown, Nigel Winterburn, David Seaman, Ray Parlour – all of those guys told me what it was to play for Arsenal Football Club. That was very important because they know the history of the club, because they genuinely loved Arsenal. I remember when I arrived they knew the names of everybody at the training ground, at Highbury, and the name of the fans sometimes. I was like, 'What? You know that guy?'

'Yeah, yeah,' they said. 'He used to travel all the time and is always there.' So, it was a family club, but being a family club didn't mean less competitive. It was about winning and only about winning, and they were letting you know.

They had been part of something special. You can never say never but to be able to reproduce what happened that night in 1989 is virtually impossible. Everybody's watching that game. To have two teams going for a title. First versus second. The only game on TV. No one else is playing. You have to win 2–0 away at Anfield – something that wasn't happening at the time. Even then you would only win the league because of the amount of goals you scored over the whole season. You thought you blew it. You come back to take it to the last day of the season. It's you against them. Nothing else. I don't care what people are saying, that's the best ending ever of any league I've ever seen. Period.

When you watch the game you can clearly see that Arsenal thought that they could do it and that Liverpool were more thinking, let's not lose it. It's weird because you would like to think that the Liverpool side would know how to close the game out, especially at home. Anfield. Sometimes the fear of winning is bigger than the fear of losing. Anyone can get trapped in it.

People do forget that Alan Smith scored in that game. People remember Michael Thomas at the end, obviously, but to be able to score that crucial second goal you need to score the first one. When Michael Thomas goes through in stoppage time, with a situation of that intensity, the best thing is not to think about what's at stake. There was a ricochet and then he goes through. He's in front of the goalkeeper. When you don't think sometimes it's way better.

When I arrived at Arsenal I was always playing against these guys in training and at first I didn't understand what the boss was trying to do. I thought, is he trying to expose my weaknesses here? What is he doing? But then I soon understood that he wanted me to play against the best to get better. Those guys are not going to greet you with 'Oh hello, you won things before. Welcome. Do you want a cup of tea?' No. Now we're going to try to see who you are. Can you play here? We saw that you can play somewhere. Here is different. I remember some games where I wasn't putting my foot into challenges the way some of the senior players wanted me to. If I was in France it would have been all right but in England then it was not the right way to go into a challenge and so they were letting me know. At half-time. After the game. Pretty much in your face.

In training I had those guys playing against me and I said to myself, if you can deal with those guys you can deal with everybody. I took it as a challenge every day in training to be able to beat those guys and that was like a competition. They used to kick me. I used to look at them as if to say, you can kick me but it doesn't matter. Go on, you won't stop me.

The point is them playing at their best made me the player that I became. When I was waking up I knew I'm going to face Lee, Martin, Tony, Nigel and you can add Sol Campbell a bit after that. You have to be ready. You have to wake up early and be ready for that one. I took it as a challenge. They were testing you. Can you play with us? Can you wear the Arsenal shirt? You find yourself in a situation where that's the only way you can find out. I think you always have to train in extreme conditions to be able to survive in the game and they were giving me every morning extreme conditions. Can you take an elbow in your face and are you going to moan about it or are you going to play? I'm going to leave something on your ankle, or on your knee. That's the way it is. Get up and fight and play.

The cannon on the shirt means everything. First and foremost when you go into a club you need to understand everything in order to be able to feel something. If you don't, you're not meant to be in that dressing room and that's what those guys taught me.

INTRODUCTION

by Amy Lawrence

Three decades down the line, two yellowing sheets of lined A4, handwritten in the spring of 1989, reacquaint me with my 17-year-old self. Dismal haircut, rolled-up jeans and baggy tops, Walkman and carefully collated mixtapes, traipsing up and down the country to watch football, last year of school, head full of big ideas. I was never a regular diarist but when something felt unmistakably important I would grab a biro and everything spilled out. The first sheet is dated 23 April. The second is dated 26 May. The two dates are inextricably linked. On both occasions I visited Anfield and traversed a rite of passage. There is of course a third date that is necessary to understand any of this – 15 April – but I did not feel capable of finding any words, least of all the right ones, back then.

On 23 April I was supposed to be revising for A levels, but found it impossible not to be drawn to the small red rectangle of card then in my possession. It was my ticket to the match between Liverpool and Arsenal. Away terrace, £3.50. The ticket would go on to represent something seismic. But that day it evoked only a profound sadness.

The game had been postponed. Football was in mourning for the brothers and sisters, sons and daughters, fathers and mothers who had been killed at the Hillsborough disaster the previous weekend. Although it was Liverpool's tragedy, with the cities of Sheffield and Nottingham also entwined, everybody who cared for English football felt connected to this devastation.

I had never been to Liverpool and wasn't sure how to articulate my sympathy, how best to show my empathy, but I knew I wanted to go to Anfield that day. I had planned to be there for the match and felt compelled to go anyway, drawn by the sense that the least we could do as fellow football fans was to metaphorically link arms and wrap the bereaved with support. It was a Sunday morning. I phoned Liverpool Clubcall to hear the recorded announcement that Anfield would be open all day to the public and headed to Euston to catch a train to Lime Street.

At the ticket office I met Kevin, a Liverpudlian working in London who was going home for a few days to make his own pilgrimage to Anfield and to attend a friend's funeral. We sat together on the journey. I noticed how he became more nervous and subdued the closer we came to the train's destination. Three of his friends, Peter, Ted and Jimmy, met him at the station and they insisted on taking me to Anfield with them. They took me under their wing and looked after me all day. A couple of them went to get fish and chips and came back with some for me, which they wouldn't let me pay for. Later that evening they phoned my house to make sure I had got home safely.

We spent almost four hours queuing for a couple of miles in the streets outside Anfield. It was the most thoughtful and respectful queue I have ever seen. I would later describe it, and note down every club I saw represented, in my diary entry. 'There was an incredible sense of unity and strength of spirit. Fans of what must have been every league club spanning the whole of Britain intermingled and waited together, clutching flowers, scarves, messages and personal mementos they were going to give in honour of those who died. The walls were covered with messages and many had written poems and stuck them up. It was totally overwhelming. People had laid down treasures, given up in memory of their friends and relatives, and many messages of reassurance that Shankly will look after those in heaven.'

So that was how I found myself at Anfield on the afternoon of 23 April 1989. At the exact time that I should have been watching a football match, I stood on the visitors' terrace looking at a field of flowers that stretched over the halfway line in front of the Kop. At the exact time that I should have been immersed in those tribal instincts as an away supporter entering opposition territory, I lay down my Arsenal scarf on the Liverpool turf in a small act of solidarity. It all felt unbearably poignant. I took a taxi back to Lime Street and the driver, an Evertonian, refused to take my fare.

Little did I know, or even much care at the time, that the ticket would still be valid for the rearranged game that would take place on 26 May, still bearing its original date. I returned to Liverpool to take up position in the away terrace, feeling incredibly lucky to be at the match and still mindful of those who weren't. That particular day has gone down in football folklore as, in the words of commentator Brian Moore at the time, 'maybe the most dramatic finish in the history of the Football League'. That 'maybe' was a good hedged bet with a few seconds to go but there remains no doubt.

The genesis of this book had been brewing for many years but began to take this particular shape during the creation of the documentary, *89*. This was a film that deconstructed an iconic football moment, built around testimony from players and central figures, mixed with rare archive footage. I was part of the production team, and it became obvious in the editing process, when so much golden material hit the cutting room floor, that it would be a waste to leave so many fascinating memories hidden, so many powerful thoughts unspoken. That prompted the idea not just to salvage them but also to search out even more voices, enabling this book to expand and bring extra layers to the story.

The other aspect that was so striking during the interview process was how vivid, how crystal clear, the memories were. Talking about that time, particularly with George Graham and the players involved, there were often moments when it felt like nobody dared to breathe, so caught up were we all in the clarity of the recall. It was strange, like watching the protagonists go back in time in their own minds and appear to be there. Details. Conversations. Feelings. Things that were nearly 30 years old catapulted forwards into the present as if they had been perfectly preserved in a time capsule.

An oral history felt like the best way to portray that energy, that sense of people talking intensely about memories that stayed so intact because they meant such a lot. While the book focuses on the inside track, the desire for the ripples of this moment in time to also be felt encouraged me to seek recollections from anyone and everyone who felt moved by it, who remembered their exact circumstances. Where were you? Who were you with? What did you do? The hundreds of people who took time to tell their own versions of events, from pitch-side to far flung places, emphasised the powerful effect that can be distilled into one event – in this case one goal.

The snapshots build a collage of the time. How David O'Leary wished his son happy birthday on the morning of the game. How Nigel Winterburn's wife's sister-in-law kept phoning up with a sixth sense about what was about to happen. How the staff back at Highbury rolled up the banner that had been ordered for the open-top bus and hid it under a desk ready to throw away on Monday morning. How the players had to fight for their places on the team bus because so many bigwigs suddenly wanted to take official transport to Anfield. How the physio told George Graham that Michael Thomas's knee tweak meant he could start the game but probably wouldn't finish it. How the referee needed a nod from the TV reporter to be able to relax about his decision on Alan Smith's goal come the end of the match. How the photographer behind the goal worried he would run out of film in stoppage time. How Lee Dixon ended up in a Liverpool chippy with his club suit on.

It soon became apparent, seeking stories from way beyond the people on the pitch, that this event somehow reverberated with people as a kind of footballing JFK moment. Outside of monumental international news, or personal milestones like the birth of a child, it is not often something hits you with such force you can conjure up all the tiniest details for years to come. The more stories came in, the more the fascination grew. I heard from a new British Army recruit who drove through the night in East Germany to pick up a VHS, an ex-pat in Oman searched for the BBC World Service broadcast in 38-degree heat, a faraway fan eventually found a newspaper days after the event in Tasmania, Australia, a boy peered through the net curtains of a stranger's window in Guernsey to catch the TV pictures . . . Closer to home, some quit their jobs or abandoned exams to go, others tried to bunk in, or smuggled portable TVs into work, kissed strangers, heard from old friends, fell in love, fell out of love – in all cases they scaled the extremes of emotions and that is why they remember exactly what they were doing when Mickey Thomas scored in the final seconds of the season.

I am very grateful to everyone who wanted to contribute, particularly those from the Liverpool perspective who looked back on a period of great pain. If the voices are predominantly one-sided that is out of respect for those lost at Hillsborough and their families who fought so long for justice. There are definitive accounts about the tragedy I would urge anyone to read. It did not feel appropriate to go into depth with those from Liverpool about the final game without the context of that season, so the choice was made to recall events from a different perspective, from outside the city looking in.

As for me, that time remains a touchstone. It feels extraordinary that the two most extreme football-related emotions I have felt in over 40 years absorbed by the game took place within a six-week timeframe. Every reminder of Hillsborough to this day remains heartbreaking, and there we were, so soon afterwards, acclaiming a footballing miracle. I am old enough that I ought to know better now but I distinctly remember the serene feeling on 26 May 1989 that life would never get any better. That seemed strange and impossible and yet it was fine.

ARSENAL SQUAD 1988–89		Division One appearances (and sub appearances)
John Lukic	'Lukey'	38
Lee Dixon	'Dicko'	31 (2)
Nigel Winterburn	'Nige'	38
Tony Adams	'Rodders'	36
Steve Bould	'Bouldy'	26 (4)
David O'Leary	'Paddy'	26
Gus Caesar	'Gus'	2
David Rocastle	'Rocky'	38
Michael Thomas	'Mickey'	33 (4)
Paul Davis	'Davo'	11 (1)
Kevin Richardson	'Richo'	32 (2)
Brian Marwood	'Brian'	31
Alan Smith	'Smudger'	36
Paul Merson	'Merse'	29 (8)
Perry Groves	'Grovesey'	6 (15)
Niall Quinn	'Quinny'	2 (1)
Martin Hayes	'Hayesey'	3 (14)

Manager: George Graham

ONE

Naked Ape

George Graham (manager):
I used to watch old cowboy films with John Wayne in and he used to always say, let's get in there, do the business and then get the hell out of there.

Paul Merson (forward):
We went up there the day of the game. You know, that's a bit weird. You're playing Friday evening, the biggest game for Arsenal in the last 18 years, since they played at White Hart Lane and won the league. To go up there the day of the game was just phenomenal. I think George was like, if we go up the day of the game, the players haven't got time to think and get nervous.

George Graham:
I was into coaching big time and I started to get a lot of books from America. Coaches of American football. Basketball. I started to learn from people who had been successful in the States, reading up to see if it would help me. It's really about being in charge of other people. In charge of a bunch of players. How do you handle them? There are a lot of ways to do it. I just thought it was fascinating.

Somebody recommended *The Naked Ape* by Desmond Morris and it was about territory. It was about why, in the animal kingdom, if it's somebody else's territory you would be fought off. Get out of here. This is my territory. Get out. I tried to relate that to football and footballers.

I always remember previously when I was a player going to Anfield and you would go up the day before the game and get into the hotel and all the people working at the hotel would say, 'Excuse me, what are you doing up here? This is Liverpool. You should get back to London where you belong.' When you've got a group of players, there's a number that are very confident of their own ability and there's some that are not so comfortable. When you go into a situation where you need warriors, you'd like the whole 11 players to be warriors but it doesn't work out that way. You usually have two or three really strong characters who carry the rest of the boys. When you go away from home you need your leaders who love the challenge, the battle. There are people who are much stronger mentally within a group of players. When I was a player I was not strong mentally. Not as strong as I maybe should have been. Frank McLintock was the equivalent of three people. We used to think, cor! With Frank and another couple of others, how can we lose?

I knew we had a lot of warriors in that team. It's not a secret who we had. Nigel is like that. He's no meat on him at all and Nigel would kick anybody. Bouldy, Tony, even Lee, who was a gentleman – he didn't like kicking people but occasionally he would. David Rocastle had it. We had a strong back bone to us and sometimes you think nowadays some teams lack that. If you've got too many who are mentally not as strong then you go to some grounds and it's more difficult to win matches. Liverpudlians are very, very passionate about their own city. They're very, very intense about their game and their team especially. Nothing against Liverpool or the people up there but I didn't want to be staying in a hotel for a couple of days with negative vibes. That's why having read that book, *The Naked Ape*, I suddenly thought we'll go up the morning of the match. Have a light lunch. Off to bed to have a rest and then the game in the evening. The

Desmond Morris idea definitely convinced me I wanted to take the team up there as late as possible near the game. Then play the game and get out of there as quickly as possible, obviously with the right result. I'm glad I did that.

Steve Bould (defender):
Surprisingly as a group we were all very calm. I don't know whether that's because we didn't have too many expectations, or we actually believed George's story. He told it like it was a Western. Get in and get out of town quick with the rewards. He used to quote that kind of thing regularly.

Lee Dixon (defender):
Did I wake up thinking this is the day we win the league? I'll be honest with you; not really. I didn't sit there going this is it. I wasn't pumped up like that that early. Because there was still all that stuff going on around Hillsborough for me. Even during the prep in the dressing room, it was like another game but there was still that feeling of, you know, should we really be here?

David O'Leary (defender):
It was my son's birthday. I went away that day thinking it would be nice to bring him back a medal, wouldn't it? I wished him a happy birthday. He was six at the time. Later on he was too tired to stay awake for the game and went to bed.

John Lukic (goalkeeper):
It's a good job I got there early because there were no seats on the bus. Everybody and his brother was on that bus going up to Anfield. Even people I didn't know were on the bus. It was packed.

Perry Groves (forward):

The first team coach is sacrosanct. No one goes on it unless you're in the squad. No one travels. I remember getting on the coach and it was full of VIPs and I thought half of them actually were barely alive, aged about 70 or 80, cobwebs coming off them with their old blazers. But the thing is they sat in our seats and broke an unwritten rule. When you're a regular in the first team you always sit in the same seat. It's a rite of passage. You have to earn your right. Some officials from the club were sat on our table so we're like, what are you doing? I said, 'Sorry, chaps, you've got to move' and they went, 'You can sit down there.' We said, 'No, no, you don't understand. You have to move. That's where we sit. Every single away game that is my seat. That's where Bouldy sits. That's where Alan Smith sits. I tell you what, if we get beat tonight or we don't win the title it's your fault. If you don't move we've got no chance.' Because footballers are very superstitious. Very superstitious. In the end we got them out of our seats.

Lee Dixon:

I remember playing cards on the coach like we always used to do. We used to play hearts at the back of the coach and it was really relaxed.

Gary Lewin (physio):

There was a bed at the back of the coach. It all started because Charlie Nicholas got badly injured in Nottingham on my first game as first team physio in September 1986. We had nowhere to lay him after the game on the way home. I went to the coach company to ask if one of the tables could drop down on springs to make a bed. They adapted it and it was designed for when players were injured, the table would convert and we put a mattress on top. But of course people like Mickey and Rocky used to go for a sleep all the time.

Michael Thomas (midfielder):
Travelling up that day we were all in a good mood. Good spirits. Get on the coach, a summer's morning, I was thinking, oh yeah, this should be a nice little journey. I used to be at the back all the time. On the bed. Ha ha ha. Horizontal. We used to fight for it. It was me, Rocky and Tony Adams. I could sleep anywhere. Obviously I woke up a few times. Merse, Nigel, Dicko and Bouldy were playing cards and joking. It was great. Then reading all the press. Lambs to the slaughter. Graeme Souness from his hospital bed and you think, oh here we go. Everybody writing us off. We thought, OK. Obviously no one thinks we were going to win. We'll just show them.

John Lukic:
The press did us an enormous favour really by saying we were written off. A lot of players made a mental note that day.

George Graham:
Well that's just life, isn't it? You look at the situation and you say what's the best way to handle it? And whether you liked it or not the build-up to that game was unbelievable because everything, in every paper, was all about how Arsenal were going to lose. Liverpool are going to win it. Blah blah. So the players were going to go through it anyway in the media. I just thought, let's have a relaxed attitude to the whole situation. I knew they'd perform because of the way we worked midweek. I was always confident we would do well. Whether I was confident enough to win two-nothing is a different matter.

Alan Smith (forward):
We saw the now infamous Graeme Souness interview and he'd obviously come down on the side of his former team. He said they were the much better team, play the much better football and the headline was 'Men Against Boys'. So, one of the lads said, look what Souness

has written here. Up on the noticeboard. Everyone has a good read. Somebody brought it up on the coach with us. We were really chirpy on the way up. It was a good atmosphere. Lots of chat and looking forward to it. We had the card school at the back, which I was never part of. I hated cards. Bouldy, Merse, Rodders would be there. I was kind of in the middle, with some of the boys like David O'Leary and Grovesy and we'd just have a chat.

David O'Leary was my room-mate at the time. We got to the Atlantic Tower hotel where we were due to stay for lunch and a kip and a pre-match meal, which is right on the water down by Albert Dock. We had our lunch and we all went to our rooms. That was the strange thing because quite often with a night match you go to your rooms and you can't really go to sleep. You're obviously thinking about the match. Tossing and turning. But that day me and Paddy were out like a light. We had a good couple of hours' kip.

Gary Lewin:
Me and the kit man, Donners, went to the ground to put the kit out around 3 o'clock. I usually went for a run around the pitch. Partly superstition and partly just to get some nervous energy out. I did it everywhere. In those days you would go into an empty ground and get a buzz. Anfield had that. We stayed in a hotel shaped like a boat. We got back and I did the alarm calls at 4 o'clock, calling the rooms, and if they didn't answer the phone I would go and bang on the door. Pre-match meal wasn't a buffet like they have now. On a Thursday I would go round to every player: 'What do you want for your lunch?' It would be steak, chicken or fish. 'What do you want for your pre-match meal?' It would be omelette, beans on toast, scrambled eggs on toast. I would stand at the entrance to the dining room with a list to hand out the right meal. As they came in, 'That's for Steve Bould, that's for Paul Merson . . .' We didn't have a travel manager so that was my job.

Alan Smith:
Woke up. 'Cor that was nice, wasn't it?' We got down for our tea at 4. Everyone was saying, 'Sleep well?' 'Yeah, yeah, slept like a log.' Everyone had a really good sleep. There was something about it. People were relaxed, felt energised. The old flip-chart was out after tea and toast and the gaffer's going through the set-pieces and he did everything as he always did. Gives us a little pep talk.

Right, lads, gather round. The tactical side of it was about the importance of not conceding a goal, stressing that if we concede then we've got to score three, which would be impossible. As long as you keep a clean sheet you're always in with a shout. Then it's going through who's marking who at set-pieces. Smudge, I want you to mark Gary Ablett. You stand at the near post. Make sure you stay with your markers. Do your jobs properly. At the end of that he gets to the Churchillian stuff, just setting the night in context. The importance of not wasting the opportunity. The importance of not leaving anything out there. Giving it your all. Having no regrets.

John Lukic:
The team meeting was the interesting thing. Obviously because George had changed the formation his team-talk was quite enlightening. Once he'd named the team, he outlined his plans for the evening, which revolved around keeping a clean sheet until half-time and then early on in the second half play a little bit freer, hopefully score a goal which will put Liverpool on edge and then towards the end of the game we'll get the winner. Pretty straightforward stuff really.

Tony Adams (defender and captain):
It made sense for me. Two of the biggest teams in the country, away from home, you're going to go and play five at the back and it was a good option. George kept us normal. It's just another game. Just perfect. As I remember it he called every shot right.

Lynne Chaney (Arsenal box office in 1989 – present day media assistant):
I started working at Arsenal in 1987 and I worked in the box office and that's where I was in 1989. There were 25 Travel Club coaches for the fans; and me and Jo, we were giving out raffle tickets. Charlie George came down and he drew the raffle ticket and it was so ironic that he picked number 18 and the person that won it was on coach 18 and it was 18 years since we last won the league and everyone was thinking, oh my God, is this an omen. It lifted our spirits, didn't it?

Jo Harney (Arsenal telephonist in 1989 – present day office manager):
We stood there and waved everybody off and then went back to work for a couple of hours. After work we went up to the old Cocktail Lounge in the East Stand where a few staff would watch the game together. I didn't stay though. I went and sat in a tiny flat in Finsbury Park with six guys and some peanuts that had been put on the table.

David Miles (Arsenal assistant club secretary in 1989 – present day club secretary):
The club was a big family. The whole system has changed now but in those days the players like Dave Rocastle, Mickey Thomas, Martin Hayes, Paul Merson all came through what was called then the apprenticeship system and part of their apprenticeship was that one afternoon a week they actually did work experience in the offices. As an example in the box office you'd have Kevin Campbell and Paul Merson opening envelopes and selling tickets, which is quite ironic when you see how the young players are treated now. It was a real camaraderie because we all grew up with the players. Now it's totally different because the players are at the training ground and you don't often see them. But these lads from the age of 16 actually spent quite

a bit of their lives here at the club because they trained a bit at the club at Highbury and did work experience here.

MICHAEL THOMAS:
It was a family for us. We had families at home but this was a real tight-knit family with this group of people. We all grew up at the same time with all the people around the club. The tea ladies were so special. Midweek you'd be bored, you'd finish training, why go home? Go to the ticket office and help out with the tickets or answering the phones. We knew everybody. We'd go for lunch with them, go across to Highbury Corner and get something to eat or just meet up because that's how it was.

JO HARNEY:
They'd sit on desks for hours after training. I remember George would come in and say, have you not got homes to go to? They literally didn't go. They just sat and chatted and it was like your friends.

LYNNE CHANEY:
Mickey would come in for the biscuits. I remember him actually hiding under a desk when George come along.

DAVID MILES:
We just thought that it would be great to spend that last night of the season together. Celebrate the season. Didn't think we'd do it but nevertheless we were going to make a night of it. I would guess there was about 20 staff and it was a complete range. It was everyone from the groundsman, the plumber, the electrician, box office staff. We went out for a meal on Blackstock Road and all came back into one of the rooms at Highbury. There was a regular TV in what was then called the Ladies Lounge but it was probably 20 inches and we thought, well there's 20 of us, so we phoned up a local retailer and

hired in for the night something we thought was very swish. It must have been about a 36/38-inch TV. We hired some drinks in.

We had ordered a big plastic banner that was due to go on the front of the open-top bus just in case and it said 'Arsenal FC League Champions 1989' and it had been delivered during the day. I just rolled it up and put it behind my desk and I thought, I'll throw it away on Monday morning and just get rid of it.

Penny Smith (Alan's wife):
Alan got up in the morning and off he went. I was in work for 8.30 at a beauty therapists. In those days it was no computers, the appointment book was written, so I'd put in fake appointments for the afternoon, moving ones that I could get done in the morning to the afternoon so the takings were all in the till regardless. My friend was manager of the salon and she had done the same so we were hoping to leave for Liverpool at lunchtime with her boyfriend. Just as we were about to go upstairs to get changed out of our uniform, our boss turned up. Oh my God. He'd come to collect the takings and was chatting away and we were desperate for him to go. We had to hide my friend's boyfriend in one of the treatment rooms because he shouldn't have been there anyway. Eventually off we went in his beige Ford Escort estate. The aerial had been snapped off, and he'd put a coat hanger in to make an aerial. Because we were late and got stuck in all that traffic, trying to pick up what was happening on the radio with a wire coat hanger as an aerial was quite difficult. It was very crackly.

Roy Dixon (Lee's dad):
I had a ticket but I was so nervous I couldn't go. I was so uptight and worried about it I gave my ticket away to Lee's uncle Albert, who was over from Australia. That's the way it goes when you are a parent. I decided to watch it on television by myself in the house.

Paul Johnson (Arsenal Travel Club manager):
I was in charge of team, directors, reserves and supporter travel. We had 26 coaches going up in convoy and we were all late. I was on coach number 1 with Roberto, the coach driver, who took us up the hard shoulder to try to get us there. It became obvious the M6 was completely jammed. I was very worried. We had borrowed a phone for the journey as there were no everyday mobiles then. I put a call in to Ken Friar, Arsenal's managing director. I then go through to Peter Robinson, the secretary of Liverpool, and to put this politely he said, 26 coaches or not we are not delaying the game. In the end there was a ten-minute delay but it wasn't enough.

Mark Leech (photographer):
We were supposed to meet at 1 o'clock at Toddington Services and were a bit late. We had to average about 40mph, said that would be a breeze and I think we were around Walsall at half past five with my friend and fellow photographer Andy Cowie driving his Peugeot 405. He was due to go to Hampden Park the next day for the Scotland v England game. Having to get back to London to catch the flight the next day he kept wondering if it was worth continuing or better to head back. Every ten miles we thought, we're not going to make it. We're not going to make it. Then the traffic moved for about three minutes and we'd say we've cracked it and then it would grind to a halt.

Andy Cowie (photographer):
Well it was probably one of five times we said, look shall we just watch it in a pub?

Mark Leech:
Andy had been covering Liverpool all through the late 70s and 80s and I remember him saying to me, 'Well it's just Liverpool picking

up another trophy shot. I think we've done this enough times. Do we need another one?' And I digested this for two whole seconds. It made sense and then I seemed to grab him by the lapels. 'Young man, we're going to photograph a team in yellow. Drive!' Some of the fans must have been in Stoke-on-Trent at kick-off.

David Dein (Arsenal vice-chairman in 1989):
I'm always a supreme optimist so I thought we had a chance. I didn't think we were going to do it but we've seen enough football in our lives to know that anything can happen. Going to Anfield that day I remember we hired a private jet, the board and a couple of friends. We didn't want to chance driving up and getting involved in congestion on the motorway or a problem with a train that doesn't run to schedule and then we're going to miss the game. We wanted to make sure we were there on time. We got there and the Liverpool board were very nice, always very social and accommodating, and I think they felt inwardly confident that the league was theirs for the taking.

Dave Hutchinson (referee):
I was the first one there. The first thing I did in this case was to go and see Peter Robinson, the Liverpool secretary, to tell him he's got a referee and then ask him if my colleagues are there. They eventually arrived. I had to get to know them and form some rapport with them. It's the first time I've worked with them as far as I can remember. So, it's a question of me weighing them up and seeing who's nervous and who's not. The last thing we talked about probably was the match. About an hour and a half before the game I say, 'Right. OK, we've got work to do now.' I always went out on the pitch with my two linesmen and I wanted to walk around the pitch and give them instructions about certain situations rather than do it in the dressing room, because it's a funny thing at football grounds but everybody wants to

come and knock on the referee's door and have a word with him. If I'm out on the pitch then the only person who's likely to come out is the one that says there's a cup of tea for you in the dressing room. So, we went out on the pitch and we walked round and we stopped off, deliberately stopped off in this case, in front of the Kop. Even an hour and a half before, it was filling up quite full. It's a question of getting the lads used to the atmosphere. We walked further round and stopped here and stopped there to emphasise certain points. Walk them through the position they should take for a goal-kick and for penalty kicks and stuff like that. It used to take about 45 minutes.

They know how to signal a throw-in and so on but it's getting the teamwork correct. It was very difficult. You've got three things to consider as a linesman. Is the ball in or out of play if it's coming from your left-hand side? Is there an offside situation? Or is there any foul play going on in that quadrant just in front of me? As a referee, I don't want too much flag but I do want help. So the way I used to describe that was to say if a foul is just in front of you that if you were a referee you would blow the whistle for, please don't flag automatically. Just count: one-two, and whilst you're counting one-two make eye contact with me and you'll see one of three things. I shall either be saying nothing, letting play on, and if you've put your flag up and I'm saying play on, I've got to knock you down in front of 45,000 people, which is not good for teamwork or for your morale and it gets me worried about you as well. The second thing is I'll be saying play on, advantage. Not so bad if you have put your flag up because I can take the brunt of that one. The third possibility is that I'll be looking at you and my eyes will be wide open and written across them in red block capital letters, six foot high, is the word HELP. That's when I want the flag.

Perry Groves:
When you're on the coach to the ground you talk about the game, what's going to happen, when you're in a group together. Players today can't talk about the game and what's coming up because they've all got headphones on. How can you then talk about situations you might find yourself in? We'd have Lee Dixon talking to Tony Adams about the distances they're going to play for each other if the winger gets it. If John Barnes gets it, Dicko's going to close him down and then they'll shuffle across and he'll try and bring Barnes inside. Kevin Richardson's saying to Michael Thomas, if you go forwards you've got to make sure you get yourself back in. Merse and Smudge talk about when the ball comes forward and they are going to split. There are conversations with everybody that's going to be around you. I don't see how that happens today because of the headphones.

Paul Davis (midfielder):
There were a lot of us in the changing room because everybody was up there for this game. Myself, Niall Quinn and Brian Marwood weren't playing. We were all in our club suits so it came to a point where we knew we were going to need to leave the changing room and let the boys get on with it but we were waiting around for our tickets. Where were we going to sit?

Niall Quinn (forward):
There was no room on the bench. It was a sunken bench so you couldn't just put chairs behind it because you would be blocking people's view. There were no seats in the grandstand behind the dugout. There was a bit of confusion. It was suggested the safest place to go was in the section where the Arsenal fans were segregated from the Liverpool fans. Footballers weren't as fussy then. We just followed orders.

Paul Davis:
The boys were getting ready now about an hour before kick-off. We wished them all well, said our goodbyes and good luck, went out of the ground and walked outside to the entrance for the away fans and came back into the ground. So we were behind the goal in amongst the Arsenal fans. They couldn't believe that we were there.

Dave Hutchinson:
The official visitors were the team managers. So, anything you wanted to say or get across you said then. Experience tells me that you might just as well talk to a brick wall because they're as emotionally tied up in the game as I am and once that game starts anything that you've said is most likely not going to be taken care of. But they were both experienced managers in this case. George Graham and Kenny Dalglish. There appeared to be lots of respect between the two of them. That's great. I got the impression that they were trying to make me feel comfortable, which helps. It's a bit like the boxing referee. Give me a good clean fight and get on with it.

I should think it was one of the biggest certs in the season to most people in terms of Liverpool being favourites but that doesn't come into our thinking as match officials. That's the last thing. I was aware of the maths.

I wasn't nervous. I was conscious of the responsibility that I'd got as the match official. I desperately wanted it to go without any controversy and that meant I'd got to be on top of my game. It was the only game being played in the Football League that night and everybody who was a football fan was either at the match or watching it live on television. So there was a very special atmosphere and you could feel it and of course it was an emotional situation too. We're all aware of the background to the game and the reason why it had been postponed, so all those factors add to the atmosphere.

Jim Rosenthal (ITV pitchside reporter):
I can tell you about arriving at Anfield because the last time that I'd been there the whole pitch was covered in flowers on the back of the Hillsborough disaster and that was a very, very emotional time for everybody. I can remember particularly Kenny Dalglish during that time. The way he'd conducted himself and the inspiration and the help he gave to so many people. He was a phenomenal figure during that immediate aftermath of the Hillsborough tragedy. The image of the flowers all over the pitch was very hard to get out of your mind.

It was the first time in a hundred years I believe – and it'll probably be the first time in the next hundred years – that two teams played each other on the last day of the season and the title was at stake so of course it was unusual. Did we build it up in the way that we would have built it up now? We didn't. It wasn't that sort of era. I remember doing the interviews beforehand and I can remember George being really calm. Kenny was tense. I think one of the reasons was I don't think they quite knew how to play the game – where you can lose 1–0 and you're going to be champions.

Bob Wilson (Arsenal goalkeeper in 1971, goalkeeping coach in 1989):
I would have loved to have been there at the ground. I was sitting glued to the television. I was doing every bit of superstition that I thought possible. Anything really. I always have certain things close to me that link me to the club. It's the old motto Victoria Concordia Crescit; victory through harmony. In recent times it's as simple as a key ring with the Arsenal badge on it. It will be hidden somewhere on part of my body. It might be in a shirt close to the heart. It might be in a shoe. It might be wound round my finger. I know it sounds ridiculous. It's a little key ring with the Arsenal badge on it and if we're in trouble I sort of press this thing and it

doesn't always work but I'm trying everything to turn the tide, you know. My wife gets upset anyway when I start to lose the plot, shouting at the television, giving instructions. So she went out to meet some friends at a restaurant and I stayed at home and would meet them later.

This was the time of the explosion of television. Suddenly people were beginning to realise there is a mega audience out there and it's something then that creates that piece of history. The difference between reading it in the newspaper the next day, like when we went to Tottenham in 1971 and won the title on the last game of the season, was significant. Obviously it has grown and grown but I think it was one of those early iconic moments in television.

JEFF FOULSER (ITV FOOTBALL EXECUTIVE PRODUCER):
Anyone under the age of 40 would be astounded with the way television is now compared to the way it was then. In 1988–89 it was the first year of live football on television, apart from the FA Cup final and the odd England match, and that season we covered 21 league matches. There were people in football that said this is going to kill the game. They just thought no one's going to turn up. They'll just watch it on TV. Now you can probably watch 21 matches in a week. So, it was a completely different landscape. We were getting audiences of 7, 8, 9 million on a regular basis on a Sunday afternoon. The average rating these days for a live Premiership game is probably 1.5 million.

We had a pundit booked for the night and we only had one pundit because there's no point having a couple of people if you've only got three or four minutes to talk. They pulled out last minute and I knew Bobby Robson, who was the England manager, was going to be at the game and I cornered Bobby in the directors' entrance at Anfield and said, 'Look, Bob, we've got a real problem here. We haven't got a pundit for the game.' He just wanted to watch the game and I said,

'Please just watch it with us.' He was a lovely bloke and said, 'Of course I will.'

David Pleat (co-commentator):
I went up on the day and met up with Brian Moore, who was the most fastidious, genuine, nicest man you could imagine. Although it was such a big game and we all knew it was going out on terrestrial, he was very good at relaxing people. I remember going up the stairs. At Liverpool you had to clamber along these planks to the gantry position, along the rafters with your head ducked down. There were only a couple of camera crews. The commentary position was good but there wasn't a lot of room.

Ian Wright (Crystal Palace striker in 1989, joined Arsenal in 1991):
The estate where I lived in Brockley, where David Rocastle grew up, locked down. I moved the television and had six cans of Foster's. We all knew Arsenal were going to Liverpool that night and it was live on the telly. Everyone was talking about it. All of a sudden the cars stop driving down the road. There is nobody milling around. Everybody is inside. Come kick-off there is not a soul out there. It was amazing to think David off the estate was playing in one of Arsenal's biggest games in their history. You could hear people in other flats jumping and screaming. That's how exciting it was. I cannot emphasise enough how proud we were that we had somebody from the estate playing in one of the biggest games in English football.

Lee Dixon:
In the dressing room George was philosophical. He was determined that he wanted to go out to win it. He talked about the game, how he wanted the game to go. He didn't normally do that, spelling out each

part of the game. So, I think he had a vision in his head about the best way to try and beat Liverpool 2–0 at Anfield.

GEORGE GRAHAM:

If they score a goal first, in the first half, which they normally do, then we had to score three goals at Anfield. It's never been heard of. Especially with that team at that time. So, I said to the boys we've got to keep it 0–0. We mustn't go out there thinking we've got to attack. Because the papers were full of it. Arsenal's got to win 2–0. They've got to go out there and have a go at Liverpool. Hello! I don't think so.

Managers always look at your own team, your own structure, the way you play and the way the opposition play. You know, what are their strengths? What are their weaknesses? You try to exploit their weaknesses and try and force your strengths on to them and that's the way most coaches sort the game out before kick-off. I had it all organised to play Liverpool and even though they won 5–1 in their previous game and were clear favourites, I still thought it was the right way to play.

PAUL MERSON:

Do you know it was 16/1 on the last day to win 2–0? There's one for you. It was 16/1 to win the league in pre-season and we were 16/1 to win 2–0 at Anfield 37 games later. Ha ha ha.

I just couldn't see it. I remember his team-talk. I remember sitting there like, what? I was thinking, as long as we don't start getting beat 3s and 4s, that's all right. I was thinking, he's on what I'm on, isn't he?

ALAN SMITH:

The mood in the dressing room would have a pattern. George was centre stage. Theo Foley, his right-hand man, would do his bit individually, going around making sure we were OK. Feeling all right.

Feeling confident. Tony would do what Tony did, the shouting bit and in those five or ten minutes he'd be getting louder and louder as kick-off approached. I think it's as much to get himself wound up as anybody. Everybody has different methods before a match. I'd quite often disappear to the toilet and read the programme. People are banging on the door. Smudge, are you finished yet?

Steve Bould:
Playing with the back five was a major risk. We had done it before as a sort of one-game special. But in those circumstances, having to win 2–0 away against such a great Liverpool team, it was brave. Had it gone wrong, there'd have been major questions asked.

Alan Smith:
In the minutes leading up to kick-off it was a fantastic team-talk from George. I think he freed your mind. Concentrate on your individual jobs. You might never be in this situation again. Don't waste it. Just go out there and do it. You've worked so hard this season. Do it for yourselves. Do it for your families. Don't pass up the opportunity. After the speech he had given us in the hotel this was a bit more ramped up, with more passion. It was one of those where we went, 'Phew, that was good.' He shook all our hands on the way out, which he never did. He was stood by the door. 'All the best.' We got our bouquets of flowers each.

George Graham:
Ken Friar [the Arsenal secretary] told me, 'George, we're going to get the players to walk out with a bouquet of flowers each and take them into the Kop and the Liverpool supporters and give them to the crowd.' I thought it was a fantastic gesture by the club.

Paul Johnson:
I had already been up to Anfield on a pre-visit to make arrangements about the new date for the game and had laid flowers down on behalf of the club. I got a phone call from Ken Friar saying we had to make a gesture at the game and he suggested flowers for the players to take out to the Liverpool fans. I ended up arranging 20-odd bouquets with a local florist. I think they thought it was a wind-up but we arranged it and it seemed to go down very well.

Tony Adams:
It was a great idea and it was the way Arsenal used to do things in those days. I think we had our finger on the pulse with compassion and with empathy and we knew how to respect other people as well as ourselves. Given the pain that the Liverpool people had gone through it was important.

Alan Smith:
Obviously, we'd been watching the Liverpool lads and Kenny Dalglish attending funerals. It was very emotional and you could feel that in the ground.

John Lukic:
It's the football fraternity. Liverpool obviously suffered more than anybody else but I think all football suffered and we just wanted to show compassion. I think gestures sometimes do fall by the wayside but I think that one hit home with a lot of people. By the time all the lads had run off the only spot that wasn't catered for was down at the Kop end and I had to run all the way down to the Kop and run all the way back up again and that's the furthest I'd ever run in my life so I was knackered by the time I got back. That moves the moment on into the game and the reason that you're there and what you have to do on the night. It's the flick of the switch.

Nigel Winterburn (defender):
Talk about emotions. In the pit of your stomach knowing that you probably should have won the league title two or three games before is pretty annoying and everybody is writing you off and saying it's a fitting end to the season that with the Hillsborough disaster Liverpool are going to do the Double. You realise that if you can pull it off you're going to upset a lot of people. The flowers still stick in my mind. I knew exactly where I was going when I went out on that pitch before the game. I was going to take those flowers down behind the goal. Then you've got to switch that off. You've got a game of football to play in. It's difficult.

Lee Dixon:
I've always had that feeling about the Kop being a really special place. As a kid I was a Man City fan and my friend was a big Liverpool fan and his dad took us to Anfield. City were playing Liverpool at Anfield and we went and stood on the Kop and I had a blue and white City scarf on, a bobble hat. All the Liverpool fans were taking the mickey out of this little cocky Mancunian with his bobble hat on and putting me on to their shoulders. Passing me down the front. Like the old stories. It was brilliant. It was one of the most amazing experiences I've ever had at a football ground. So when we were taking the flowers out I really wanted to give my flowers to someone on the Kop.

My superstition was always to go out on the pitch third behind the captain Tony Adams, the goalkeeper John Lukic, and then me. Arsenal's tradition was to line up on the halfway line and salute the away fans before we went and did our warm-up. So we were all lined up with these flowers and when we'd done our wave I remember sprinting off to the Kop end. There was a lady near the corner flag and I ran over and gave them to her. I remember the emotion of actually passing the flowers over. The minute I let go of the flowers it was like I had this flood of 'Right!' My game face came on immediately. I sprinted back to my position before kick-off and I was full of energy. Ready to go. It was almost like a handing over of emotion. It was: right, we've done that. Now we'll go and play the game and that was the first time I can remember thinking, we can win this. We're going to win this.

TWO

Gorgeous George

George Graham:

I learned the word 'standards' at Arsenal when I was a player, especially under Bertie Mee, who was very strong, very tough, very honest. That was his favourite word. Standards. Whether it was behaviour, performance on the pitch, attitude on the training ground, the way you dressed when you were going to matches, mixing with the public – there was a certain standard around the club and I think there is still. I think Arsenal has still got it.

The club I walked back into in 1986 was quite a famous club without doubt. Still one of the best. What I would say is for a club as big as Arsenal, it was struggling. So it was, in a perverse sort of way, probably an easy task to actually improve them. Coming into a new job you think, right, where's your assets and where are the problems? You do a lot of homework and even before I met the players I did a whole lot of decision-making. Even for the players who had to go I thought, my mind can be changed. It's up to you. It's as simple as that.

I spoke to a few people around the club at the time and I just thought there were a few different groups of players. It wasn't a unit. So the first thing I thought was, I've got to get everybody on the same wavelength. I wanted a new set-up at the club where everybody was equal. There was no star system. As soon as they came through the gates at the training ground, equality was the word I used. I remember the first day of training in the summer when I went there and I'd got my team behind me and all the boys sat on the ground and I introduced myself. I said, 'I'm the new manager. I'll give everybody six weeks to prove their worth and then I'll make decisions. It's going to be hard work.' I was very honest with everybody and I told them there'd be no favouritism because one's got a bigger reputation than the other. I think it worked very well.

Bob Wilson:
I think one of the most extraordinary things about George Graham was the difference as I saw it between George the player – his nickname was Gorgeous George, he was a good-looking boy – and the manager he became. George was a team-mate of mine. We played in the Double season in 1971 and the year that we won the Fairs Cup in 1970, the first European success, which broke the spell of 17 years without a trophy. He was a great team-mate when I was selected for Scotland. George and I shared a room. As a player I would have said throughout the 71 Double squad there were three I would predict would never be a manager – Peter Marinello, Charlie George and George Graham. He never showed any interest at that time in coaching badges or really seriously thinking about the game tactically. George was a fantastic dresser. Still is. Immaculate. Mannequin. He loved that style outside the playing side of the game.

Pat Rice (defender in 1971, youth team manager in 1989):
When George was a player he was always laughing and joking in the dressing room. But he developed this focus that it's about winning, which made him a tremendous manager. I mean it's no use playing your career just to play football. You want to win games and that's it – you've got to have that hardness.

Bob Wilson:
As a player he hid the desire and passion of wanting to win and maybe that's why I was always uncertain about what was behind the mask of George. I'm not sure I ever knew what was truly going through George's mind. He was ruthless. He would smile with a sort of disguised smile. I never saw George celebrate quite as much as some of us did in stupid ways. George was always seemingly under control.

David Dein:
I remember the discussions about who to appoint very well. I had the temerity to suggest Alex Ferguson. Ha ha ha. But we got George in. Today the average longevity of a manager across the 92 league clubs is 12 months and I always say that the biggest decision a board has to make is that one of appointing the manager. If you get it right, your life's easy. If you get it wrong you're on the roundabout again in 12 months' time. You weigh up. You do your homework. He was an ex-player. He had a track record at Millwall. You could see that perhaps he was one for the future. So that's how it transpired.

Nick Hornby (supporter):
In terms of expectations, Arsenal had just appointed the manager of Millwall to run the team. It wasn't what we were hoping for. So it wasn't like we got terribly excited about him taking over. The excitement really didn't start until the team began to play and then the beginning of 1986–87 they were fantastic. The first half of that season they had this young team and they were very vibrant and I can remember the queues outside the North Bank getting longer and thinking, wow, there is something happening here. People are coming back and they want to see these players and that hadn't happened for quite a long time. I stood on the North Bank, slightly on the edge,

and I think there was a very deep connection between fans and players. I was telling my kids the other day how when the players went out on the pitch everyone sung a song for each player until they acknowledged the crowd and that never happens any more. There's not that same kind of link between one end, behind the goal, and the team.

The 1980s had been a very difficult decade for football. Because of the Heysel disaster first of all, people were drifting away from the game. One of the reasons Highbury felt so dismal in the 80s was because this was not a team who could do anything. So when George Graham took over in 86 the crowd starts to go up again and then you got that old intensity back.

Things started changing straight away. First game of his first season in 1986 we beat Manchester United 1–0. I remember the interview with him afterwards on the radio where he seemed a bit sniffy about the performance of the team and I thought, wow, we've just beaten Man U and he doesn't think they played very well. I thought, I'm interested in this. He wanted to play direct football. He wanted to play fast football. He wanted wingers and centre-forwards and there was nothing not to like.

ALAN DAVIES (SUPPORTER):
Don Howe had been manager and he was much loved. We thought his treatment had been quite shoddy. Howe quit because he felt he was being undermined and there were a lot of people on Avenell Road complaining, including me, that he'd been badly treated. I actually wrote to the chairman of the club. I remember we played Watford twice in two days, unusually, and everyone went to Vicarage Road thinking we were going to lose just to stick up for Don Howe. That's how much he was loved. They appointed George Graham, who by all accounts interviewed very well. This wasn't a glamorous appointment. They tried to get Terry Venables. Bobby Robson's name

was always being touted or would we get someone from abroad? And we get this guy who had managed Millwall, who was an Arsenal legend because he'd been part of the Double team of 71. But his nickname was Stroller and he seemed a bit vain and how's he going to be a manager?

David O'Leary:

It needed a change. It needed a broom to it. It needed a freshening up and George came in and certainly gave it that. He called everybody in, first meeting, and let you know what was expected, how things were going to change. He was very forceful. This is the way we're going to do things from now on. When you have people at a club for a long time, people get set in their ways. I probably did as well. You took too many things for granted. Now we had a new boss to prove yourself to and get you back on track. It was certainly good for me. The impression he left was: the door is open but if you don't want to stay we can always find you a home somewhere else. He addressed it to people like myself more because we were the bigger players. I took it on as a challenge. I thought to myself, this is a man who wants to win things at Arsenal. I want to win things. George came at the right time. The club needed him and felt his impact straight away. Friday night after a long journey he'd look down the coach and he'd say, lads, put your tie on, button your shirt up.

George Graham:

We used to always have to wear a blazer and nice grey slacks or a suit as our uniform. We needed a new tie and I asked one of the hierarchy if I could I get a few dozen ties made by a guy that I knew in London who was in the rag trade, who offered to make some beautiful ties, red and white stripes with a nice cannon at the bottom. I never got the OK for it so I paid for them. I gave one each to the players and I gave one to the directors. After that we used to get the ties for nothing. Ha ha.

PAUL DAVIS:
Before George came along we were going nowhere and it didn't look as though anything was going to happen really. We had a lot of older players who seemed comfortable where they were, didn't seem as though they were hungry for success. We had some horrendous times, crowds of 11,000, 13,000 were turning up to watch us play and we were mid-table. So it was a tough time to be at a club like Arsenal because we were expected to do things. George came in with a real strong attitude straight away.

He very quickly got rid of some senior players to bring on and encourage the younger guys. I came between the senior players and the younger players. I was right in the middle so I didn't know where I was or what his attitude towards me was.

TONY ADAMS:
A massive gamble. I know they interviewed a few other, more experienced coaches. But George got the nod and I think that was brave of the club at that period. I don't think it would ever happen now. George wouldn't even be a candidate, you know. Millwall. Scottish. Second Division. Going to manage The Arsenal.

The first pre-season, I remember he got the clipboard out and went through rules and regulations and having played at The Arsenal before he knew a little bit about the way that they did business. He instilled that from the very start. George was extremely lucky that he had a group of international-quality kids coming through. Myself, Rocky, Mickey Thomas, Paul Merson, Quinny. George did two things, for me, that instantly made a success of the club. One was laying down the law and throwing all the big-time players out. Two, he got lucky with players that were coming through. So that's the secret for George Graham at the very start.

John Lukic:
Some people might say he was professionally ruthless. He had an idea in his mind. He had his own authority. George arrived in the summer as my contract was up for renewal. I hadn't met him at all and I remember going down to the ground. I had an appointment to see George and my wife was with me in the car and said to me, 'Well what shall I do?' I said don't worry, I won't be long. I literally went in and came out and that was it. It was very short and sweet. We didn't really see eye to eye. But I just got on with it. Having said that, I've got a huge amount of respect for him because of what he did and what he brought to the football club.

I do remember starting pre-season training and for some reason I started calling him Gaddafi. Don't ask me why but I did and it sort of stuck. So I must apologise, George. It was me.

George Graham:
The youth set-up at the club was first-class. In fact, it was probably the best in the country at that time. The class of 92 that flourished under Alec Ferguson* at Manchester United and was at the top for a couple of decades, well I had that a few years earlier. I don't think anybody realised it apart from the people inside the club. At Arsenal, when I look back and I see Tony Adams, David Rocastle, Mickey Thomas, Paul Merson, Niall Quinn, Martin Hayes – they're looking great. I thought, what a chance I've got here if I can just improve these boys. Play them in the first team,

* As a Scot, George Graham always referred to his compatriot Alex Ferguson as Alec.

blend them in with a hunger that I was hoping to get from the players that I bought.

DAVID O'LEARY:
If you have home-grown players it gives the team some real caring about the club and all those young players came in and had that passion. I chose Arsenal some years before and I got into a team with players who had this belief and love for the club. Those lads that came in were top-class players who had that love. There was a real togetherness.

PAUL MERSON:
People say I was called Son of George. I mean he gave me a million chances. If it wasn't for him I would have been thrown out of football years ago, especially at Arsenal. So I'm always thankful to him. We were fearful. If we were laughing and joking in the dressing room and he walked in – 'Shhh'. That was it. There was no messing about. Training was serious. In this day and age the players half dictate it now with the money they get.

You had to work very hard. If you didn't work hard you were out the team. I remember we used to do this squeezing game in training where you'd have five in one square, five in another square and then another five, and two had to go in and get the ball. You had to keep it in the square for five passes and flick it over to another group. But if you lost it you had to go as quick as you could across. I gave the ball away once and I jogged and he went 'Hurry up' and I literally laughed. I just giggled and I carried on. I never played for about two months. He didn't say a word. Saturday the team goes up. Not in the team. And that's what he was like. He would chop his nose off to spite his face. He was hard but I always say if it wasn't for George Graham I don't think we'd have won anything. I really don't.

He took a big gamble. Top players – you're talking Viv Anderson,

Kenny Sansom, Charlie Nicholas. He come in and he went: bang. You go and play in the reserves. You're completely out. Now he was the man, Charlie. I'd rather a good footballer than a hungry footballer if I'm being honest but George took that chance. He wanted to rule with an iron rod and he didn't want people questioning him. So the younger the players he got in the more we were going to listen and it worked a treat for him.

TONY ADAMS:
It was fun and we had the naivety of youth. We were young, determined and ruthless and we stuck together. We went out together. Me and Martin Keown went to Ilford Palais and Martin was going through a phase of wearing the same colour socks as his T-shirt and it was brilliant. So if he had yellow socks he had a yellow T-shirt. We liked different music. Mickey was talking about the Lyceum, and Rocky was into lovers rock. I come from the East End. Martin Keown was in digs. Rocky was South London. We all came together and trained Monday and Thursday nights and it was great fun. We got lucky that we got a good teacher, a good coach, in Terry Burton and we developed at a very quick rate.

MICHAEL THOMAS:
At that time it was a great time to be around football, especially at Arsenal. Arsenal only picked the best. It wasn't about quantity, it was about quality. So if you had three good youth players, they'd just pick three players and play them in a higher team. At that time we had quite a few of us who came through together and it was just like family really. I remember seeing Merse play before I came to Arsenal. I came to watch a schoolboy game down at London Colney with my Sunday football manager. Little Merse was so small, smallest on the pitch, with his big Arsenal shorts. He was just running the show. I met Tony Adams at a district game and I was in awe. This guy was so

tall and he was commanding everybody around the pitch at a district game and it was like, who is this man? He played like he was a professional. Then finding out it was Tony Adams who plays for Arsenal. Wow. Tony was making ripples in the football world being so young. Everybody knew about him. I never knew that Rocky played for Arsenal as a schoolboy until the first day when I came in. I walked through the Marble Halls and the next minute in the dressing room Dave Rocastle was there. I said, 'How come you didn't tell me you were training at Arsenal?' David was quite quiet then. We had belief in our own ability and belief in each other. Playing in the youth team we were playing free-flowing football and like a lot of the nation I loved watching Brazil play. That was my thing, watching Brazil. I was a full-back and I used to love to attack all the time. I had Rocky in front of me so when I'd attack he'd defend. Or we'd both attack together.

NIALL QUINN:

We were all trying to make the grade together. I know Man United and the class of 92 marketed themselves brilliantly and went on to do spectacular things, but in our own little way we had that special feeling amongst us. There was a lovely connection. It was probably more innocent when we came through compared to the class of 92 when things were already getting a lot more modern. Nobody had an agent. We found our own trouble to get into as normal teenagers or young adults do. We had some magical times together. After training we'd hop in the car and head to Sandown or Windsor races and throw away what few quid George was paying us. You almost live together. You learn to win together. You learn about losing together. When there is a crowd of you in that spell everybody blossoms. We propelled each other on.

I had two sets of friends: my football friends and my Irish lads. I used to go to the dogs with Donners, as we called him. Behind the scenes Tony Donnelly, our famous kit man, was from the same parish as me, Crumlin in Dublin, and his wife Ethel was our famous laundry lady, who ran all the big washing machines with a ton of stuff going in every day that we would bundle up for her. My first landlady across the road from Highbury was Irish. Pat Galligan, the groundsman, was a great character. I started to find out a bit too much about the pubs of Holloway Road. The fun we had. Not a great reference for a young professional footballer but I think I knew a barman in every pub on the Holloway Road.

PAUL MERSON:
You watch players when you're in the youth team who get a lucky break and they're in the first team and you're so pleased for them and it gives you that faith. If I do well I've got a chance of playing for Arsenal here.

MICHAEL THOMAS:
As schoolboys you could see how good we were. We all complimented each other. It was like a race. Who'd be the first one in the first team? Obviously, Tony Adams was the main man. He was the first to get in the team. From then it was Martin Keown and after it was David Rocastle and next was Niall Quinn and Gus Caesar. Then I came and Merse come after me. It was a great feeling. I was chomping at the bit.

ALAN SMITH:
Mickey Thomas and Dave Rocastle were still quite young but were already quite important players in that group and you did feel, despite their youth, there was a character – a sort of inner city vibe – that came from them. There was that clutch of lads. Strong boys physically as much as anything. Big personalities. Funny lads. Rocky and Tony obviously, the cheeky Essex chappie, as he was then. But a leader even then, becoming captain aged 21. You could sense there was this

kind of groundswell. There were these boys coming through that were hungry to do well and you always want there to be that core of home-grown players. Certainly fans do and even as a team-mate I think you like that. The fact that they've come up through the Arsenal ranks and they were part of the club. You know they feel part of it.

ALAN DAVIES:
It used to be important who you had who was kind of your own. It was a big thing in football. We had Brady. Tottenham had Hoddle. West Ham had Brooking. These were our players. The idea that you would go and buy everyone's best players and assemble some super team, well, that was for Manchester United to be doing, which was ironic because they had their own history of producing players. But we had a whole raft of them and they were genuinely outstanding footballers. Particularly Rocastle, Merson and Paul Davis.

AMY LAWRENCE (SUPPORTER):
Not that we realised it at the time, but there was something more natural about the way you could connect with players then. If you arrived at Highbury early enough, or hung about afterwards, you could see them in the street and grab a quick chat about nothing special. If you were keen enough to attend youth or reserve games you would see the same old faces and get to know people who worked at the club or players who were coming through. In more recent times I noticed the crowd that wait around outside the Emirates surrounding one of the cars emerging from the bowels of the underground car park. A tinted window was lowered just enough for a hand to poke out to sign an autograph. Players don't have that freedom to just wander about football grounds now as they did then, without being driven completely mad. It must be suffocating, unhealthy even. Back then, as nothing more than a bog standard ordinary fan, you could

have an almost normal connection with a player you idolised. The group of young players coming through were only a couple of years older than us so we were into the same fashion or music, cultural references or places to go.

Gary Lewin:
I was appointed first team physio at the start of George Graham's first season. It was a small staff. George was the manager, Theo Foley was assistant manager, Tony Donnelly the kit man, I was physio – we were the only full-time staff. We had part-time doctors, Dr Crane and Dr Sash, and a part-time goalkeeping coach, Bob Wilson. Steve Burtenshaw was chief scout. That was it. That was us. We would talk all the time, non-stop.

I was always an Arsenal fan and had signed associated schoolboy forms at 14. I was released in 1982. I didn't know what I was going to do and Fred Street, the physio, asked if I was interested in going into physiotherapy. He arranged for me to spend a day at Guy's Hospital. I got a feel for it. I worked at Guy's Monday to Friday 9–5, covered training four nights a week, Saturdays I did the reserve team, Sundays the under-16s. I qualified in July 86 and got offered the first team job in September 1986, so I went straight from uni into the first team job. As someone who had come through the academy and had been working with these youngsters for three years in the reserves, for me it was really exciting. You had a passion driven into you for the club from a young age. You knew if they had a sniff of the first team the only thing that would stop them from staying there is talent. The commitment was second to none. We had so many home-grown players in the team alongside players with that hunger who had come through the lower leagues. Put that together with George's discipline, tactical nous and will to win and you felt something special was going on.

GEORGE GRAHAM:
When I was at Millwall I had to do a lot of shrewd buying because a team like Millwall hadn't much money in the transfer market. Going to Arsenal, I was still aware of the players I liked in the lower divisions and I thought to myself, I wonder if they could perform in the top division? It was desire as well as technical ability that I wanted from the players that I brought in.

PERRY GROVES:
He signed me from Colchester and he said, 'You're very raw. We've watched you.' He watched me when he was manager of QPR's youth team and I played for Colchester youth team and we got beat 7–0 at the old Loftus Road with the plastic pitch. He said he remembered me from then. I thought I must have played quite well and he went, 'No, no, you just ran around moaning at everybody. But when your team was getting beat you didn't stop. You kept going and going and going. It wasn't as much your ability, it was the desire you had to keep playing even when your team was getting battered.' With the youngsters and players from the lower leagues like myself, Lee Dixon, Nigel Winterburn, Steve Bould, Alan Smith, his whole thing was: now I can mould you. I can mould you into how I want my team to play. He knew we were so grateful to be at Arsenal that we would do anything. If he said, oh look there's a field of thistles over there, we'd have run through a field of thistles.

NIGEL WINTERBURN:
A couple of weeks before I signed for Arsenal I was at Chelsea for talks and they'd broken down. I was feeling pretty gutted anyway. But then I just got a call from my manager at Wimbledon, Dave Bassett, saying they've accepted an offer from Arsenal and did I want to go over and meet them? I mean when a club like Arsenal comes in for you you're not going to say no. It was a massive step up for me and

then going to Highbury to meet George Graham. I didn't have an agent. I just went myself and you sat in that room and you realise what George is like. He's very commanding. He's very dominant. I think as soon as I sat down I was going to sign. I was that petrified of him.

George Graham:
Each town and city around England had their own paper so I knew that there was a local journalist who would have a whole page to himself every weekend. I knew that that journalist or reporter would be well in with the manager of the local club and he would get all the good stories. So every Monday morning, my secretary would always bring in this pile of papers. In the Midlands it was the Pink *Argus*. In Sheffield it was the *Green 'Un* . . . I used to just read that one page and throw the rest of it away and it would enlighten me to the players that the manager rated. That's how I got Lee Dixon and Stevie Bould because of getting good write-ups. I was going to watch Lee because he won player of the year at Stoke in two consecutive seasons. When I see a full-back winning player of the year two years on the trot I think he must be good, I'll go and watch him. So I went to watch him and I saw Stevie Bould, centre-half. Liked him as well. Then Nigel Winterburn from Wimbledon. Kevin Richardson from Watford. I wanted these people with desire. They must think, my God! Arsenal! Arsenal want to buy me.

Lee Dixon:
Mick Mills, my manager at Stoke, says we're going down to Watford Gap to meet George Graham. Do the deal. I'm a little bit nervous at this point. We get in the car. We drive down. So I say to Mick Mills, what sort of money do you think I'll be likely to be offered down there? Because I was a little bit naive. I was on £350 a week at Stoke. So Mick says to me, oh, you've made it now. Everything's sorted. You'll definitely get at least £1,000 a week. I was blown away. £1,000

a week seemed an awful lot of money to me but it was Arsenal and it was the First Division. So we drive down to Watford Gap service station. We pull up. George Graham's sitting in his Daimler next to us. Mick gets out the car and goes in for a coffee. Leaves me to get in the car with George, who is sitting there as smart as anything, club blazer on, looking a million dollars. I shake George's hand. At this point I'm absolutely petrified and all I've got going on in my mind is £1,000 a week. £1,000 a week. Big move to Arsenal. George said to me, 'Welcome on board.' As if the deal was already done, which it was really as far as I was concerned. 'I'm going to build a team. We're going to get rid of the prima donnas. We're going to introduce hungry players. We're going to go and win the league.'

So he gets out the car and starts walking away and I thought, hang on a minute. We haven't actually talked about money yet. So I said, 'Mr Graham, can we just have a little chat about the wages?' And he looked at me a little bit strange as if that's a bit inappropriate to talk about your future like that. He offered me £500 a week. That threw me a little bit. I said, oh. He said, 'Is that not enough?' I had Mick Mills in my head and said I was kind of looking at £1,000 a week. He shut the door in my face and started walking off to the service station.

George Graham:
I think he wanted petrol money!

Lee Dixon:
I start filling up thinking, what have I done? I've ruined the deal and it's all over. I think I cried all the way back to Stoke.

George Graham:
Lee was obviously asking for way too much. Way too much. And I thought, he's got to be joking so I say, Lee, we're not talking the same

language. I've got to go, I'm busy. So I got up and left the car and he came chasing after me.

LEE DIXON:
The next day I said, I can't leave it like that, so Mick phones George up and I speak to him on the phone and ask for a second chance. I went down to London on the train. As I'm walking up the marble steps at Highbury, Herbert Chapman is looking at me. As I open the doors I had that feeling right then of: I'm not leaving this place until I've signed a contract. I told George I would sign. George replied, 'I tell you what, I'll give you £700 a week.' I signed on the spot.

GEORGE GRAHAM:
Eventually he saw common sense. I knew from when I was a player you always want to ask for something. You probably know you're not going to get it but you've got to ask and you've got to negotiate. But no, I didn't have any problems with the players. I'm sure they might think differently. Ha ha ha. Brian Clough had a wonderful saying, 'We talk for 20 minutes and then we decide I was right.'

STEVE BOULD:
I travelled down there and just took one look at the place. It's just one of those clubs that once you join you're there for ever. I felt it straight away. George is very classy, dressed smart, spoke well. He said I wasn't gonna get paid as much! Which was par for the course. But he sold it to me. He said, 'We're very close to doing something good.' And he was absolutely correct.

ALAN SMITH:
When I signed I was shown round the ground by Steve Burtenshaw, the chief scout. George was away in Portugal with the team. He showed me round the pitch and he went, 'Alan, a lot of number 9s

have played here but not many have done well.' I thought, oh my God. You smelled the history. The expectation. The added scrutiny. It was much different to Leicester and you could understand then why some good players can't make the step up. It must have been the first day of pre-season that I saw him. I obviously heard he was quite a strict manager. I'm one of his big new signings and I'm on board with him. He was a tracksuit manager, always there every day of the week. He loved that side of things. Loved his team shape. His tactics. He always pushed us hard.

PERRY GROVES:
His mantra – I can remember him saying it: 'World-class players aren't lazy.' World-class players don't just walk around and not close down. Your team spirit is cultivated on the training ground and on the football pitch. That's where your team spirit first comes from because you're all in it together and nobody is lazy and if someone is lazy then they're dug out. You don't carry any passengers.

ALAN SMITH:
I remember Kevin Richardson coming. We used to call him Albert Tatlock, the old bloke out of *Coronation Street* who didn't stop moaning. He'd obviously had success at Everton, where he got a title winners' medal, so he'd had that feeling of success. Then he'd gone to Watford and George bought him in for £200,000. You could see straight away he was a good player, a scuffler with great positioning, always encouraging people, telling them where to be and having a moan if somebody needed a bit of a kick up the backside. He was the type of player the gaffer would really appreciate.

MICHAEL THOMAS:
George loved the togetherness of the team. He didn't care if you hated him as long as your team stuck together. Sometimes when he

said he wanted young hungry players I think he just wanted to cut the wage bill really. Ha ha ha. Pay us in shillings for the job we did. But George was so tactically astute. He knew the game inside out. He watched the first half from the stand and within ten minutes he'd change the game.

George Graham:
Everybody in football knew as a player I wasn't the one that worked the hardest, that's for sure. I used to try and skip every opportunity in training that I could and I used to say, 'For heaven's sake, get the balls out! Why are we doing all this working?' I never ever thought in my wildest dreams that I'd ever be a coach of a football team. Terry Venables gave me the opportunity at Crystal Palace to start coaching the youth team. I just took to it. I loved it. Couldn't get enough of it and then when you're working with a youth team the kids do what you told them anyway. There was no question. Nobody ever argued. So I thought, I can do that with a first team, with established players. I'll make them work. But it was not just physical work. It was intelligent work. The players were fantastic. I pushed them a lot. Especially the first year, 18 months. I was wanting to get the defence right. When I first arrived the right-back was Viv Anderson, the left-back was Kenny Sansom, the centre-halves were David O'Leary and Tony Adams. The two full-backs were international players with many, many England caps. But they got a shock, because they didn't realise how hard I worked the back four. When I joined Arsenal I had this vision that I wanted two top players fighting for every position.

It was very, very important to me that the players coming to The Arsenal under my management were hungry and would die for success.

THREE

Desire

John Lukic:

George arrived at the club in 1986 and we got to the Littlewoods Cup final in that first season and won it. It gave a lot of players including myself a lot of self-belief. During that run we went through three semi-final games against Tottenham – home, away and a replay. To come out victorious in those was a major, major turning point. The belief grew from there. Then we beat Liverpool in the final. It was an interesting scenario because you don't expect a manager to get you to a cup final in the first year. Particularly given the way the team had been playing in the past five years.

Tony Adams:

The significance of that game was huge. The first trophy for George and for us. The club was a very different animal then. We had won the FA Cup before that, in 1979, and didn't win anything much since, which was eight years. Liverpool dominated the country. They were winning everything in sight. Kenny Dalglish was player-manager. He is probably the best player I've ever played against. He had an enormous arse and he used to stick his bottom in and turn you and he was very aggressive. It was an era where you could actually come through the centre-forward. But he used to hit you first. I remember I was 17 or 18 playing at Anfield and as he goes to receive the ball – smack – I couldn't breathe for about ten minutes and he just dropped off and, of course, he'd turn and pick his ball. Unbelievable. Physical, strong, intelligent. They went ahead in the Littlewoods Cup final through Ian Rush, knowing they had this stat behind them – they never lost when he scored. So to turn that around gave us enormous confidence to go on and keep winning and winning and winning.

Perry Groves:
For that final in 87 George's team-talk told you a lot about his ideas. He had a flip-chart and went through the whole Liverpool team – you're talking seasoned internationals who had won titles and championships – and for every player he highlighted a weakness . . . I think we can get at the two centre-halves – they're not quick enough. Charlie, you back in, you'll be all right. In midfield they're not going to be mobile enough. Jan Molby is a brilliant player but if we can get around him we can break . . . So instead of talking about all their strengths, he highlighted their weaknesses. You come out of that and think, basically, they're human. Just footballers. George was very good psychologically as well as tactically. We closed people down, we showed people inside and everybody knew what to do.

John Lukic:
The new boys coming into that environment were just thirsty for knowledge. Everybody embraced it from very early on.

Lee Dixon:
My first day I remember going in and the first people I saw in the dressing room were Kenny Sansom, David O'Leary and Tony Adams. I walked in and I was like, what am I doing here? If I could have given the money back I'd have done anything to go back to Stoke at that moment because I was just thinking, I'm so out of my depth. I really want to just go into my comfort zone of playing in the Second Division. But you need to be pushed and you need to push the boundaries and I said to myself, no, come on, this is where you

need to be right now. The first day's training I was all over the place. On a Tuesday we had a 'phys' – a physical. There was a red gravel track round Highbury and George used to run the players round there. The lads said, 'We run all morning and then we go into the gym and do weights. We don't play any football.' That was it. We did have a little kickabout in the gym. The lads were putting the ball through my legs. 'Wahey! We've got one here!' I remember Dave Rocastle nutmegging me after about 20 seconds. But it was good. It was character-building.

We were a bit apprehensive about all these big players leaving the club. That heaps the responsibility on your own shoulders. You're thinking, we've got to carry this club now and I'm not Kenny Sansom. He played 80-odd games for England. It was quite daunting to know that you were now in charge of pushing the club forward but on the other hand it was exciting because we were in the side and George was all about that hunger.

David O'Leary:

One thing I'd noticed over the years at Arsenal is that you can sign players who look really good at other clubs but they can come to an environment like Arsenal, a big club, and not flourish. When you're signing players for the top clubs you've got to think, can they cope with the intensity, the expectation, the demands? All those players like Lee and Nigel and Bouldy and Alan Smith could. They relished it. They loved that pressure being put on them and I enjoyed that. That's what kept me on my toes.

Lee Dixon:

I certainly wasn't thinking about winning the league. I'm just thinking about staying in the team. But George wanted the players to think we're going to beat everybody. We're going to be a team. We're going to create something. We're going to challenge the best. That's drilled into you from day one. Tony Adams had been there and he was Mr Arsenal so he educated us on what the club was all about. Day one, you realise why it's called *The* Arsenal because they do things in a certain way and there are certain responsibilities as a player. Remember who you are, what you are and who you represent – that was drilled into me by David Rocastle. He used to say it all the time, bless him. When somebody says it to you it makes your shoulders go back. I get goosebumps thinking about it now.

NIGEL WINTERBURN:

If you were not doing your job 100 per cent out on that pitch you would be told. Someone would tell you and you had to take it in the right way and sometimes it got physical. There might be some pushing and shoving but when a game was finished, or the next day in training, everybody was best mates again. There were no grudges held within that dressing room because the desire of each player to win a game of football was so, so strong. You needed to know very quickly if your standard drops; it wasn't going to be the manager who was going to leave you out the team, one of your team-mates is going to let you know that you need to pick your game up considerably. Tony was quite good at doing that. He was so annoying because he used to come and tap you on the backside and say, 'Come on. I know you can do better.' Yes, I know I can do better. I don't want you tapping me on the backside and letting me know that. That's for sure.

LEE DIXON:

The philosophy was: you train like you play. You don't have days off in training. That's not what training's about. You can't just come in and freewheel because on a Saturday you've got to be full on, so you're full on from Monday to Friday. Every now and again, very rarely, George would have a meeting or he wasn't there and Theo Foley would take training. That was like a bank holiday. The next day he'd be back in and Theo would tell him that the lads had been messing about so we'd work double hard. The whip was cracked again. We didn't have any other options because he was teaching us from a base level: this is how you win games and this is how you go and challenge Liverpool and the big teams. I thought, I'm buying into this. It hurts every day being almost hit with a stick, saying do this, do that, run here, run there. You get used to it after a while. It was full on. Train. Train. Train.

Players just need to see a bit of success for all their hard work. We're doing back four work again and we're running on a Tuesday and we're going to do the weights. We had the odd day off on a Wednesday and maybe a game of golf or something like that, but not that often. George was a really tough manager to play under. He was a disciplinarian. He was fierce at times. I was scared of him. I would do anything I could for him to look at me and not have a frown on his face. That for me was gold dust because it meant he wasn't on my back. The treat for us was he educated us. The treat was three points on a Saturday. The one bit of candy you got was, 'Well done, you have won the game.' Our treat was winning.

Michael Thomas:

It was a battle of wills with me and George. He always wanted to get something over on you and I was like, no, I'm not having it. If we'd do something wrong in the training session or if we missed a chance you'd have to do press-ups. I was doing press-ups once and I thought he wasn't looking so I'm pretending. He sees me and he goes, 'Come on, do it.' I said, 'I have done it,' and he says, 'No, no, you're not getting up until you do it.' Here we go. So I had to do it and then he lays on top of me and I had to do a press-up with George on my back. Are you kidding? But that was George.

Alan Smith:

He actually clambers on top of Mickey and he's kind of sitting on him trying to get him to go all the way down. It was dangerous really. The sport scientists would have a heart attack. But Mickey just decides 'I ain't doing that' so his arms are locked and the gaffer can't get him down because that's how strong he was.

Paul Merson:

Mickey was the most laid-back player. Honestly, he could sleep on a clothes line. He was so laid-back he wasn't allowed to play five-a-sides on a Friday. He'd have to go in because he'd just mess about. He wouldn't run around as much as everybody else so George wouldn't let him play. Mickey was a cool dude.

Alan Smith:

George used to join in little five-a-sides. He'd have a little shimmy and move the ball about and if he scored he'd let us know and do a little celebration. He was a really good header of the ball and he used to give me a bit of one-to-one coaching. 'Alan, this is how you head it. You get the old neck like that and go tsch.' He'd always make the sound effects. Tsch.

David O'Leary:

George had his buffer in his assistant Theo Foley. Theo used to drive me mad at times. He used to drive me round the twist. All he talked to me about was Dublin all the time and I would think to myself, you know, just because I'm from Dublin, I've been living over here a long time. We can speak about other things you know, Theo. But Theo was good for him and us because he wasn't as serious as George.

George Graham:
Theo was a lovely personality and the players loved him. We'd got to know each other when I joined Queens Park Rangers as a youth team coach and he was a reserve team coach. Then we got on great at Millwall when I asked him to be my assistant. When he came to Arsenal he was fantastic. It was the good cop, bad cop situation. It was always good for me to bounce ideas off him. Theo, what do you think here? What do you think there? Because he was a coach longer than I was.

Lee Dixon:
George used to sit in the stand first half of every game because he'd get a better view. The second half there's not a lot you can do so he'd sit down on the bench. He always used to write stuff down on a piece of paper from his seat in the directors' box. At Highbury the doors open into the dressing room and there's a massage table there and he used to be standing, hands resting on the massage table, with his piece of paper. I used to come in and have a look over his shoulder because inevitably my name would be on there. If your name was on the paper you were getting it. It wasn't a well done. He'd start with the defence. Top of the list, Dixon. I'd go straight towards the toilet so he couldn't tell me off and then he'd go, 'Lee, come on, sit down.' I would sit down. 'Right, you're not doing this and you're not doing that . . .' Nigel never got anything said about him. He used to love Nigel and Tony Adams. But me and Bouldy used to get it all the time.

John Lukic:
At half-time he'd be tearing the wallpaper off the walls at times. He'd praise you but not that often. Being on the edge gave us the impetus.

Paul Merson:
If we lost the game literally you'd put a towel over your suit so when he came in, when the cups and the tea went everywhere, it wouldn't go all over your suit. It was unbelievable.

David O'Leary:
George would always linger and want to pick your brains about this or that. I remember him doing that at the start of the 88–89 season. Tony had come back from bad times at the European Championship for England and he was being treated badly by the press. We'd bought Steve Bould and George said to me, 'Tony's having a bad time, David. What do you think about it?' I said, 'Well I don't think you'd be right to leave him out because I think that would be the final nail in the coffin.' So a couple of days later the team was announced and I was out of the side and Steve Bould and Tony were in. I remember going to see him on the Monday about it. He said, 'Dave, I wanted to play Bouldy. I wanted to give Bouldy a chance now to see what he's like. You told me it would kill Tony to leave him out . . .' I absolutely went mad with him. It was probably one of my only proper go-to-see-the-manager fall-out times. I was very wary of offering advice after that!

Nigel Winterburn:
With George there was the impression of: address me when I ask you to. If you want to talk to me you've got to make an appointment. It wasn't really like that but that's what it felt like. I always felt that Tony was the link to the manager and that if you had a problem, you go and speak to Tony and he'd speak to George. Or if the team had a problem and George wanted to feed something out to the team he'd probably go through Tony. But away from that his attention to detail as a manager, particularly in the way that he wanted you to play and the way that he analysed the opposition, was absolutely sensational.

Tony Adams:
I was scared of George. You could say he was a father figure. My own father gave George permission to father me as well. My own father said, do as you're told, son; George knows best. My dad handed me over in a football context and George was a very dominant father figure. We used each other I think. George was good for me and I'm sure I was good for George and we were after the same end result. We were after winning things. He was a manager of that time. He did get lucky with the amount of young talent coming through but I also think that he was brilliant in the way that he worked them and organised them and formed a character. George did an unbelievable job for The Arsenal.

George Graham:
When I was on a coaching course up at Lilleshall in the old days, all the coaches one afternoon were watching the England youth team play a practice match. Everybody was discussing Tony Adams, this young lad who hadn't played in the first team but did soon after. He was outstanding. He had leadership then and everybody knew it. Bossing people. Talking to people. He was just a young lad. Oh my God, who's this boy? When we had to have a new captain, even at 21, he was a natural leader. It was a simple decision to make him captain.

Lee Dixon:
My education as a defender was all down to George. He taught me how to understand winning the ball back, to make that a pleasurable thing for me as opposed to it being a chore. It was like, wow. Clean sheets. Cor, we used to love clean sheets.

Nigel Winterburn:
I think the good thing about it was, even if we were winning by two or three and it was near the end of a game, if we conceded a goal that

used to eat me up all over the weekend. If we lost a game, you can ask my wife; I wouldn't go out. I hated it. I felt as if it was failure and that's what really hurt me. I look back now and think you've got to feel the hurt of the supporters who are working all week to pay to come and watch you play. You've got to feel the pain that they're feeling. I hated losing. I'd say all the back four did.

LEE DIXON:
The back four was purely George's idea. He wanted to build a side from a solid base. You had to do it every single day and at the time you don't appreciate it because training was boring. Same thing. Same thing. But it put us at an advantage – not all the time, because obviously we conceded goals. You can't stop goals sometimes because it is just brilliant play or a mistake – but in general the team knew what they were doing when we didn't have the ball. There's a lot of the game when you haven't got the ball so let's be good at that. We can be expansive when we've got it but when we haven't we have to constrict the space and win it back early. So the high press that everyone's talking about in modern day football, trying to win the ball back in the first few seconds? We did that in 1989. George wanted that: as soon as you lose the ball, the first player who's closest to the ball goes to close down and then you drag everybody with you and everybody has to go. If you see a player go, it doesn't matter what's happening behind you; everyone goes together. It's amazing how if you all go together, how easy it becomes to win the ball back. It is joked about with George having a piece of rope across the training ground tying us all together. That didn't happen but in the training sessions he put on we did imagine there's a piece of rope. So if Lee goes over there you know Tony has to come because I'm pulling him with me, and he's pulling Steve Bould with him and Nigel's having to come because he's got hold of the other end of the rope. So there are no gaps.

STEVE BOULD:
Training was certainly different. At Stoke it was 11 v 11, no coaching. I came to Arsenal and it was all individual unit work, constant, every day.

NIGEL WINTERBURN:
George used to come out with a ball. He would take the back four and we would be on a line on the edge of the box and he used to move around the pitch with the ball in his hand. Every position that he went into we would have to move individually and collectively to stay as a back four. We'd do it for half an hour, 45 minutes. The ball would not even be on the floor. You ask professional players to do that today. They would probably just laugh at him. The reason behind it was he wanted to keep the distances between each player exactly the same no matter where the ball went and he worked at it and he worked at it and then he would introduce the apprentices to play against us. He knew if he brought in the young kids they'd run everywhere. You were expected not to make a mistake. So you always got yourself into a good defensive position. If you show the winger inside, as we did a lot under George, you knew that the centre-half around the edge of the box was going to come out and take absolutely no prisoners whatsoever.

JOHN LUKIC:
It really was monotonous. Just going through it continually. It was long afternoons. We used to be up at London Colney, the five of us there. Everybody else had gone home to have a cup of tea and we were still out there. But it served us well I think from a defensive point of view.

GEORGE GRAHAM:
I absolutely loved it. The thing in the English game is that everybody thinks a defender just is a destroyer. Just loves the physical contact side

of the game. No! Definitely no. You've got to *think*. You've got to make decisions on that pitch and that tests if you're a good defender or a bad defender, not if you're going to win a tackle. When are you going to win a tackle? When do you sit back? When do you play offside? There's a lot of thought put into defending. Today's game could do with a lot more of it. I have nothing but admiration for my defenders. There were millions of sessions. Sometimes I would have the youth team take on the back four – the whole team. They wouldn't get a shot in.

We didn't man-mark. We covered space. Those back four were always linked together. If we push one of the full-backs forward the other three spread the width of the pitch, so really instead of a back four it would be an outstanding back three.

Alan Smith:

George would say in the morning, 'OK, lads, we're going to work on the back four today', and everyone would go, oh no, not again. We'd hardly get through. A shot would be an achievement. We were trying to break down this back four while the gaffer was organising them and they held such a good line and they were so in tune with each other after a bit that you had to make a perfect run and the ball had to be perfectly timed in order for you to get round the back of them. You'd say individually that's not the best right-back in Europe or the best left-back in Europe . . . But as a unit, they were by far the best rearguard I've seen so that just goes to show what can be achieved with hard work.

Tony Adams:

We worked as a unit and the unit was bigger and better than the individuals. Boring Arsenal? I took that as a compliment.

Paul Merson:

It was very groundhog day. In November I could tell you what I was doing on a Tuesday in March in four months' time. Every single day you knew what you were doing. But it worked a treat. We were Ashford & Simpson: we were 'Solid'.

NIGEL WINTERBURN:
We knew within our group that if we did our job the front players we had could excite the league. You could play it into Alan, he'd link up the play. Merse had individual ability. Brian Marwood was whipping sensational balls into the box. You'd got the driving runs of Mickey Thomas, who was as strong as an ox. Then we'd usually have Rocky out on the right-hand side with his ability to go past players. I always used to call it dancing.

LEE DIXON:
Up front we had magic Merse. He could do anything with a ball. Absolutely brilliant player, one of those enigmas. What's he done? How's he got past someone? He just used to run and balance and know where the gap was. And Smudge wasn't underrated at the club but outside was an underrated player. He was just brilliant. He did everything. I remember my dad saying to me, is Alan Smith right-footed or left-footed? I want somebody to say that about me one day. He scored some great left-footed shots and was brilliant in the air and his hold-up play was second to none. He wasn't particularly muscly but he was wiry and he had really sharp elbows. In training he was always catching you. You didn't want to mark him in training because he was bony. He'd sort of hit you with his knee. He was horrible to play against and a gentleman on the pitch.

ALAN SMITH:
Merse was my favourite strike partner. He was an unselfish person to have alongside you and such a skilful player as well. If you made a move he knew where you were and would try and find you with one of those little dinks. Brian Marwood was really important for me.

We built up a good understanding. He was one of those wingers that didn't need to beat a man, a much different style to Rocky on the other side. He was very clever at shifting the ball and just curling it round the full-back into the box with that left foot of his. Back then you didn't count assists but he would have had a lot of assists that year. He gave us great balance.

George Graham:
I always remember one team meeting and I said, 'Look, in an ideal situation in this club, I would like my back four to play until they're 30 at the top level. I want my midfield players to play until they're 28 and I want my front players to play until they're 26.' They all looked at me as if I was stupid. Why? Because my front boys are going to work harder than midfield and my midfield are going to work harder than my back four. They all looked at me as if I was crazy.

FOUR

The Team of the 80s

TONY ADAMS:
Liverpool were the Barcelona of the day. Winning everything, so renowned, they passed the ball so well they kept it. At Anfield most teams were beaten before you even went up there. I remember going up with the England team when I was 20 for Alan Hansen's testimonial. They absolutely destroyed us because the England team wasn't a team. Liverpool would just destroy you, make you feel very lonely and Anfield was an enormous place.

LEE DIXON:
Liverpool were the epitome of a brilliant, brilliant team. Every department of their team was special, with iconic players. They had the history to go with it. They had this aura about them that you don't get very often in football. I always felt that you were half a goal down against Liverpool before you even kicked off. Especially at Anfield. Alan Hansen was the one that stands out for me because I'm a defender. I used to look at him and think, his game is so easy. I want to play like that. I want to be him.

TONY ADAMS:
It was a conveyer belt of players in the Liverpool way. Central defenders. Goalkeepers. Right midfields. Right-backs. They went on and on producing players and recruiting brilliantly. John Toshack, Kevin Keegan, then Ian Rush.

NIGEL WINTERBURN:

You just have to go back and look through the scrapbooks. Look at the history. Liverpool were the team to beat. They had already won the league six times in the 80s by the start of the 88–89 season. They won the European Cup four times by then. It's the ultimate test, isn't it? Playing against the team that's so dominant. So powerful. Looking at the team-sheet. Looking at the players' names. What they've achieved in the past and then you're pitting yourself against them in real life. Real time. You want to try and make a statement. They're saying to you: show us what you've got. That's what we were trying to do. We were trying to beat the best. Liverpool were the best.

ALAN SMITH:

Going to Anfield was a big deal because hardly anybody got out of there alive. When I was with Leicester we were their bogey team. Once there was quite a lot of interest in me and the papers were going it's Ian Rush versus Alan Smith, it's a showdown. We lost 3–2, which isn't a bad result. I got two, Rushy got a hat-trick and they went, 'Rush wins the showdown.' I thought, that's a bit strong, I got two goals at Anfield.

ALAN DAVIES:

Liverpool always won the league and they always came to our ground and beat us and the thing about Liverpool was they played a different brand of football to anybody else. I remember them coming to our ground in the mid-80s and they won 2–0. Dalglish ran the game. I went to Anfield a couple of times. That really was an extraordinary experience. That was a heaving, packed ground and they were crammed in and the noise of the place shook. Whenever a Liverpool player had the ball Dalglish would appear and get it to his feet, and it was very unusual for a team to play into feet like that. They could because they had Dalglish. He was that good. He was the Messi of his day. He was better than anybody else and they were a formidable outfit. They were hard as nails. Jimmy Case was the most frightening footballer there ever was. Dalglish was nasty.

Liverpool won the league most of the time from the mid-70s to the mid-80s. Then they had a bit of a wobble and found themselves caught up by Everton, who had an outstanding team. So they went out and spent a fortune and they bought the two best players in the country, which was Peter Beardsley and John Barnes. In 87–88 they played the best football that anyone had ever seen in England. The best. No one played football like that at that time. The ball was on the floor all the time. It was fast. There was no one better than Beardsley. Barnes was fantastic. He was footballer of the year. He was unstoppable. They only lost two games. They should have won the Double but they somehow contrived to lose to Wimbledon in the FA Cup final. They couldn't play in the European Cup for reasons that are well known but they would have won it. They were amazing. They were winning every week. They were scoring three, four, five goals. They were the best team that anyone had ever seen.

NICK HORNBY:

It's a bit like that Gary Lineker line about the Germans. It was true of Liverpool. Football is a game where 22 men kick a ball around and then Liverpool win at the end. They won everything. A home defeat used to get on the news. Every now and again somebody would challenge them but the rest of the decade belonged to Liverpool and it felt like they were unbeatable. As a football fan it felt that you were in a parallel universe. How do you get to this place where teams like Liverpool win the league? It felt like Arsenal would never be able to cross the tracks. It wasn't like you ever thought, oh, it will happen one day.

Alan Davies:

Arsenal never got anywhere near the title. Nowhere near it. We were runners-up in 73. The highest position we ever had when I was going there as a kid was third in 1981, which was a freaky season when the title was duked out between Ipswich and Aston Villa. But there was something, there was a feeling that maybe we could do it in the 88–89 season. We really did have a side and we were top for quite a long time. We felt like we could do it. We had a League Cup tie against them at Anfield and we got a 1–1 draw and we felt like actually we're as good as they are now. We've got to this level. So it was all a matter of can you get it over the line?

Lee Dixon:

We played Liverpool a few times in the first half of the 88–89 season. Those games not only validated us as a team to ourselves but also to Liverpool. I think they realised we were a top team to play against. It gave us that confidence that all young players need.

Tony Adams:

We had five games against them during a ten-week period before Christmas as we had a couple of replays in the League Cup and a tournament to celebrate the centenary of the Football League as well as the league game at Highbury. There was one that felt particularly important. We drew with Liverpool at Anfield in the Littlewoods Cup. Rocky scored a great goal. You know that you can compete with the big boys and actually play them off the pitch. It gives you enormous confidence. They're not that terrifying all of a sudden. The psychological barrier has been broken.

Michael Thomas:

Liverpool were the greatest team we had ever seen but George gave us this feeling that if we played against them we could beat them. When we beat them in the Mercantile Trophy, which was for the centenary, we had no fear of them.

PAUL MERSON:
They did give us a real hiding, though, in the second replay in the League Cup at Villa Park. I scored early in that game and then we got ripped to shreds and I mean seriously ripped. I was embarrassed.

ALAN SMITH:
Then they came to Highbury in the league and we drew 1–1 and I scrambled in our goal. Everybody knew about Liverpool's ball-playing skills but they could mix it as well if they wanted to. There was always a few things said in the tunnel beforehand. Them shouting. Steve McMahon would shout one or two things. He called us bottlers at one stage after a match and you'll always remember that. Don't forget what he said. Let's show them this time. They were always great tussles. We were trying to reach their level so we were going to try and win the scrap. It was important to try and make a statement that we're not going to roll over.

DAVID O'LEARY:
If you're assembling a new team and you talk about going places, the teams you really want to test yourself against or get nearest to are the teams that you're trying to emulate. Liverpool were the ones that we all respected. But our team were not afraid. I'd look at them in the dressing room before the game and think, these lads want to go out there and play on the big stage against this team and not be in awe of them and believe that yeah, we can take this team on. I think we always felt we were getting nearer to them all the time.

89

Tony Adams:

Winning feels so much better and every time we lost it was a reminder. We had won the Littlewoods Cup against Liverpool in 1987 but losing the final against Luton in 88? You can learn so much by those experiences. Feel the pain. We don't want this next time.

FIVE

Sign of the Times

David Dein:

The 1980s was not a good time for football in England because there was hooliganism. There was trouble in the grounds, trouble outside and really television didn't want to know about football. In fact, there was one period during the 1980s when television actually pulled the plug on football. When you consider how much football we have on TV today, it's inconceivable to recall that for six months football was off the air.

Nick Hornby:

All that stuff about football being for yobs is complicated. There was a huge percentage of people who went to football in the 80s who wanted a fight and you had to have your wits about you and if you went to away games you had to be extremely careful. The authorities believed that home fans would want to stand in the home end and away fans would want to stand in the away end and that was all you needed to do to keep them apart and, of course, it didn't work out like that. Big teams would go in the home end and the mad lot were up the away end the other half of the time. So there was always a very febrile atmosphere. What happened after the Heysel disaster is the half that didn't want to fight started to drift away from the game. People who just wanted to go and watch a game and have no hassle decided it wasn't really worth it. The stadiums were old, not really safe.

I just loved it. There was something about the atmosphere that added intensity to an otherwise dull week. So there was nothing that could have kept me away, but I was getting aware of the fact that it wasn't such a smart thing to do. I remember being invited for dinner somewhere in Finsbury Park and this woman saying, 'Oh, do you know the street?' I said yeah, yeah and she said, 'Well how come?' I said, 'I walk down there a couple of times a week pretty much because I go to the football' and she said, 'No really, why?' Ha ha ha. She couldn't believe that anyone that she talked to about anything at all, politics or books or films, would go inside a football stadium.

Alan Davies:

People didn't go to football because there was fighting. Because it was disgusting. Because people were urinating everywhere. There was considerable bad language and that was what football was. It was just: if you like football, you like football and it was a bit sad. Socially, to be a football fan then was to be generally not treated very well. That was the general experience and you got treated worse and worse and worse. If you were an away fan you got treated particularly badly.

You were herded into horrible grounds with terrible facilities and the travel was an experience. Going on trains was quite fun, but you'd get the worst trains that were pulled out of some yard somewhere and labelled 'football special'. It was great to go to the big grounds because you'd seen them on TV. You wanted to see them for real. Anfield. Goodison Park is my favourite. Villa Park is amazing. Maine Road. But you'd quite often have to go through Crewe and when you got to Crewe there'd quite often be two or three football specials all in the same station. I remember once there was some banter with a train full of Wolves fans that got quite ugly. Once going back to the train station at Nottingham Forest there was some bloke just going around punching Arsenal fans. Just running up and punching them in the head and people saying, come on then. Walking to the station after a game it was the police you were frightened of. The police would throw you up against a bus shelter without a second thought. You were frightened of the police. You couldn't trust the police. If you saw something happening, you couldn't go to the police and say there's something happening because they'd say, bad luck.

I remember coming out of Stamford Bridge and they shut the road outside on the way down to Fulham Broadway station. They insist on having all the fans on the pavement queuing for the Tube even though the road is empty. So in the road there's a load of police horses and coppers standing about and on the pavement you're just hemmed in and I remember having my hands up against the shop window, a plate glass window, thinking, I'm going to go through this in a minute. Because I'm using all my strength not to be crushed right up against it. I come out the other end and there was a copper with a cap. I'm middle-class. I never had any fear of the police. I never had any dealings with the police. If I thought the police were misbehaving, I'd jolly well say so. I went up to this copper and I said, what's going on? You're crushing people against the shops. I've nearly gone through a window. He goes to me, 'Do you want to be nicked?'

Going away, it was the first time for me hearing any of these accents. I remember going to Anfield and hearing a programme seller and thinking, oh my God. What did he just say? You didn't speak to anyone and you were terrified of anyone asking you for the time or asking for a light.

NICK HORNBY:
I wrote in *Fever Pitch* that one of the first times I went to football I can remember someone shouting at one of the players, 'A hundred quid a week! A hundred quid a week!' in disgust and disbelief because he was earning 20 quid a week. So there's always been that mismatch. The really big thing that's changed in football is how much you pay

to get in. In the 80s the price of admission to the North Bank was never a factor in going to football. It would have been the same as a packet of fags or a couple of pints and everyone could afford to go. So there wasn't that sense of expectation in quite the same way. I don't think the fans felt owed in the way that they do now. If you're paying £1,000 for the cheapest season ticket you're going to feel let down all the time by players you know actually are substandard before the season even starts. Back then what the fans wanted for their not very much money was honesty and they got that from that team in particular. They worked their socks off and they were young and hopeful. David Rocastle, Michael Thomas, Paul Davis, Tony Adams, Paul Merson, the people who had come through from the youth team, were very loved. Even the players they bought for not very much money came from not very glamorous teams.

Alan Davies:

I was a season ticket holder on the North Bank and I'd go to away games when I could. Back then it was all terraces and there were quite a lot of fences. When Arsenal started to do well a lot of away fans would go, and the opening day of the 88–89 season we were at Plough Lane. Plough Lane was tiny. Wimbledon's old ground. The best view at Plough Lane was from inside the toilet, which was a Portakabin. So if you got to a urinal, there was a little window and from there you had a clear view of the whole pitch. So people would go in there and urinate for 45 minutes and then they'd come out, get a pie and go back in. So I saw quite a lot of the game in there. Out on the terrace you couldn't see much but we won 5–1 and it felt very significant that we'd done that. Because they weren't a bad side, Wimbledon. They'd won the cup the year before and they had some decent players. But we really took them to the cleaners.

AMY LAWRENCE:

The 1988–89 season was my first going away. It felt like a notable rite of passage, that you somehow proved your worth as a supporter by travelling, by being outnumbered in someone else's domain. At the back of the narrow terrace at Villa Park I accidentally kicked one of the line of policemen behind us by clicking a bad knee, which made my Dr. Marten boot catch him on the shin. Suddenly I felt a threatening hand on my shoulder, whose owner probably wouldn't have given me the benefit of the doubt had I not been a teenage girl. I recall going to the Baseball Ground, Derby's home, and searching for the ladies' in the away end at half-time only to find there wasn't one.

NICK HORNBY:

It felt actually much cooler to be supporting Arsenal than a lot of other teams. Arsenal felt quite a safe and tolerant place compared to watching teams where you knew that the fans gave black players fearful abuse. Arsenal had had black players for a few years by that stage. Viv Anderson, Chris Whyte, Raphael Meade. Brendon Batson was at Arsenal you know, right at the end of the 1960s and beginning of the 70s, and it felt like Arsenal were streets ahead actually in that way.

AMY LAWRENCE:

An incident at Goodison Park in 1989 remains seared on my mind. It was not known as particularly liberal-minded in those days but what we heard from the Everton fans was shocking. Arsenal played with Rocastle, Davis and Thomas, full of zest and invention in midfield, and Gus Caesar got a rare game in defence. When the team went ahead the response from the home support was to start a chant in repulsive language about (and I will leave the terminology to your imagination) shooting black people. The communal disgust from the away fans was obvious – manifested in lung-busting songs in honour of our players. The noise was angry and defiant as everyone bashed their wooden seats down on the frames in the seated section. Afterwards, hanging around the players' entrance in the hope of an autograph, I remember an exchange with piercing clarity. David Rocastle came out and an Evertonian, while asking for a signature, asked, 'Rocky, why don't you come and sign for a big club?' Rocky looked him in the eye and quick as a flash replied, 'What, and get shot?' before walking calmly off to the team bus.

Arsenal's crowd were not angels but it did feel more mixed, more cosmopolitan, than the sights and sounds encountered elsewhere at the time. There were always plenty of faces from various communities who were rooted in North London. Everyone could belong, which was not the case around football generally then. Although football was a male preserve it was not a big deal for a girl to take up position on the terraces – although you would have to be prepared to brush off 'while you're down there' comments if you ducked down to clamber underneath a crash barrier.

Dermot O'Leary (supporter):
I grew up in a very Irish, very Catholic family, pretty much all Arsenal fans, and it became linked with my identity. There was something very identifiable about the Clock End, which was sort of different to the North Bank as well. Possibly because you were so close to the away fans, there was a siege mentality about the Clock End and I just fell in love with Highbury. In terms of the demographic of our fan base, we are a very black club, we are a very Irish club, we are a very Greek club, we are a very Jewish club, and I loved that. Where I sit now I've got a High Court judge here and a plumber there and we're an all-sorts club really. I've always really been proud of it.

Paul Davis:
I did feel conscious when I started that I was probably the only black player in the first team squad. There were some older players that had

some jokes or some behaviour that I didn't really agree with. So I had a couple of run-ins. I actually confronted one of them. But other than that I didn't have any real issues at Arsenal. The fans at the club in general were fantastic. I didn't feel as though I wasn't welcome or there were any problems around my colour. Obviously playing other teams as a black player was horrendous sometimes. You would go to some of the grounds and be really singled out because of your colour. Places like Sunderland, Everton, West Ham, Chelsea; so that was a big thing at the time for me because that's something that you can't get away from.

Stamford Bridge was particularly tough for a black player back in the early 80s. To have 40,000 really having a go at you for your colour wasn't great but I was trying to work it all out and deal with it because you can't shut those things out. You can hear it. Then I saw one of their players, Paul Canoville, was warming up on the touchline and they were giving it to him and I thought, wow, that is really pretty strong. Because I couldn't imagine if I was playing at Highbury and I got that from my own supporters how I would have been able to deal with that. I felt for Paul Canoville. Consequently he wasn't able to deal with it. His career and his life went on a different trail.

MICHAEL THOMAS:
I grew up at Chelsea from the age of 11 and I was there when Paul Canoville was. I was in the stands. I felt the abuse. I was only little, a teenager, and I'm seeing this. I remember when John Barnes came along the abuse he got. That was tough and that was part of my big decision – when I left Chelsea and came to Arsenal. Arsenal were very stable and when we played in the first team with Dave Rocastle we thrived on it. Intense. Playing at Millwall, West Ham, Newcastle. Everton had no one and when we played at Everton we used to get so much stick. We didn't care. We loved it. We just enjoyed the fight in us, to put one over on these people.

89

Paul Davis:

I felt a big responsibility. I took it on myself to think that for the younger guys coming through I know what they're going to face and I want to be there supporting them if they need that support. I just wanted to help the younger guys to feel comfortable in the team. Michael Thomas and Dave Rocastle came from South London, which is where I came from. I felt a bit of a bond towards them because I knew their backgrounds, the areas they grew up in, and they did turn to me for support, advice or just watching, seeing what I was doing. It's quite nice because they used to call me Pops. I was a little bit older than them so they saw me as their father figure within the football world.

Mickey grew up a couple of miles from where I grew up. Mickey loved his football. Loved his flair. He wanted to play. He wanted to go forward. He wanted to show what he could do. He was hard to get to know; he would think about things very carefully before saying things freely. David on the other hand he was always bubbly. He was always somebody that wanted to be in the middle of what was going on. Had a lot to say. He had a great smile. He could do anything. He could dribble, he could defend, his mental approach to every game was: there's nothing that we can't do here. We'd be 2–0 down and we could still win it 3–2 as far as Dave was concerned. There was nothing unachievable. He had a fantastic mindset. Between the two of them they were great lads to be around. Fantastic enthusiasm for football, for Arsenal. Together they came into the squad with something new. Inner city boys.

Ian Wright:

Seeing that was massive. When we were growing up in the 70s and early 80s you had Cyrille Regis, Brendon Batson, Laurie Cunningham, Viv Anderson breaking through, but in the main it wasn't happening. In black communities you would support the teams with black players in them. You would naturally gravitate to that. West Brom. Luton. When you fast forward and Rocky and Mickey and Davo were a focal point, right amongst it, and doing well, it is very inspiring stuff. This is where my Arsenal allegiance came from. They gave people a chance. They gave my little mate a chance.

Michael Thomas:
Obviously being a black player I used to look at all the great teams at the time and think, how many black players have they got in the team? Spurs had Chris Hughton, Crooksy. Fantastic. Used to look at Liverpool. You know, they had no black players but then Howard Gayle came on to the scene. Man United, Paul McGrath. Paul Davis came through at Arsenal while I was only a schoolboy. He lives round the corner from me. I used to walk through the bus garage, then go to the sweet shop and Paul was there in his sky-blue Escort. He plays for Arsenal. It was like wow. To this day I still look up to Paul.

Alan Davies:
I do remember Paul Davis punching Glenn Cockerill. It's difficult to talk about because to this day none of them will say what was said. He was my personal favourite player and one of the reasons was because he was prepared to do that and he would never say why. I thought: that shows a lot of class. But something had happened because he never punched anyone else in his whole career. David Rocastle and Michael Thomas and Paul Davis were not to be trifled with and we loved them for that and Davis was the most mild-mannered, a quietly unassuming but tough player. It was unexpected that he did what he did.

Lee Dixon:
I remember he was on *News at Ten*. This was sensational, the first time a player had got done by trial by television. It was just so out of

character for him to do something like that. We all knew something had happened for him to do that. Because Davo was tough. He would look after himself. How he never played 50 games for England I will never know. He was just a sublime footballer. But he suffered because of such a long ban. Nine games then, it was a record, and he struggled to get back into the team that season.

PAUL DAVIS:
I think I am calm generally speaking but I can look after myself as the guys in training will know. Any footballer that gets to that level has something deep inside them that's going to do something ultimately if it comes to it. That was my moment where I saw some injustice going on, happening to me, and the referee didn't see it and wasn't taking any action against it so basically for me I felt I was being trampled on, elbowed, stood on and there was nothing, there was no retribution being taken by the referee in terms of yellow cards for Glenn Cockerill. I took it upon myself to pay some retribution, which isn't the right thing to do.

I hit him in the face and he went down. This was off the ball. The ref didn't see it but obviously Glenn Cockerill is on the floor. The game comes to a stop and he gets attended to by the physios. Everybody's thinking, who has hit him? Why is he on the floor? I'm about 10 or 15 yards away. The referee doesn't see it so he doesn't book me or send me off and the game goes on. At this stage we're winning the game but all their players are after me. We got a penalty. As we were taking the penalty someone came up behind me and gave me one whack behind my back on the back of my legs. To be fair to George I think he recognised what was going on and he just pulled me off.

GARY LEWIN:
The Southampton physio had two players to treat at the time as someone else was down and I went on to treat Glenn. I said, 'I think

he's broken his jaw.' He said, 'Nah, he's all right,' threw some water on his face and Glenn carried on. We had an X-ray machine at the club at the time and after the game it transpired he had broken his jaw in two places.

PAUL DAVIS:
I remember coming out of the FA hearing feeling very, very, very despondent. Nine matches is a long, long time to be banned and £3,000 was a lot of money back then. The fact that I missed those games had an effect on me. I would have loved to have played more games in this particular season but it is what it is. That was probably the hardest situation in football for me to deal with personally because it did change my footballing career. I was on the verge of the England set-up at that point and after that my England situation tailed off.

SIX

Oh What Fun It Is to See The Arsenal Win Away

ALAN SMITH:

We started the season at glamorous Plough Lane. The dressing rooms were about five foot by five foot. You got crammed in there. The pitch wasn't the best. The old stands. They had John Fashanu up front and the Crazy Gang and you had to compete with them physically. We conceded the first goal as John Fashanu snuck behind Steve Bould on his debut. Tony said afterwards, 'Everyone's thinking, God, who's this we've bought? He's just let his man go and score!' But we came back and I got a hat-trick, which I was delighted about. We were up and running. I always remember being interviewed by the press in the little poky corridor just outside the dressing room. 'Alan, do you think you'll be top scorer this season?' 'I don't think so. I'm a back-to-goal kind of player. I'm not really one of those who's going to get 25 or 30 goals.'

LEE DIXON:

Our second away game in 89 was White Hart Lane. I wasn't ready for what happened. I was just minding my own business putting my shin pads on and getting ready to go out and I looked up and a couple of the players are looking at me across the dressing room. I'd been there a while now so we're mates. Tony Adams was staring at me. Paul Davis was too from the other side of the room. I was looking down at my kit thinking, have I put my shorts on back to front or something, because it was a bit of a weird look and then we all kind

'It's hard to explain how or why but everything felt brilliant that day. Standing outside the coach convoy in the blazing sunshine. So much naive hope in the air.' Amy Lawrence (Spot the author in the photo)

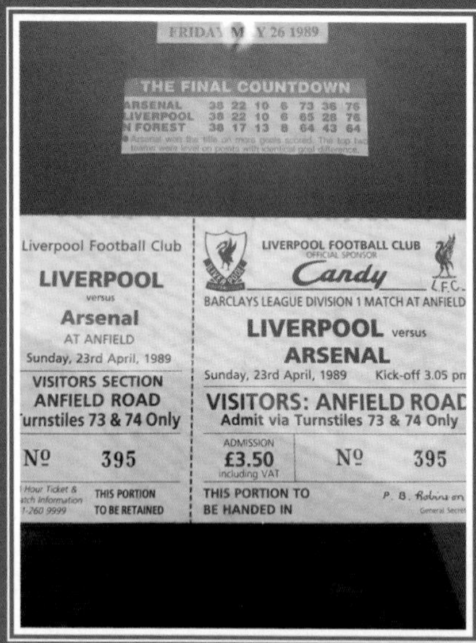

'There was no room on the bench. It was suggested the safest place to go was in the section where the Arsenal fans were segregated from the Liverpool fans. Footballers weren't as fussy then. We just followed orders.' Niall Quinn

'We were all lined up with these flowers and when we'd done our wave I remember sprinting off to the Kop end. There was a lady near the corner flag and I ran over and gave them to her. I remember the emotion of actually passing the flowers over.' Lee Dixon

'There was always a great atmosphere at Anfield. It was doubly so that night. It was just charged.' Alan Smith

‘I might be built like it but I’m not really a physical person. I like to nick balls and try and win balls but not that way. I used to like watching Rocky smash into people. Ha ha ha. It was good to see him and Tony and Bouldy. Oh, they were immense.’ Michael Thomas

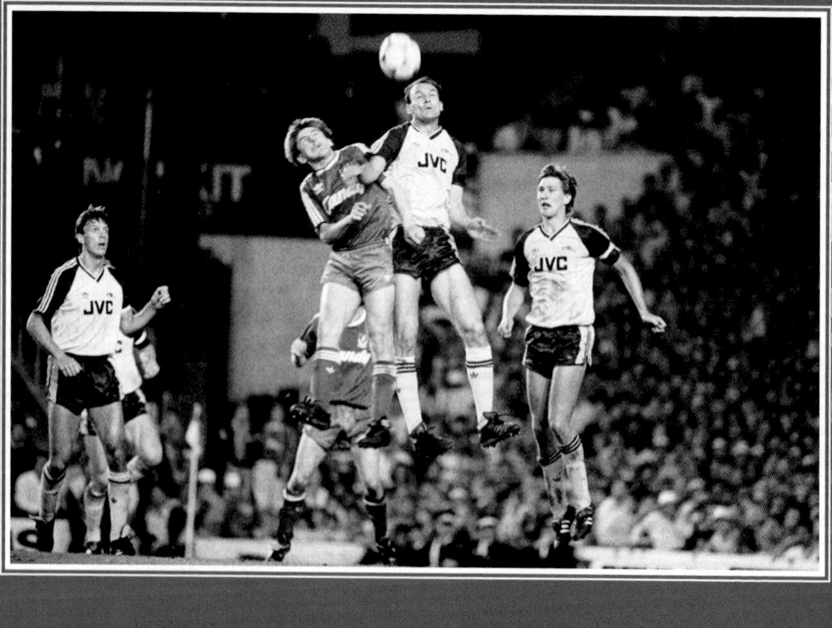

'We'd practised that free-kick so much in training and it had never worked in a match. Nigel swings it in with his left foot. Then me, Bouldy and Tony are lined up. I lost my man and got my head to the ball. I followed through, bumped into Steve Staunton and swivelled round to go to the crowd. Ah! Our section going absolutely ballistic. Oh my God.' Alan Smith

'I'm thinking now, this is my time. I'm going to score this. Ray Houghton was so close. I had no idea he was that close. It is scary. My heart beats even now with the tension every time I see it.' Michael Thomas

'If there's one player in the whole of the team that you would want to go through one on one with the keeper with a minute to go when he's just missed a sitter ten minutes before, I would say Mickey Thomas. Because if he did miss he wouldn't give a shit.' Paul Merson

‘I’m off. It hasn’t even gone in the net. Whoomph. Straight across the goal. I’m already celebrating.’ Nigel Winterburn

'It was nice to be a part of history in the making. It meant so much to us all. We fought together, cried together and this one was obviously a big one – to win it and to feel we were all part of it. It's a brotherhood. Nothing ever better for me.' Michael Thomas

PHOTOGRAPH CREDITS

Page 1. Tony West. Page 2. Top left: Peter Antonioni. Top right: Mark Leech, Offside Sports Photography. Bottom: ITV broadcast, 26 May 1989. Page 3. Tony West. Page 4. Top: Mark Leech, Offside Sports Photography. Bottom: Bob Thomas Sports Photography/Getty Images. Page 5. Top: Tony West. Bottom: Mark Leech, Offside Sports Photography. Page 6. Top: Mark Leech, Offside Sports Photography. Page 6 Bottom. Action Images. Page 7. Top: Mark Leech, Offside Sports Photography. Bottom: Doug Poole/Darren Epstein. Page 8. Doug Poole/Darren Epstein.

of stood up. Mickey Thomas had a little glance and Dave Rocastle is looking down at me. I just thought, I'll ask what's going on. But I didn't have to ask them because then they had me up against a wall before we went out saying: 'It's the North London derby. You're a northerner. You don't really know what this is all about and we just want you to know that you've got to play well today and if you don't you'll be in trouble.' Tottenham away seemed to be the one that everybody wanted to play in.

ALAN SMITH:

The boys that had already played in some derbies would talk about some of the previous matches. They would always bring up that famous 1987 League Cup semi-final at White Hart Lane, when they were advertising for Wembley tickets at half-time and how the boys were fired up in the dressing room because they could hear the announcement. We couldn't have wished for anything better at the start of the season than winning there. I remember Gazza losing his boot and then kicking the hoardings.

TONY ADAMS:

We wanted to win – sometimes more against Tottenham than the other clubs. It was normal I think. We were driven. We were passionate. We were strong and we liked the feeling of winning better than losing and I think it becomes a drug.

The new boys slipped into the culture of the club quite well, being northerners and all that. They were naturals. Lee, Bouldy, Kevin Richardson. Hard-working lads. Working-class boys. Very similar to what we were in the East End of London. We had good pre-seasons. We had good end of seasons. We had good weekends. We had a good Tuesday club. On the pitch and off the pitch we worked hard and they fitted in very nicely. But if they didn't have the talent to back it up I think we would have quite easily knocked them sideways and put them into

89

touch. Dicko and Nigel were flying up and down the flanks and Bouldy was so solid, a classical Jack Charlton central defender. They had the talent.

Alan Davies:

We'd go to places and batter teams, which is nice if you're in the away end because if you're three up with 20 minutes to go it's a proper party. It's noisy. It's funny. There's a lot of songs. There's a lot of abuse. The home end is emptying – the more it empties the better it gets. It is really exuberant. There is nothing quite to compare. Everyone's together. It's loud. I remember winning 4–1 at Forest and Tony Adams crashed in a corner, ended up in the net. Adams was a big part of it. There was just that drive from the back. He was a phenomenon. He was not going to give up on any ball at any time and there was a real feeling of something happening.

Tony Adams:

I loved it away. There was something special about the away supporters of Arsenal for that period as well. Towards the end of one season we went up to Man City and got beat 3–0 and they were doing the conga round the stadium. Well, there were a lot of other bad things in football: gangs, fights and this type of thing. But there was a camaraderie with the away supporters of most clubs in those days. It was really enjoyable when you go into the lion's den, someone else's home, and turn them over. You'd go to your fans at the end of the game and it felt so brilliant. I always relished those encounters and those challenges. We rolled up our sleeves and won most of the time. The feeling with the supporters was reciprocated. We drunk with them. We went out with them. We socialised with them as well as playing for them. It was very much one family at that period.

90

JOHN LUKIC:
Going away was more intimidating then because football stadiums now are pretty generic. You could be anywhere. If you didn't have the colours you could be in any stadium and you wouldn't have a clue. In those days, everything was close. On top of you. Right next to the pitch. I was a lot closer to the fans than most people were, so you got everything that was coming your way in terms of verbal abuse and all the other bits and bobs. You certainly couldn't be a shrinking violet. But football grounds have characters and as a player if you are going to Millwall or Old Trafford or Anfield you have to be big enough as a group of players to not succumb.

For any championship-winning team away form has got to be spot on because your home form takes care of itself. Away form is what wins you things. We were pretty formidable. Everywhere we went the opposition knew that they were going to be in for a game. We went to Nottingham Forest and it was live on TV and we scored four goals against a top team managed by Brian Clough.

NIGEL WINTERBURN:
When you produce that sort of performance it don't half make you feel good after. In a way you're putting down a statement. Not only to the team that you've beaten but to the rest of the league.

GEORGE GRAHAM:
The boys developed fantastic camaraderie. That was important. I learned that from Arsenal when we did the Double in 70–71. You had to have a team spirit. You had to have it all-for-one.

LEE DIXON:
We got to the stage where we were looking at the league a little bit more carefully. We felt in the dressing room there was a bit of a change. George emphasised the importance of the festive period,

with a series of games in such a short period of time. You can tip one way or the other very quickly and we were conscious of that. We won 3–2 at Charlton on Boxing Day and 3–0 at Villa Park on New Year's Eve and suddenly we went above Norwich, who had been the pace-setters and we were top.

STEVE BOULD:
They had the old tradition at the club that every week in the Marble Halls they used to pin up the league table within the inner circle. Very old-fashioned. We used to go there on a Tuesday and you'd see it up on the wall. It was the first time I'd ever seen my club top of the league and it was surreal. Completely mad. George promised it would happen, and it did.

PAUL MERSON:
To go top of the league is a big thing. Especially as Liverpool hadn't started too well and were quite out of the equation at that point. They were fifth in the table, nine points behind us when we went top for New Year. They weren't the team who were chasing us down so you start thinking, we've got a chance here. They're nowhere near us so who's the team that's going to be a threat to us?

LEE DIXON:
Make no mistake I told everybody. Top of the league. I was Lee Dixon of Stoke, Burnley, Chester, Bury. Now all of a sudden I was top of the First Division. It was a relatively new experience for all of us. That was my first full season in the First Division. Nigel had come from Wimbledon the year before. Bouldy was at Stoke with me. It didn't last long, though, because as soon as you go into training George is like, 'I don't want anyone looking at the tables.' You don't want to say too much as you don't want to jinx it.

NIGEL WINTERBURN:
I always looked in the papers. It's a great position to be in in the league. We had some sensational results away from home. We won 3–1 at Goodison Park in January. Kevin Richardson scored at his old club. He was my best pal when he came. Because he lived 150 yards away we travelled into training a lot together. Mr Moaner. There was always something wrong. Never anything right for Kev but he just did his job very simply and intercepted all the tackles. You find out much more about a player when he's playing away from home at a big ground. When you've got 40,000 people and a large majority hate you, probably 2–2,500 supporting you, you get to find out about individual players and a team's character. It sums up our characters within the team and the collective character as a group of players that we didn't fear anyone anywhere. When you have big wins away from home you're making the rest of the league look at you.

ALAN SMITH:
Everton away stands out. I just remember the end of the game the Goodison faithful clapping us off and as a player that sticks with you. We'd not only won, we'd played some really good football and for them to appreciate what they'd just seen gave us even more confidence. We all said in the dressing room, ooh, did you hear that?

TONY ADAMS:
Then we went to the Den. We didn't know the referee was miked up for a documentary. I had a goal disallowed but it was over the line. Looking back, I loved the way he told me off. Typical. Bless him. 'Mr Adams, stand up.' But he's not a cheat. He just made a mistake and we're all human. But in those days unjustified anger was a biggy. It was over the line. I was fuming.

Alan Smith:

The ref, David Elleray, was a schoolmaster and he refereed like that. 'Don't talk back to me, young man.' He was very strict.

Lee Dixon:

I remember seeing the television programme afterwards. It was just hilarious. But we didn't know. They should've told us but there was a breakdown of communication somewhere. To this day I don't know whose fault that was. Nobody's owning up to that one. But it was quite obvious when you see the footage of Tony Adams when the goal was disallowed and hear his language that he didn't know. But I think it epitomised the spirit of the team. The fact that we had goals disallowed and we came back into that game and won the game.

Tony Adams:

What I really remember about this game was when I was in the bath with Dave O'Leary after the match in the old Den. We both looked at each other and David went, 'I think we'll win the league. When you can come to places like this and grind out results, it might have just won us the league.' We had lots of games to go but I'll always remember that. In the bath that day he was convinced we had a hell of a chance. It is interesting I'm still holding on to that memory, to reflect on that 30 years later. It's a powerful moment. He had never won a league and he was getting feelings – maybe this is it. But I was so young and naive to think, well why can't we win it? What's stopping us? Why can't we win every game that we ever play in?

Lee Dixon:

There always seemed to be controversy attached to the team somewhere regardless of the football. George would have a crisis meeting saying, right, everyone's waiting for us to get beat. I remember at London Colney we used to come out and there was a big wall with some benches where you put your boots on. We were almost lined up against this wall ready to be shot from George and he used to come out and have his little piece of paper with his set-pieces on and he'd start banging it on his hand saying, everyone's waiting for us to fall again. But we're not going to. This is The Arsenal. This is where we link arms and be strong. He always seemed to be able to rally the troops. We took that mentality on to the pitch.

ALAN SMITH:
George would give you a hard time. He'd bollock the lads in training, half-time, full-time, on a match day. So once he's gone you'd all have a little laugh and joke about it and as a group you do need that. We had a great team spirit at the time. We were really together. There was never a dull moment in the dressing room.

LEE DIXON:
I remember thinking at one point, we're going to win this and I think that was probably the day where we started having a wobble. We lost at Coventry and then at Highbury we lost against Nottingham Forest and dropped points against Charlton. George tried to get us to keep our focus but it's not easy. It was like, oh, what's going on? It was all unravelling and we hadn't got the experience to deal with it. We weren't Alan Hansen.

NIGEL WINTERBURN:
We got annihilated by Nottingham Forest at home. George decided to try something different. No one was going to question it. But I suppose it takes some belief as a manager to change tactics – not only am I making the right decision but also I need to convince the players. I'm going to change my back four and convince them that our style of play is going to be the way forward.

George Graham:

We were always famed for having the famous 4–4–2 but with a very important couple of away games coming up towards the end of the season I decided to try a new system, which didn't really go down well with the players at the time. But I knew how important it was. I'd done a lot of work with my staff on how we were going to beat Liverpool because they were the major threat. I fancied playing a back three. I was very impressed with John Barnes on the left, who was sensational, one of the best players in the country. Ray Houghton was on the right, who I was a big fan of; in fact, I tried to get him to join Arsenal.

I thought about it and thought about it. We'll push Lee Dixon tight because you don't want to let John Barnes get the ball. You have got to be on top of him all the time. It was the same on the left with Nigel pushing in on Ray Houghton. We wanted to eliminate these two because the centre-forwards, Ian Rush and John Aldridge, were great goal-scorers. We had to stop where the danger was coming from by trying to nullify it from the wing positions. Then our three at the back would look after their two strikers. It was as simple as that. When we've got the ball we have three defenders and the two wide boys push on and become midfield players. When we lose the ball then they retreat and make it into a five if need be.

That was the plan but I don't think the boys were very keen on it because we were doing well in the league with a back four and they think, why are we changing? I could feel it in the response that I got but still, that's the way I decided to go and Old Trafford gave us the perfect game to try it out. I don't think they were very keen when I introduced it. But the idea was to tackle two away games which were really, really important for us.

At the training ground I could hear the mumblings. I think it was Tony Adams who spoke up about it. He said, 'Boss, we're doing well. Everything's working well. The back four is really successful. Why do you want to change it?' I said, 'Because we've got to think bigger than that. We've got an opportunity to win the league. If we just tweak here and tweak there to improve the team we have to do it.'

LEE DIXON:
I always had 100 per cent belief in George knowing what he was doing. I was in. It's like looking up at your dad when you come home from school and he says, right, we're doing this tonight, and you go, OK, because it must be right. George earned the respect from the players. We'd jump through walls for him. We'd certainly play a different way. OK, I'm wing-back. I'll just run up and down all day long.

DAVID O'LEARY:
Top managers make the right calls at the right time. George threw the gauntlet down and the players relished it in that way. I don't think it was a system that was going to stay for ever but he felt that time of the season he could change things up a little bit to freshen the team up or give it some sort of a different focus. It was a big call to make at a big stadium. I thought to myself, as a back five we'd be able to handle this fine at Old Trafford. Let's see what the rest can do further up but don't worry about us.

STEVE BOULD:
It was revolutionary from George's point of view because every day's training was back four, back four, back four, back four, back four, and then he threw this back three in and we all thought, wow, that's a move. But I think it suited us. Dave O'Leary was great as a sweeper and Tony and I could get tight and tackle and close down.

JOHN LUKIC:
The change came out the blue. It shows the manager had huge belief in his players to be able to do that. Because had he not had any faith

in the defensive unit it would have been suicidal. He certainly paid respect to the players by doing that.

ALAN DAVIES:
I remember Brian Glanville writing about it in a very disparaging way. This greatly respected football writer was a lover of Italian football and the idea that you could play with two hard-nosed defenders and one elegant sweeper. But this wasn't what Arsenal were doing. They were just playing three centre-backs. O'Leary came in and Brian Glanville thought it was misguided and catastrophic and it was going to be the end of the title. It was a big mistake. You've got a team that works. Why are you changing it now? It's a terrible error. But it turned out not to be an error because it freed up Dixon and Winterburn to go and play in midfield and really what we had then was a 3–4–3 when we had the ball. It just worked. It was smart and it was about getting the best people on the pitch and utilising O'Leary's experience. O'Leary was calm and it was a good thing to have at the back. He brought that. It was an interesting way to use him. I thought it was very clever.

TONY ADAMS:
I was happy because they're both fantastic players, David and Bouldy, and our full-backs were amazing offensive players, magnificent at getting forward. I think it was more their strength than defending at that point in their careers. It made sense.

ALAN SMITH:
Not surprisingly we worked hard on it in training. It wasn't something he sprung on us on a Friday. We'd work on shape. We all thought, why is he doing this? But he had Liverpool in mind and in the meantime it worked OK at Old Trafford.

JOHN LUKIC:
That was an interesting game. It finished 1–1 and Tony scored at both ends. I remember the equalising goal was late on in the game and it came off Tony's shin, looped up over my head and I do remember thinking to myself, this is not going to end very well. I just got a hand to it and because it was so wet couldn't get any purchase on the ball at all.

TONY ADAMS:
The only thing I was bothered about in this system was I had to play on the left side. I was on my left foot. At that point I kept on putting it in the stand. I remember Alex Ferguson on the sideline. 'Show him the left foot! He can't kick it with his left foot.' I actually put one in my own goal. So I blamed George. You should never have played a back five and I should never have swung at it and looped the ball over Lukey's head and I should never have been a donkey and all my problems would have been fine.

ALAN DAVIES:
We all loved Tony. Tony was talked about from a very young age as being a big prospect and he made his debut against Sunderland when he was 17 and he made a mistake and we lost and he seemed really ungainly and scrawny and skinny. But everyone talked very warmly of him and he made a big impression early and he got in the England team age 20. I remember him saying they give you two shirts: one to keep and one to swap, and he kept them both. He was patriotic. Lionhearted. He was an impressive character. But he'd gone away to the European Championships with England in the summer of 88 and England had played really badly and he'd had his trousers pulled down by Marco van Basten. Van Basten was perhaps the best player in the world at that time apart from maybe Maradona. Adams came back a bit chastened from that experience. He was Arsenal captain

and, it transpired, drinking a lot. We didn't know about any of that. But he comes back from that having had that experience and because he'd been made to look bad by Van Basten, he's a target for Tottenham fans, Chelsea fans, United fans, everybody. They want him to fail now. The *Mirror* did a splash on the back page and put donkey ears on him. The donkey chant wasn't exclusively for Adams. Eeyore, Eeyore from the away end was any time, anyone. Air kick. Miskick. Do something rubbish. You'd get a donkey chant. The *Mirror* pinned it on Tony Adams. Made him the donkey and it felt very unjust. It was just one of many things in Tony Adams's career that he'd bounce back from.

PAUL MERSON:
I lived about ten minutes from the training ground. Coming back from Old Trafford Tony asked, 'Any chance of staying at yours and coming to that pub you go in?' Because we wouldn't have got back till half ten so the pubs were nearly shutting, but the bloke in the local always used to give us afters. I said, yeah, all right. I'd just moved in. Brand new one-bedroomed house. I rang up my girlfriend at the time and asked her to put the sofa bed out for Tony; we're going to go to the Rose & Crown. We get in about four in the morning. Next day the missus wakes me up. She's been downstairs. Tony's still asleep. She's got the paper. Donkey Adams. Headlines. I thought, oh my God. She said, 'Are you going to tell him?' I didn't want to. I thought I'd better let him buy it at the garage. The amount of stick he took for that was bordering on pathetic. He'd done nothing wrong that day. It was ridiculous.

LEE DIXON:
We kind of knew he'd be OK with it because it was Tony. He was a big character, George used to call him the Colossus. He absolutely loved what he stood for. The way he, at such a young age, was captaining the side.

David O'Leary:
I'd seen Adams grow up at the club. I used to watch the youth team and I'd see what young players are coming through and he was always this young kid who had this way about him. I'd come in on a Monday morning and he'd be this big apprentice on the side and go 'All right, David? How's the wife and kids? Did you have a good weekend?' And I thought, who is this? But that was his way. He had great determination, willpower, steel about him. A leader.

Lee Dixon:
Having spoke to him now, knowing the clean and sober Tony Adams, you know he's a vulnerable human being. Back then I think part of his problems was all that stuff he was carrying around. We thought, yeah he's fine. He's Tony. He'd come in sometimes a bit worse for wear on a Thursday and wouldn't do much training on a Friday and then we'd play Everton at home on a Saturday and he'd be awful. Me and Bouldy and Nigel would be cleaning up after him, last-ditch tackles, and Tony would be like, 'Oh, sorry, lads.' Then at the end of the game, a minute to go, the announcer would go, 'And today's man of the match is Tony Adams!' We'd all think, are you kidding me? The crowd loved him. The sponsors loved him. Everybody loved Tony because he was just this amazing big strong Arsenal captain. The weight of the world was on his shoulders at the time and Tony played hard, drank hard off the pitch. He had a lifestyle that the lads didn't know an awful lot about because he'd go off and he'd go on these binges. I read his book and it's a fascinating insight into him. I thought I knew him and realised I didn't know him at all.

In a successful team striving to achieve something, if you perceive somebody to be all right then that's all right. You move on to who else needs looking after. Nobody really tells you how they are feeling or who they are as a person. It doesn't happen in football

89

because it's a very testosterone-driven situation. You don't show a weakness to anybody. It's sometimes quite difficult to deal with because you're not all right most of the time because of the pressure.

TONY ADAMS:
It is well documented now but in those days I didn't feel things and I just got drunk really. It hurt deeply but I didn't allow myself to feel. I got drunk at the drop of a hat so that was my way of dealing with things. So all those horrific feelings about humiliation just fuelled my drinking and self-loathing and confirmed my self-destruct button really. But that's another story. At that time I used to say, well, as long as they're having a go at me, at least they're not having a go at Rocky or the players that are doing the damage. But it was hurting. I've not heard it for a long time now. I went to a funeral I suppose about seven years ago in Hornchurch and a cabbie just jumped out. 'Oi, Donkey!' I think that was the last time I heard it. But there you go.

SEVEN

96

15 April 1989
In Memoriam

John Alfred Anderson	62 years
Colin Mark Ashcroft	19 years
James Gary Aspinall	18 years
Kester Roger Marcus Ball	16 years
Gerard Bernard Patrick Baron	67 years
Simon Bell	17 years
Barry Sidney Bennett	26 years
David John Benson	22 years
David William Birtle	22 years
Tony Bland	22 years
Paul David Brady	21 years
Andrew Mark Brookes	26 years
Carl Brown	18 years
David Steven Brown	25 years
Henry Thomas Burke	47 years
Peter Andrew Burkett	24 years
Paul William Carlile	19 years
Raymond Thomas Chapman	50 years
Gary Christopher Church	19 years
Joseph Clark	29 years
Paul Clark	18 years

Gary Collins	22 years
Stephen Paul Copoc	20 years
Tracey Elizabeth Cox	23 years
James Philip Delaney	19 years
Christopher Barry Devonside	18 years
Christopher Edwards	29 years
Vincent Michael Fitzsimmons	34 years
Thomas Steven Fox	21 years
Jon-Paul Gilhooley	10 years
Barry Glover	27 years
Ian Thomas Glover	20 years
Derrick George Godwin	24 years
Roy Harry Hamilton	33 years
Philip Hammond	14 years
Eric Hankin	33 years
Gary Harrison	27 years
Peter Andrew Harrison	15 years
Stephen Francis Harrison	31 years
David Hawley	39 years
James Robert Hennessy	29 years
Paul Anthony Hewitson	26 years
Carl Darren Hewitt	17 years
Nicholas Michael Hewitt	16 years
Sarah Louise Hicks	19 years
Victoria Jane Hicks	15 years
Gordon Rodney Horn	20 years
Arthur Horrocks	41 years
Thomas Howard	39 years
Thomas Anthony Howard	14 years
Eric George Hughes	42 years
Alan Johnston	29 years
Christine Anne Jones	27 years

Gary Philip Jones	18 years
Richard Jones	25 years
Nicholas Peter Joynes	27 years
Anthony Peter Kelly	29 years
Michael David Kelly	38 years
Carl David Lewis	18 years
David William Mather	19 years
Brian Christopher Matthews	38 years
Francis Joseph McAllister	27 years
John McBrien	18 years
Marian Hazel McCabe	21 years
Joseph Daniel McCarthy	21 years
Peter McDonnell	21 years
Alan McGlone	28 years
Keith McGrath	17 years
Paul Brian Murray	14 years
Lee Nicol	14 years
Stephen Francis O'Neill	17 years
Jonathon Owens	18 years
William Roy Pemberton	23 years
Carl William Rimmer	21 years
David George Rimmer	38 years
Graham John Roberts	24 years
Steven Joseph Robinson	17 years
Henry Charles Rogers	17 years
Colin Andrew Hugh William Sefton	23 years
Inger Shah	38 years
Paula Ann Smith	26 years
Adam Edward Spearritt	14 years
Philip John Steele	15 years
David Leonard Thomas	23 years
Patrick John Thompson	35 years

Peter Reuben Thompson	30 years
Stuart Paul William Thompson	17 years
Peter Francis Tootle	21 years
Christopher James Traynor	26 years
Martin Kevin Traynor	16 years
Kevin Tyrrell	15 years
Colin Wafer	19 years
Ian David Whelan	19 years
Martin Kenneth Wild	29 years
Kevin Daniel Williams	15 years
Graham John Wright	17 years

THE END OF INNOCENCE

by Laura Lawrence (Sheffield Wednesday supporter), first published 15 April 2012

I've been reading *Hillsborough: The Truth* by Phil Scraton. Truth is subjective and personal according to a person's agenda. Even in the preface Phil Scraton says, 'I was determined that the disaster itself and the investigations which followed should be subjected to external, independent scrutiny.' Scraton is an academic. He is also a Liverpool supporter, so can his truth be objective?

I was ten years old on 15 April 1989. In a novel, that would make me an unreliable narrator of a story, but I can only tell you the truth of what I saw that day.

I'd spent the morning colouring in scraps of paper that my mum had given me. I loved making things. Today I was making a banner to hang in my bedroom window. I coloured the scraps in red and white, which would normally have been a travesty in my family but today I had decided I was supporting the local team. Today I was a Nottingham Forest fan.

As I hung the banner from my window I watched the cars pulling up and parking on the street as they would on any other match day. In the distance I could see the blue of the South Stand between the new leaves on the chestnut tree across the road and a sea of red flowing down the street. A minibus pulled up on the junction of the road and out jumped a rabble of happy and vocal Liverpool fans. I can remember feeling disappointed because I'd made my banner and I hadn't seen any Forest fans to wave it at.

When I went downstairs Des Lynam was on *Grandstand*. Des

was always there on a Saturday in our house. Today was no exception. In fact Hillsborough was on the TV so the draw was all the more exciting. Between Des and the buzz on the street outside I remember being enthralled.

Now, my nan always sat in the nosy chair. It's the armchair that faces the television but it's also in the bay window. If anything happens outside you can guarantee that Nannan knows about it first. At about 2.50 p.m. I remember her saying quite openly, 'Look at this lot. They're going to be late.' About 10 to 15 Liverpool fans were walking down the road with crates of lager in their arms, all of them with a can in hand. Pissed and loud. It's a 15-minute walk to Hillsborough from my parents'. With dozens more following down the street, she was right. They were going to be late.

It was 3 p.m. now. Kick-off had begun or so we assumed.

The next thing I remember was Des saying, 'We're getting news from Hillsborough,' and then the footage coming on to the TV. There were people on the pitch and no one seemed to know why. I could tell from my parents' faces that whatever it was there wasn't going to be any FA Cup football today.

An ambulance drove on to the pitch and my dad went outside.

The news was coming through that people were dying. We could see the ground from where we were and the reporters were saying people were dead. I don't think I fully comprehended what that meant until later that day. I'm not sure I really understood what death was.

Over the next hour or so people started to make their way back to their cars but the happy vocal fans were now silent and weeping. They were like zombies, not knowing what to do with themselves. The overriding image of that day will always be my dad out on the street bringing people into our house and mum making them cups of tea and getting them to contact their families. It's amazing the mundane things you remember. I remember we had a burgundy push-button phone in the dining room and there was almost a constant queue to use it.

In the family we have an enormous steel teapot that's used for family celebrations. My mum had taken it down from the top of the kitchen cupboards and was making tea for around 30 Liverpool fans, who were now sitting in the living room watching the events unfolding only a mile down the road.

I'd never seen a man cry before that day. I'd also never heard my dad swear. In one five-minute period I saw and heard both.

Standing at the bottom of the path my dad was talking to people and ushering them into the house to get a drink when a man wearing stonewashed jeans and jacket, across the road, just fell to his knees in the gutter. My dad ran across the road to bring him into the house. The man almost howled as he wept. He just wanted to be left alone. He was almost fighting with my dad, shouting at him to 'fuck off' and leave him alone. But he didn't leave him alone. I heard my dad say, 'Get in that fucking house and call your family because somebody out there thinks you're dead.' The man just looked at him and cried. Dad brought him up the stairs and into the house. I remember talking to him in the garden as he drank a cup of tea. He was a nice man but he was broken.

Now every stereotypical image of a Scouser is the curly perm and tache but I really did meet a Liverpool fan like that on that day. He was tall and rotund. I could see his belly peeping out from under his red Liverpool shirt. We were in the garden and I was listening to conversations and delivering cups of tea. I'd heard other Liverpool fans saying how many people there were in such a small space. So when I took the Scouse stereotype his tea I felt knowledgeable enough to join in the conversation.

I gave him the mug and said in my most confident voice, 'They should have let the Liverpool fans have the Kop because you've got more fans.' He looked down at me and then back to his friend and said to him, 'Out of the mouth of babes.'

Remember the minibus that pulled up on the street when I was hanging my Forest banner? Now they were all sitting in the living room watching the TV. All except for one. A member of their group was missing. His name was Billy. In between other people calling home the members of the minibus were ringing all the hospitals and anyone they could think of to try and find him.

As the death toll began to rise everyone was thinking but not saying that Billy may be gone.

After what felt like hours but it couldn't have been more than two, screams came from the living room but they were screams of relief. Billy was being interviewed on *Calendar*, the ITV local news programme, and he was in the hospital. He'd broken his leg and was describing to the reporter what he had seen. It was the first time since they climbed out of the minibus earlier that day that I had seen them smile.

In the days and weeks after, my parents received a lot of cards from the families of the Liverpool fans. We even received one from Billy's family. The card read, 'Strangers are friends that we haven't yet met.' The lads from the minibus also came back and brought my mum flowers the next time Liverpool played at Hillsborough.

If mobile phones had existed I would never have had this experience. Our plastic burgundy phone was a lifeline that day and the source of comfort for many families.

I don't remember when the house emptied but I know it was dark. My nan had decided to stay the night so I was sleeping on a camp bed in my brother's room. It was very late when my dad came upstairs and I was still awake. He peered through the banister and asked me if I was OK. I wasn't sure but I knew I was safe and there were others out there who weren't. Suddenly things felt different.

So there you have it. The residents of S6 are the silent witnesses to what happened on 15 April 1989.

This is my truth of what I saw and heard that day, nothing more, nothing less.

Alan Davies:

On the day of 15 April Arsenal played Newcastle at home and we were going for the title and it was a big day. In those days the semi-finals were played at 3 o'clock on a Saturday just like all the league games were. I used to go on my own and stand in the north-west corner of the North Bank and I'd quite often take a little radio. Loads of people had a little pocket transistor, especially if something was happening like the cup semi-finals, which were a huge deal. The Cup Final is the biggest game of the season and so I had the thing to my ear and so people would say, what's the score, mate? Any scores? All the time. But word was coming through that there was something going on and the Liverpool match had been stopped. The immediate reaction was there must have been crowd trouble because there was a lot of crowd trouble in the 80s.

Then it came through that someone had been killed. One person. And it changed the whole atmosphere on the terrace. By the end of the afternoon, by full-time, we won the game 1–0. Marwood scored. It was another three points, you know. We were going for the league but the whole atmosphere in the ground was strange. People knew that something was going on but they didn't know what and by the end of the game the word was that seven people had been killed, which seemed like the most appalling tragedy you could think of. Little did we know what was unfolding.

Nick Hornby:

I was at Highbury. It started to come through on people's radios that something had happened. I don't think I knew precisely what had happened until I got home afterwards and turned on the TV. I don't think anyone in the ground knew a lot of people had died. I remember the Ibrox disaster when I was a teenager and you just couldn't see how they could keep doing this. Herding tens of thousands of people into spaces which were basically concrete steps with a bit of fencing at the bottom. Arsenal weren't allowed to host a semi-final because they wouldn't put fences up and it was the fences that killed people. A few years before, I'd ended up going on the pitch because there was a riot behind me in the North Bank. It was West Ham fans and everyone surged forward and ended up going on to the playing surface and the referee called the game off. I was standing in the penalty area waiting for a corner to come over. We were taken down the other end where there was a bit more room. I think there was that sense of – I think we all had it – that could have been us. You look back on all the times when you feel you might have been crushed and somehow there was always this sense that someone knew what they were doing. Of course, no one knew what they were doing. It was all desperately unsafe and, of course, we've found out loads of things about the police behaviour and so on since. The biggest problem with what happened at Hillsborough was the way that we watched football. It was uncontrollable.

Bob Wilson:

It was a cup tie, Liverpool versus Nottingham Forest, and Des Lynam was the number one presenter at *Grandstand* but he was presenting from Hillsborough that day. I used to fill in for Des so it fell upon me to be in the chair on that day on *Grandstand*. Five hours, no script, and we were going between the world snooker at the Crucible and the semi-final at Hillsborough. That was basically the content of the programme. Very soon after we'd gone on air it became clear that we had to go to Hillsborough. In my ear I was hearing there's something dreadful happening. Then we got the information through and I'm hearing a lot that the people at home didn't hear. The producers of the programme and then the head of sport came on to me and said to me, 'Bob, do you realise there are bodies there?' It was only towards the end of the programme they said: be very careful in what you're going to say. I had no idea that it was going to be 96 lives lost ultimately. I remember coming up with the words: 'If you're really concerned with your loved ones if they're at the game, this is the number to ring.' That was all I was allowed to do at that particular time before we went off air. We had no idea of the eventual horrific situation. We came off air and we always used to go for a drink and I think most people had a bit of a cry. I heard the news just afterwards and the numbers were rising with the next news bulletin. We knew that Downing Street was in on it. I went home and had a good cry.

How can you go to a football game, how can you go to any great entertainment, and lose 96 lives? For football it was a defining moment. There was no question that it made the authorities sit down and say, look, what are we going to do here? How did this happen? How did they allow so many people into there? How did the crush develop? Why did they not listen to Bruce Grobbelaar, who was so close to it in goal and was screaming: 'Open the gates.' I'm sure a lot more people would have survived if they'd listened to Bruce's screaming because he knew that people were losing their lives in there.

John Lukic:

In football stadiums you pick up things off supporters. You can pick up vibes and that probably sounds strange but there was definitely a sombre mood as our game against Newcastle went on. It got a little bit more subdued and more subdued and more subdued and then at the end you get to find out what actually happened. Sport doesn't mean anything when it comes to life.

Tony Adams:
It's obviously devastating. It's hard to understand and to empathise with the horrific thing that happened on that day. It was beyond comprehension. I can only imagine how the players there were feeling. It must have been absolutely horrific for everybody involved. Unless you're there and having that experience you can't understand the pain of what happened.

Lee Dixon:
I think we'd all played in games in our careers where there'd been crowd trouble and people getting on the pitch. So it was always in the back of your mind that some trouble might happen. You're always aware of the crowd. People always say to me, do you hear the crowd? Do you hear what people say? You hear a lot. You block a lot of it out because you're concentrating but it comes in and out of your consciousness. After the game more and more information comes out and I just remember when the shock of what happened came out thinking, that's it. The season's over. I genuinely believed that it wouldn't carry on. Why would you? Ninety-six people have lost their lives. Why would you carry on playing football? That was my initial thought, not as a footballer but as a person. Football was just irrelevant then at that point. Quite rightly so there was a real concentration on the relatives of the people who had lost their lives and football didn't matter.

Alan Smith:
I watched our game from the paddock because I was injured. I had a depressed fracture of the cheekbone from a collision with one of the

youth team players in a training ground match. I'd headed the ball and he'd come and headed my cheek and it had all caved in. The paddock was the area behind the dugout where some of the youth team players and those not involved would sit. At half-time I went up to the halfway house, which was the old players' lounge just halfway up the tunnel there on the right and I saw some of the scenes unfolding at Hillsborough and reports that people were injured. I went up to the dressing room and said to the lads, oh there's trouble at Hillsborough. They reckon there's crowd trouble and people have been hurt. But they're obviously thinking about the match and the second half. We won the game against Newcastle and then I went back up and told them more. Stories were coming in all the time of deaths and it was an awful, awful day and it got worse as the night went on. Everybody went home and watched *News at Ten*. Just awful.

NIALL QUINN:
What I won't forget is going down to the halfway house after the game to find out what happened in Sheffield, knowing that I had got two tickets for that game for friends of mine who were Liverpool fans. It is something I can never shake off. That moment of fear. I didn't find out until my mother heard the news the next day that they were OK. I remember the journalists being there for interviews just outside the halfway house and I said, it's not a day for talking about the football. Everybody packed up their notebooks and went away. It was dreadful. Steve Burtenshaw scouted at the game as we were due to play Liverpool shortly after. I remember speaking to him two weeks later and he just started crying. It was tough stuff. It was a time that went on to change the game but it was such a dark, terrible time. Football can never afford to forget those who died.

Nigel Winterburn:

I remember putting the television on and seeing those scenes. It's so difficult to describe. It absolutely makes you feel numb. I can still see it now. I can still picture that end at Hillsborough. I can still see all those supporters. Some of them being pulled up. Some of them being pushed over the top. The ambulances come in. People ripping up the hoardings. Stretchering people away. That just can't happen at a game of football. But it did. Sitting here thinking about it now is upsetting. I don't think you realise what has happened really internally unless you're part of Liverpool Football Club. It's impossible. We don't understand. It's so hard to talk about. So I don't know how they carried on after that. Maybe they felt that they had to as a mark of respect. You've got to somehow block it out but it's there.

John Lukic:

You understood the enormity of what had actually happened and for that to have happened in a football stadium on a day which should have been a joyous day, it's just one of those days that sticks in your memories. For all those poor families that suffered losses. It was a very, very sobering experience to go through. It didn't directly involve us but it did from a footballing fraternity point of view. It does rip you to your core to see events unfold as they happened on the TV, it's just beyond belief and to think that there has not been any conclusion to that until recently and even ongoing now. It's just unbelievable because it's so long ago.

David Dein:

We had a television in the boardroom and just seeing the pictures coming through from Hillsborough was chilling. Nobody really knew what was going on and how serious it was until afterwards. It was only as the story unfolded that we realised what a tragedy that was. Not just for English football but it was a wake-up call for everybody around the world. Two of the girls who sadly lost their lives went to the same school as my daughter, Haberdashers' in Elstree. I was on the Football League Management Committee at the time and I offered to speak to the parents. I live locally and asked, do you mind if I just pop round and see you and just talk it through? This was only a few days after the event. They said, please do, so I ran around to see them. It was terribly sad hearing their stories about their daughters who went to the game and they never saw them again alive.

NICK HORNBY:
Looking back on it now I think I feel a little bit ashamed that I gave it two weeks like everybody else. There was no football for two weeks and then we played Norwich on a Bank Holiday Monday and won 5–0 and the sun was out. We can get back on with it now. But it probably wasn't right in the same way that it wasn't right that we all watched the game after Heysel in 1985. They just kicked off and played it and looking back at that I feel a bit kind of unclean. Why didn't we all just turn the TV off? Why didn't they stop the game? There are lots of arguments to say that football shouldn't have continued but there we are. I think there was probably a sense also in a bad way of, well, it's football fans, isn't it? They're always hurting each other. So I think there was probably a sad reason that it was off in its bubble.

ALAN DAVIES:
At Highbury, we used to have semi-finals. Tottenham played a semi-final at Highbury. I remember West Brom and Ipswich playing a semi-final and it was quite a good thing for the club. It felt good that your ground was worthy of it and we had a big capacity with the terraces. But they said, if you want to continue staging semi-finals at Highbury you've got to put fences up around the pitch, and the club refused to do it and the reason they refused to do it was common

sense. Because in the early 80s there used to be a lot of trouble, especially at London derbies, with fans going on to the home fans' terrace and trying to take the terrace. So you'd try and take the Shelf. Take the Shed End. Or take the North Bank at Highbury. So you'd sometimes get fighting and then the police would wade in and that was terrifying and they'd batter everyone and that was your afternoon. Once West Ham appeared on the terrace and a smoke bomb went off in the middle of the North Bank and the police waded in, cracking heads with truncheons, which made a sort of pop sound that was weird and everyone was running and you're trying to run away and you don't know which way to run and there's smoke everywhere and people poured on to the pitch. Hundreds of people went on the pitch to get away from the smoke. Now, had they had fences who knows what would have happened on that day. It was panic. They had games at Hillsborough because it had fences and the fences killed all those people and whoever was responsible for putting fences around football grounds and caging people in should be held to account and hopefully will be finally. The fences killed all those people. I can remember at so many grounds being up against fences. I used to like standing at the front, especially when I was a kid. Being up against the fence. Being crushed from behind. It's frightening and everyone felt it that day. It was after that they started taking the fences down.

NIGEL WINTERBURN:
Blaming Liverpool supporters and then the police are covering things up. When I think about that it sends me cold. It makes me shudder after all this time.

PAUL MERSON:
I won PFA young player of the year that year. I had to go and pick my award up that weekend at the Grosvenor Hotel. I didn't want to go. It was the most horrible thing I have ever seen I think in football. Ever.

I won probably the best award you could ever win as a youngster and I didn't want it. Football had gone out of the window for me then. I don't like talking about it now if I'm being honest. It was so sad.

Amy Lawrence:

The impressions of that day have never gone away. Anyone who loved football then felt it, still feels it, whenever those images come up. As they have done for all these years, all those anniversaries, as the families of the 96 have shown such remarkable endurance in pursuit of some kind of justice. That day, in its immediacy, it was too much to comprehend. Without the rolling news of our contemporary world, without social media and cameras on mobile phones, it was just a case of sticking together and waiting for the next news bulletin. Nobody wanted to be by themselves. Our little band of friends, teenagers, who had gone excitedly to a game that day able to afford it with their pocket money, just like 37 of the 96 did who were still in their teens, left our usual spot on the North Bank and went home to Matt's house. Nobody had any words, as we absorbed each news update and the number of dead kept rising. It felt like the world as we knew it was caving in.

EIGHT

Football Focus

ALAN SMITH:

There was a question, there was a doubt at one stage, whether the season would be abandoned. We had a break. The gaffer said, 'We're going to pay our respects and we just want to make sure we stay fit for when football does resume.' When things were finally decided our match against Liverpool was put to the end of the queue because we were supposed to play them during that period where the matches were postponed. It was just an awful time. Back in the day when there were terraces we used to see that surge forward and you'd think, oh, look at that, and you'd never really worry about the safety aspect of it. You just took it as a part of football and obviously, things changed totally after that and rightly so.

LEE DIXON:

I think a lot of people were looking at Liverpool going, what do we do? What's acceptable? Whatever you do we'll do. The way they conducted themselves, their players, Kenny Dalglish in particular, and the way that Liverpool as a club dealt with the aftermath was sensational, if that's the right word. It was just so humbling to watch them deal with that from a distance.

PAUL MERSON:

First of all what those Liverpool players did was phenomenal. After what happened they just kept on winning and winning and winning, just brushing everybody aside. They could have easily gone the other way and they didn't. They could have folded and they didn't. They showed unbelievable strength.

NIGEL WINTERBURN:
I don't know how they carried on after that. Emotionally I cannot think about what they were going through. Maybe they felt that they had to as a mark of respect. I don't think you really realise what has happened unless you're part of Liverpool Football Club. It's impossible. For us? You've got to get out and get on and do the job that you're being paid to do as well. When my kids were around I always said I was going to work. It was a job. It was a job that I absolutely loved. It is horrible to say it but you've got to block out what's happened and get on with the job that you're supposed to do. At the time our job was to try and be league champions.

LEE DIXON:
You do get on with it and it's a relief because you don't then have to deal with what's really going on as a human being. Football is an escape for the players. Because we were competing with them it felt a little bit weird. A little bit wrong at the time. What's everybody thinking? Do they want us to win it? What's the right thing? Somebody tell me what the right thing to do is. It was all really surreal.

ALAN SMITH:
As a footballer you're thinking, we've just got to tick over and we'll be led by the authorities. Whatever they think is best, we'll follow and we'll try and pick up where we left off. But you're conscious that you might not be able to. First game back you're hoping to hit the ground running again. We played Norwich at Easter. Another game on the telly and I got quite a spectacular goal for me. John Lukic pumped one upfield and I chested it, thighed it down, swivelled and rifled it

in the net with my left foot. I really caught it sweetly. It was a good game for us. It was like, OK, we're back in business. Let's do it.

LEE DIXON:
Four games to go. We went to Middlesbrough and it was a bad game, one of those scramblers on a terrible pitch where it didn't look like it was happening. It was a really hard game to get any flow going. Every time you passed the ball it hit a bobble. It was windy at Ayresome Park. It was a horrible grind. But the make-up of the team was such we knew that if we could score one we should win the game. The vital one came from the subs' bench. The goal that Hayesey scored was typical for that kind of game – bobbling and scrambled in. It didn't matter. When we scored we knew how important it was.

PAUL MERSON:
Three games to go. I thought we'd won it. I seriously thought we'd won. We've got Derby at home. We've got Wimbledon at home. We win both games it's all over.

DAVID O'LEARY:
Oh don't . . . I could have sleepless nights now just thinking about it.

JOHN LUKIC:
I suppose there's an air of expectation in the camp that you're in touching distance and you know it's a fatal place to be. It's a subconscious thing.

LEE DIXON:
The game against Derby was quite weird because we knew we had two home games and it was in our hands. I don't remember being particularly nervous going into it because I genuinely thought then that we would win the league.

Paul Merson:
I remember the team-talk. We met at South Herts Golf Club and I remember George always used to go through all the opposition's players. That's how thorough he was and he said, 'Peter Shilton. He was a great goalie. He's gone. Just keep on peppering him.'

Lee Dixon:
I remember driving in. Coming down the hill, Avenell Road, and there was a bloke selling the enamel pin badges and he had one saying 'Champions 89 Arsenal'. I remember just going, God, that's a bit premature. It snapped me with a reality check. We might not win it. I was thinking about that bloke. How much money he was going to lose if we didn't do it because he'd had all these badges made. So I wasn't complacent on the day. He was taking it a little bit for granted so I remember going into the dressing room going, come on, lads, this is a big one.

Alan Smith:
I mean we just didn't get going. I remember I had some friends down from Birmingham. It was almost like, come and see us, this is one step towards the league. It was a big occasion and we fell flat on our faces. Dean Saunders was a top striker, great finisher, and said afterwards that it meant an awful lot because he wanted Liverpool to win. He was a Liverpool fan. I got our goal. A header at the near post. We thought, well what happened there? Why were we so bad? Obviously nerves were coming into it. We were beginning to fluff our lines but at the end of that game you think, right, that's a one-off. Come on, lads, we were crap but let's make sure that doesn't happen again, and that's the message off the gaffer. We'd been superb, lads. Let's forget about that. Bad day at the office. On to the next one.

MICHAEL THOMAS:
Very frustrating. That was a big downer. I think the pressure of it all got to us. We went there thinking we could beat these. Dean Saunders, my old team-mate, crucified us.

PAUL MERSON:
There were nerves. Arsenal haven't won the league since 1971. We should have won that game by ten. It was that one-sided and if it wasn't for Shilton it would have been a cricket score. You come off and you just think it's not meant. Not meant to be. You think that's it.

LEE DIXON:
I do remember going home and I just stayed in and I had a glass of wine. I felt guilty about drinking a glass of wine so I only had half. I remember thinking, this is the time now that you really roll up your sleeves.

ALAN SMITH:
Wimbledon was next, the party spoilers. The old boom box in the dressing room thumping out the music and them slamming across into the doors and the walls. You can hear them. Always different when Wimbledon visited. You know the hallowed halls of Highbury? They didn't have much respect.

PAUL MERSON:
It was bizarre. Wimbledon were a hard team to play against and one ground they loved playing at was Highbury. Because it was lovely and tight. They could lump the ball forward.

NIGEL WINTERBURN:
I knew what it's like from my time with Wimbledon. We always felt as if teams hated us. Supporters hated us. We didn't care less. Most of

those players came from lower leagues. We were all put together, free transfers. When I signed for Wimbledon my transfer fee was a bottle of Scotch. Ha ha ha. That is a true story. Just thinking about that now is ridiculous. If you ever wanted to try and win at a big ground at a big club, you didn't want to be playing against Wimbledon.

LEE DIXON:
Nigel hit an absolute screamer with his right foot into the top corner. He smashed it straight into the top corner. Nigel? Right foot? It felt like it was meant to be.

NIGEL WINTERBURN:
You should have seen the shock on my face. I remember my teammates running up to me and shouting in my ear. 'It's your right foot!' If you asked me if I would ever take that shot on again with my right foot? No way. Not in a million years would I have tried that. Then I suppose you tend to think, maybe we are going to be crowned league champions. But you know what Wimbledon are like. Spoilers. Complete and utter spoilers.

ALAN SMITH:
They equalised; Alan Cork was great in the air. And then Merse got a really good goal. Do you remember who scored the equaliser for them and he went off on a little mazy run celebrating? They all piled on top of him. Paul McGee, who I hadn't heard of before and I don't think I heard of after as well. It was the final whistle I remember. It was the last home game of the season so we did the traditional lap of the pitch, clapping the fans. And it was kind of: thanks for staying with us, sorry that we couldn't do it this time. Hopefully next year. It was that kind of vibe around the ground. We were just so deflated that we'd had these two games at home and we'd absolutely messed it up. We were low. I thought it was over.

NIGEL WINTERBURN:
When you look back that tells you what the pressure's about. It's the pressure of trying to achieve something that you dream about. That would have been my first league title. We had a couple of games to do it really and we didn't do it. It's particularly annoying when you didn't do it at home in front of your own supporters. Just shows you what pressure can do to a team.

STEVE BOULD:
We were a really young group at the time and really inexperienced, and it was a big ordeal. We'd played so well up until Christmas and just after, and then we very nearly pulled up and faltered and fell at the last hurdle.

MICHAEL THOMAS:
Oh gosh. We all thought it was over then. That was a big downer.

LEE DIXON:
It would probably have been easier if everybody had been all honest with each other at that point during the lap of honour and we'd have gone, 'I'm really sorry we've messed it up', and all the fans would have gone, 'You're rubbish.' We'd basically just thrown it away in those two games. I honestly thought: that's it, we've blown it. We're not going to beat Liverpool at Anfield. Especially with what's happened at Hillsborough. Especially with how we've thrown the league away. Especially with all the things that have been mounting up against us. Especially that we weren't experienced enough and everyone was going to say yeah, it's Liverpool and you're just a bunch of kids and you did have it and now you've lost it so well done you. That was the feeling after the Wimbledon game. What's the point?

89

Tony Adams:
God, you non-believers. We're all doomed! I didn't feel like we'd blown it at that point.

George Graham:
What did I think? I've got the words but I can't say them. Very disappointed? That sounds very polite that. Very disappointed. Losing and drawing at home. Games we were expecting to win. I was gutted. It was awful. God, it was never meant to be easy. Football in this country, it's so unpredictable at times. This is English football. This is why it's loved all over the world. But that was awful. We had one game to put it right.

Alan Smith:
The press was saying, come the crunch the pressure got to us. We weren't ready for it. Liverpool, with their experience, had made a run up on the rails and pegged us back. They were the team. They were going to win it once again. That's what everybody thought, I think. Then they had one more home game, against West Ham, who had been relegated. It was the same night as the football writers' dinner actually. I got invited so I went along and the scores were coming in. What's the score at Anfield? 1–0. What's the score? 2–0. 3–0. And I'm going, oh my God.

Nigel Winterburn:
I sat in the room on my own. Put the radio on. I just sat on the floor, listening to that game. Praying that they wouldn't win and then suddenly the realisation's come in of our task as they keep scoring. I'm sitting there with my hands over my eyes praying and shaking my head and thinking, blow the whistle! Your emotions are going through you. In my own head I'm thinking, if they score again we've got to win by three. Phew. We might as well just give them the league

title now. It's just not going to happen, is it? No way, not with a team like that. How can it be a relief when the final whistle goes that you've got to go to Anfield and win by two goals? That's just crazy.

LEE DIXON:
I didn't want to watch it, didn't want to listen to it, so I went for a meal with my ex-wife, middle of Hertfordshire, in a restaurant way away from everything. Went in. Table for two. Thank you very much. The waiter comes over and he's got this little grin on his face, so I think, oh, he's clocked who I am. He goes, 'All right there, la,' in a Scouse accent. He was in the kitchen and every time a goal went in the kitchen door would open and he'd give a thumbs up. Yeah, thanks for that. It absolutely ruined my night. All night long he kept giving me the score. I couldn't even work it out and then the waiter came and told me, 'So you've got to beat us now 2–0. It's not going to happen is it?' And I went, no.

MICHAEL THOMAS:
Liverpool scored five. You are thinking, what do we have to do? It's over. What do we do?

PAUL MERSON:
Oh, the goals were rolling in. It was like, you've got to stop! I remember ringing Grovesy. I think I was in an Indian restaurant. I said to Grovesy, 'Oh my God. What chance we got? That's it.'

PERRY GROVES:
West Ham had their flip-flops on, their rubber rings and their snorkels up at Anfield. I said to Merse, 'We're done. We've done all right. We've come second. You know, it's not bad. We'll go again next year.'

Paul Merson:
I'm a professional footballer and a compulsive gambler; I thought it was fucking impossible. Here's one for you. It was 16/1 for Arsenal to win the league in pre-season and we were 16/1 to win 2–0 at Anfield 37 games later. Ha ha. I don't think they'd lost a game since January. We'd just been beaten by Derby and we couldn't beat Wimbledon at home. We'd let in four goals in those two home games. Now we've got to go to Anfield and win by two clear goals. Seriously? No.

Alan Smith:
It was really only when we came into training the next time that, in my memory, Mickey Thomas said, 'We've got to win 2–0, lads.' He'd done the maths. Oh, is that all? We've got to win 2–0 at Anfield? So a part of you is thinking it's not un-doable, but then the other part is thinking, at Anfield? Really? Against them on their own turf? I can't see it.

Perry Groves:
I remember the gaffer pulling us all in and he sat everyone down at London Colney on the little benches. He said, 'Lads, I fancy our chances. We're going to go up there, they're going for the Double as well, they're going to think that it's done and dusted. We're going to spoil the party. We're going to play three at the back.' Everybody just looked round at each other and just thought, has he gone mad? It didn't make logical sense. We should be playing an extra forward. But I can remember him saying this to this day: if we go there and we concede first it is virtually impossible. But if we're 0–0 at half-time then we've got half a chance.

George Graham:
We had just had a couple of big disasters at home. So it was tough. Changing shape was a tough call because Liverpool were dominant

for so many years and especially at Anfield they were magnificent and they usually won all their home matches in the first 20 minutes and then enjoyed playing football the rest. Managers always look at your own team, your own structure, the way you play and the way the opposition play. What are their strengths? What are their weaknesses? You try to exploit their weaknesses and you try and force your strengths on to them and that's the way most coaches sort the game out when they are planning beforehand. I had it all organised to play Liverpool. Even though they had won by scoring five goals the previous match I still thought it was the right way to go. Did it cross my mind to go with a back four having planned it with three central defenders and the full-backs pushing on? Never. I was very confident in the boys. I was very confident we could go up there and get a result.

BOB WILSON:
I do remember clearly one day I was blowing up the footballs before training and the guys started to come out and I remember Alan Smith in particular looking over and he can have quite a serious face anyway, Alan. The guys weren't their usual selves. 'What's the matter with you lot? This is the week you're going to win the league, be the champions of your country.' There was a look. I mean, where it came from I can't tell you and it probably wasn't with the greatest belief but somehow, I said it with confidence. No doubt about it, you know. 2–0 at Anfield. Not a problem.

ALAN SMITH:
We were sitting on the benches just outside where we'd have a team meeting, and we must have been looking a bit down in the mouth and Bob Wilson popped his cheery head round the corner and said, 'Cheer up, lads. This is the week we're going to win the league.' I said nice one, Bob. Good try.

BOB WILSON:
Even to this day Smudger does say to me, 'I'll never ever forget you saying that. I would have loved to have truly believed it but I'm not sure that I did.'

MICHAEL THOMAS:
Bob came in very happy. But that wisdom from Bob and George came in very handy. Don't worry about it, boys!

ALAN SMITH:
As the week got on and you're training and bubbly, you're gaining a little bit of belief. As the situation settles into you, you kind of grasp it and get a grip of it and then you're thinking about how you're going to do it and you're looking towards your tactics and how we were actually going to approach the task.

NIGEL WINTERBURN:
Sitting there in the pit of your stomach, knowing that you probably should have won the league title two or three games before, is pretty annoying. Everybody is writing you off, saying it's a fitting end to the season what with the Hillsborough disaster; Liverpool are going to do the Double. You realise that if you can pull it off you're going to upset a hell of a lot of people.

ALAN SMITH:
Nobody fancies you and it is a free hit to a certain extent. Go up there, do your best. If we don't win, well, nobody is going to blame you.

NIGEL WINTERBURN:
You've got to have the belief. Nobody apart from maybe a few Arsenal supporters are realistically going to believe it. But you've got to believe it. That was where George, from that moment, was sensational.

Because he's got to make the team believe that they can win. It's just the confidence he puts within the team. The way that he studies the game. The organisation. The trust that he had in the group of players he had.

LEE DIXON:
George's game face was on. He was like, 'Right, we've got to beat them 2–0. We can do that.' I don't think they'd lost by two clear goals since 1971 or something. It was just a ridiculous ask. But it was plausible and that was because of George: let's just give it a go. No pressure.

JOHN LUKIC:
I thought that he handled it very well simply because it could have gone the other way and the players could have lost self-belief. They could have probably resigned themselves to the fact that we were going to finish second. But he said, 'OK, lads, you've got a couple of days off so you go and get away from it all. Reflect and look forward to what possibly might be and then we will get back in the groove.' And that's what we did.

TONY ADAMS:
He made every single decision correctly. You know musicians when you're in the flow. Sometimes you're just winging it, baby, you're rocking. You get those moments. I think for the whole week or so George was swinging.

DAVID O'LEARY:
It was unique for the whole league season to boil down to a shoot-out. I had in my head that this situation shouldn't be coming down to us having to climb this mountain. We should have wrapped this league up by now. But George gave us a great deal of confidence. I'd

grown up at the club – it had been 14 years since I had made my debut. All those years I'd heard about how they went to White Hart Lane and won the league in 1971 and it had been thrown in my face a great deal – we'd never won the league. I had that in the back of my mind going on that drive up that day thinking we have a great chance. I know this group of players wouldn't be in fear of the occasion.

PAUL JOHNSON:
I remember during the week of the game Theo Foley came to me and said we are not going overnight and I said, 'Yeah, course you're not.' He said George wants to go on the day. 'To Liverpool? Are you mad?' The biggest game for years. What if something goes wrong with the coach or the motorway, what are we going to do? I was really worried. But we changed travel and hotel plans and on the day they went.

GARY LEWIN:
Mickey had tweaked his knee ligament the week before against Wimbledon. We weren't sure he was going to make it. We were treating him two or three times a day, every day. I joked with him he would be radioactive by the time I was finished with him and the last game came around. On the Monday we were running with him, Tuesday change of direction, Wednesday ball work, and Thursday was the block tackling; that was when he had a fitness test. He still had an awareness of the ligament. It's often three weeks and we were talking about ten days. I had to go through all the processes so I could look George in the eye and tell him how he was. I knew if he got a block tackle that it would get sore again. I told George, he's fit to start . . . but I am not sure he'll finish.

NINE

This Is the Day Your Life Will Surely Change

PART I: GOING

ADAM VALASCO:
I didn't have a ticket but there was no way in the world that I was going to miss the chance of seeing Arsenal win the title. I was in the middle of my GCSE exams and thanks to the back of the *Evening Standard* I managed to get promised a ticket by a ticket agency, so on 23 May I set off from my home in High Wycombe with the task of going to Arsenal to get my coach ticket and then stopping off at King's Cross to get my match ticket to return to my school by 2 p.m. to sit my GCSE economics exam. On paper it sounded a simple task and I left myself with plenty of time.

I arrived at Marylebone station to find to my horror that there was a bus and Tube strike. I could not afford taxis but as I was a fit 16-year-old I worked out that if I ran a lot of the way I could still be back in time. It was a scorching hot day but I managed to make good time to Arsenal to buy my coach ticket, so all good. Then something made me stop at a phone box just to confirm with the ticket agency that my ticket was definitely at their office. They told me that they had already sold it and did not have another one. I was crestfallen but determined not to give in, so after purchasing the *Evening Standard* and ringing around I managed to find another agency who had a ticket. The only problem was that they were in Pall Mall and there was just no way that I could get there in time and still make my exam, so after one second of thinking about it I made them promise to hold the ticket and that I would be there as soon as I could. I explained I was walking from Highbury. I took the mature decision not to bother phoning my school as I did not know what to say, but I left a message on my home answerphone explaining to my mum that I am perfectly safe but she might get some calls from my school as I could not go to the exam but I would explain all later.

Whilst walking to Pall Mall I realised that I did not possess the £75 they wanted for the ticket. I took every penny I had in the world out of the bank and turned up none the less. This gnarled old tout brought the ticket out and asked for the £75. I took out all my money and counted out £67.60 and then emotionally explained that I had run/walked all the way around London and that I had missed my GCSE exam and will probably be thrown out of my other exams because of it and that this really was all the money I had in the world. I also offered my cheap watch as security that I would come back and pay the rest when I had the balance. The tout looked me up and down and said, 'You know what, I actually believe you. I am too soft and will give you the ticket.' He asked if I had enough money to get home and then took £65 and said I should keep some money on me.

Later that night I finally staggered home ready to face the fury of my mum. She saw the state of me, listened to my story and my promises of taking the exam again and calmly said, 'It is your life. If you want to risk messing up your education for a football match, then it is up to you, but we are going to have to think of a good excuse so you are not thrown out of the other exams.'

I collapsed on to my bed and listened to the Liverpool v West Ham game on the radio praying for a draw at least. When the fifth Liverpool goal went in I thought to myself, I have gone through all this today and now we have no hope winning by two goals. Nevertheless, come 26 May, I set off for Anfield.

SPIRITMAN:
My friend and I went up on an Arsenal Travel Club coach from Highbury. Coach number 20. There were 25, numbered up to 26. There was no coach 13 – they knew that we football fans are a superstitious lot.

AMY LAWRENCE:
Quite a lot of the week leading up to the match had been spent in the garage at my friend Anna's house with an old double bed sheet and a pot of red paint, daubing a dainty cannon and a message our overthinking teenaged selves thought was significant – Arsenal We're Proud Of You – on to our home-made flag. The idea was that whether the team achieve the impossible or not, it was important to recognise that they had put in a phenomenal effort.

We were going to Anfield. Red Dr. Martens boots, yellow socks, 'I'm An Away Gunner' T-shirt under the replica shirt. Doesn't bear thinking about today on multiple levels but that's the 1980s for you. It's the little details that stick in the mind. Last day of school ever before exams and then the big wide world, and with whispers having got around that we were bunking off mid-morning for a football match it was a pleasant surprise to find the teachers sending us off with a wink, good luck, and pats on the back. Nice to see them recognising the school of life could be just as important as A levels. Mrs Roots, the most inspirational of English teachers, had brought in champagne for our last lesson. An omen, surely.

We marched out of school and jumped into our friend Toby's Fiesta to head for Highbury. It's hard to explain how or why but everything felt brilliant that day. Standing outside the coach convoy in the blazing sunshine. So much naive hope in the air. Setting off, the coaches snaked up Aubert Park and I remember four elderly ladies bedecked in rosettes frantically waving us off from their balcony. Then along Drayton Park, and all the kids at the local school were clambering on the orange boat in their playground, screaming and jumping about Arsenal. It felt like the whole community was buzzing, sending good-luck wishes via the fortunate ones heading up to Anfield.

GARY FRANKLIN:
I didn't think we would win, but hey, it's a day out, and I wanted to show the team that it had been a brilliant season. I wore my yellow Arsenal shirt; we were going on a pilgrimage. There were only coaches, British Rail cancelled the trains. We left at 12.45 p.m. with a police escort up the Holloway Road. Everyone was waving and standing outside the shops, people in cars, lorries, leaning out of windows, giving us support. An hour later we were not even on the M1. The traffic was murder, start, stop 5–10mph for over another hour. An accident, roadworks, you name it; our journey was painfully slow. The coaches were 'dry' but someone had smuggled a two-litre lemonade bottle on and was passing it around – it was half full with gin. The coach toilet didn't have a light and I was mid-slash when the driver decided to cut down a slip road on to a roundabout and back up on to the motorway to beat about 200 cars. Everyone cheered, but I was thrown all over the place, and came back out through the door backwards with an embarrassing damp patch down one leg.

RUSSELL JONES:
I was 18 and doing my A levels. Being on a Friday meant bunking off double French, which never went down well with the French teacher, who subsequently failed me. My older friends had organised a minibus to travel up from Grays, Essex. We stopped at Lakeside to fill up with beer. Paul was the only one of us who bought champagne. The rest of us didn't share the same faith and settled on Carlsberg.

DEAN WENGROW:

Anfield 89 was the day after my 13th birthday. I had an exam at school that day. My dad, Martin, let me off so I could attend the match. When children were recently allowed off school to protest against climate change, my father told me that he felt they should have been at school. What this tells us is that to our family Arsenal is far more important than the world ending.

BARRY HUGHES:

I was a first-year university student in Liverpool during the 88–89 season. I was in Nottingham for a night out on 15 April and remember all the shell-shocked Forest fans returning to the city. I was in Liverpool the week after Hillsborough and left my 79 cup winners' scarf at Anfield; it was such an awful time. I also remember observing an emotional minute's silence in Lord Street on the Saturday afterwards. I was proud, living in Liverpool, that The Arsenal were the first team to say they would not be playing in the immediate aftermath of Hillsborough before the league had confirmed postponements. I remember phoning Liverpool FC to make sure our tickets were still valid for the rearranged match on 26 May.

AMANDA SCHIAVI:

I was working in a solicitors' in London when I told my boss that I had to have the day off to go to Anfield. He said, 'No way, it's too short notice.' I resigned and as I was handed my P45 he said, 'Go, but I hope you lose.'

MICK WINNETT:

Around Birmingham the coaches got bogged down in very heavy traffic, and soon the driver announced that he knew a short-cut that would cut out a long stretch of motorway and save some time. So he pulled off on to some A road that wound through fields and villages, and was nearly as jammed as the motorway. Eventually he got completely lost, and drove up a narrow lane, where he had to do a U-turn in the tightest of spaces.

MAL SMITH:
I have a bit of a strange claim to fame. I was the very first person in the ground that night. Basically my dad was a sergeant in the mounted police and used to get me into matches. He told me if I wanted to go that night I had to get there very early so I got there for 4.30 p.m. My dad got one of the gatemen to let me in at the Anfield Road end and a policeman then walked me round the outside of the pitch along the Kemlyn Road stand and into the Kop, where I sat on my own for over an hour before other supporters started ambling in.

RICHARD ROBERTS:
We'd gone early with some footballs as we thought it'd be cool to have a 'Solidarity with Hillsborough' kick-around with Liverpool fans when we got there. As it happened we got to the ground in our minibus only about 30 minutes before kick-off, to be met by the police saying we were the first Arsenal fans they'd seen, everyone was held up. They gave us an escort to a parking spot just inside the gates of a massive car park. We were told we had to return to our vehicle immediately after the game as we, of course, were blocking the gates and therefore the exit. We thought, this a really great gesture. They must've assumed we'd have nothing to delay us.

SARAH TURNER:
It was a surprisingly warm day, so much so that when I left Richmond for the drive to Anfield I was kitted out in just a T-shirt and shorts. That morning I had been wearing my Arsenal top in Richmond town centre and had been surprised by the number of people who had come up to me and wished me good luck for the game as if

I, in some way, could influence the outcome of the match. I drove up with my mate Lee in his car he affectionately called Rusty and to this day I'm still amazed that car made it all the way there and back. The traffic jam was so bad that at one point I actually got out of the car on the M6 and stretched my legs.

Eventually after seven hours of driving, we found ourselves in sight of Anfield with only ten minutes to kick-off. Double parking Rusty, we sprinted to the ground and found the away end practically empty, with 25 coaches carrying Arsenal fans still stuck on the motorway.

MATTHEW LOWMAN:
I was a 21-year-old living on the Nightingale Estate in Hackney in 1989. My friends had earned their season tickets for that season by painting Highbury Stadium during the summer of 88, something I wasn't able to do as I was holding down a proper job and therefore had to pay for mine, some £75 I think. We had been to most games during the season, including all ten of the games prior to Liverpool. We genuinely questioned whether to travel and put ourselves through the misery of seeing our dreams crushed. In the end we were always going to make the trip and after a half day off work we arranged to rendezvous outside Highbury at noon. Whilst waiting to board one of the coaches one of our group decided to invest a chunk of his wages at the bookies on the corner of Gillespie and Avenell Roads – betting Arsenal would win 2–0. Off we set in a line of coaches on what would be a long, hot and troublesome journey to Liverpool. We were for the most part oblivious to the traffic problems as we happily played cards, drank our can of Coke each and ate a corned beef sandwich – which proved to be the last refreshment we would have until the following day. People started getting agitated the closer we got to kick-off, having still not made it into Liverpool by 7 p.m.

89

Mark Brindle:

The team had a large contingent of South London lads in it and they were only a couple of years younger than me so I really felt an affinity with them. We were the SLAG (South London Arsenal Gooners) army. I had taken the short straw of designated driver mainly because I had just taken delivery of a Renault 5 GT Turbo. As panic started to set in there were several trips up the hard shoulder, several detours, and eventually we hit a bit of clear motorway about an hour before kick-off and the turbo got a good thrashing into Liverpool – including driving past a police car at well over 100mph and him waving us on when he saw the scarves fluttering out the window.

Kelvin Meadows:

The traffic jam has passed into folklore. It was as if all vehicles were heading to Merseyside. As we sat there, not moving, I glanced across to the motor next to us. A blue Ford Granada Scorpio. Sitting in the back was John Radford, who was on his way to co-commentate for Capital Gold (we later found out he never made it in time for the radio) and sitting in the front was Michael Watson (he'd recently beaten Nigel Benn at Finsbury Park). We pulled into Corley service station, and at that moment I knew we would do it. I had a sign. Radford was in the motor behind and the van in front had KENNEDY written across the back. Echoes of 71 and the last title.

Mel O'Reilly:

I was travelling alone. Most of the mates I knocked about with at the time weren't really into football, more acid house, the Stone Roses, raves and failing to chat up girls from what I remember. The mood going up to Liverpool on the coach was helped along with some fierce drinking and singalongs.

DAVE HIGGS:
My sister-in-law was at Liverpool University at the time and we parked up outside her digs on the outskirts of Toxteth. We had a drink and then she gave us a lift across the city to the ground in her mum's old Escort. We queued up at the front of the away terrace turnstiles. Once in, we chose our position on the terracing about halfway back. I remember buying a meat pie from the kiosk in the ground. Still comfortably the worst thing I have ever tasted. Not sure what was in it but I didn't finish it.

TOM BROWN:
On the Friday, I remember leaving work full of confidence and chanting 'Champions' to wind up the Evertonians – one of them stopped me and said it was not over yet, to which I replied it was 'in the bag'. We set off to meet some friends in town before going to Anfield. I clearly remember seeing a penny on the pavement as I walked to the pub and thinking of the saying 'See a penny, pick it up, and all day long you'll have good luck', but I dismissed the superstition and walked on. Since that day I have never failed to pick up a coin I come across on the street. We were in the old boys' pen area (the corner between the Main Stand and the Kop) and it was full of Arsenal supporters, which was fairly unusual – I guess those were the last tickets available on general sale, but it does show how much easier it was to get tickets for big matches back then.

ADAM DWIGHT:
I am a lifelong Wolves fan who just happened to attend Liverpool University. I felt very much part of the true football community of Liverpool, which came together, united in grief, after the Hillsborough disaster in April 1989. In truth the whole football community came together because every football fan during this era knew that there but for the grace of God it could have been us standing on that

89

Leppings Lane terrace. During this era, we were all at times treated as thugs; all caged like animals. My best friend's girlfriend, also a student at Liverpool University, lost her life at Hillsborough and we queued for many hours to pay our respects on the Kop, where she too had stood. I was determined to try and get a ticket for the big match to end all big matches and so I made my way early on the Friday evening in the hope of buying a ticket. Sure enough we soon found a young Scouse lad who sold my friend and I two tickets for the Kop for £10 each and I'll never forget that the tickets were in his shoe, which he quickly replaced with the £20.

Brendan Boyle:

My biggest concern was my actual match ticket, which was for the Kop. The radio at work had been saying all day that any Arsenal fans with Kop tickets wouldn't get in. I unsuccessfully tried to get into the away end on three separate occasions, before being told I would be nicked if I tried again. On entering the Kop end it was quite moving to see the messages written on different areas, to those who had perished in Sheffield. I asked a steward if he would take me down to the so far empty away end. He said normally he would, but for this game they were not allowed, then informed me, 'Your lot are over in the corner.' I was astounded to find about 30 Arsenal fans in the corner, one guy was actually wearing an Arsenal sweatshirt! Everyone was trying to get moved up to the away end, and it was said they were going to move us en masse. About 25 minutes before kick-off with a big cheer we began moving to the top of the terrace to begin our trek to the away end. Unbeknown to us they were passing the lads to the police, who were throwing them out of the ground. Luckily for me I was at the back of the group, and when I saw what was happening, I made my way back to the corner, where only six remained, including the guy in the sweatshirt.

SIMON RICH:
We bundled off the coach and ran to Anfield. We stood near the back, just next to the Arsenal away seats. I had my bag of ticker tape I made using a hole punch at home the week before. It took me days to make enough. I don't think anyone does this any more but back then I did it a lot.

MICHAEL COHEN:
We secured a ticket from the great Theo Foley at the team hotel and hung around as players and staff mingled. I remember there was a palpable air of calm. It's hard to explain but you could feel we were going to do it. We got into the ground and I found myself sitting next to Pierce O'Leary, recognisable because he looks just like David.

EMILIO ZORLAKKI:
I was working as an Arsenal Travel Club steward. We missed the first 15 minutes of the game, but were told by a police officer, who came on our coach as we were entering Liverpool, that the game was going to kick off at 20.30 p.m. Amazingly, we didn't have a radio. When we parked up on the side of Stanley Park and heard the roars of the crowd, there was pandemonium. Fans were running to the ground as quickly as they could and I saw people jump over the turnstiles. I couldn't understand the atmosphere amongst the away fans, in optimistic mood and looking so happy. They must be mad, I thought.

AMY LAWRENCE:
As the convoy of coaches arrived with the game already started everyone sprinted to get to the entrance, the urgency to get in the ground rising fast. It became very crowded outside the turnstiles with people jostling for position. I recall one mounted policeman barking at the fans outside with piercing shout: 'Think about what happened at Hillsborough.' For a moment everyone went quiet, took

a collective step back, and got into a more orderly queue. It was a weird feeling to be simultaneously patient and impatient to move.

Alan Pickrell:

We parked on a grass verge very near to Anfield. Police told us we would get a parking ticket (which we did) but we just wanted to get into the ground as we were 15 minutes late. I remember a turnstile attendant telling us we were 1–0 up. We all cheered as we ran up the stairs – we weren't obviously (Scouse humour I guess).

Paul Austin:

We missed the first half hour and abandoned the minibus driver a fair distance from the ground, saying: be in this same spot after the game. Sure we were the last into the ground.

Carl Eldridge:

Ticketless, me and a pal tried to bunk in. We went through an open door in the Main Stand and followed a labyrinth of corridors, ever certain of gratis entrance with the match under way – finally faced with a closed door, we hesitantly opened it to find . . . the police control room. We (me and my mate Waz) high-tailed it before the assembled puzzled plod cottoned on – back to the away end turnstiles where a friendly bobby told us: 'You won't get in now, lads. Best bet is to go to the Arkles and watch it on TV.' Following a nine-hour drive from Bognor Regis on snarled-up roads with our beloved Gunners in with a smidgeon of a chance to win the bloody league title, we swerved his kind suggestion – and generally panicked. About 15 minutes into the game we heard a commotion and then the sound of people running – three coachloads of Arsenal fans – themselves held up by the horrific jams on the M6 – were frantically legging it to the game. We both stood in the middle and begged for 'any spares'. Within a minute Waz had a seat for a tenner and I told him to get himself in; a few minutes later I had bagged a ticket for a tenner, too, and in I went.

MEL O'REILLY:
When the boys in yellow and blue ran on the pitch before kick-off with the flowers for the Liverpool fans still mourning their 96 brothers and sisters who had died weeks earlier at Hillsborough, we were watching it on the coach's portable TV, until the Merseyside constabulary decided to give us a fast-track escort to the ground. Once inside, tucked into a corner, I found myself wedged up alongside a Demis Roussos lookalike (look him up, kids).

AMANDA SCHIAVI:
I got the great David Rocastle's (RIP) flowers. A man in front caught them and passed them to me. I always felt honoured that they were Rocky's flowers. I remember a few weeks before I had written a letter of condolence to Liverpool FC after Hillsborough.

TOM BROWN:
We arrived at Anfield full of confidence. We had been in great form and there was no way Arsenal would beat us. We took up our usual places on the Kop. When the Arsenal team came carrying bouquets that they distributed to people around the stadium my friend Andy pointed out that it was a nice touch, but he didn't like the Arsenal players getting on the 'good side' of the crowd.

PART II: NOT GOING

ANTONY SUTTON:
Instead of joining my mates for the journey north on that fateful day I did my round, selling pork pies out the back of a lorry round the

Surrey/Hampshire border. Beef sausages, steak and kidney pies, chipolatas, beef and onion pies. I was a good salesman but on this particular day my mind was elsewhere. I made my rounds on auto-pilot, returned home about lunchtime and had a few beers in my local before the game started. I got back home, hung my Arsenal flag up in the bedroom window, a feeble gesture I know but I had to do something, didn't I?

So I sat alone in front of the TV, just me, a six-pack in the fridge and a chicken vindaloo from the local tandoori, curtains drawn, with mixed emotions. I wanted to be there, I should have been there, I deserved to be there. Tonight would be for all Arsenal fans who had seen the dross. Walsall, York City, Oxford United, near relegation, Pat Howard, tonight would make up for all of that.

James Lukic:
Anfield 89 is legendary in our family. I was seven at the time and it is my first real memory of any game of football I have watched. My uncle John was playing in goal for Arsenal and so my dad, grandma and grandad were lucky enough to have tickets in the away end for the night. I remember my dad leaving the house with my grandma and grandad and not really being optimistic about Arsenal getting a result given the size of the task in hand.

Me and my younger brother sat in the front room of our house watching the game as my mum had said it was OK for us to stay up a bit later than normal to watch. My brother was only four at the time and so he wasn't really old enough to sit still and watch all the match but he kept sitting for five minutes and then going to play and then coming back again for five minutes. I wasn't much older but just remember being glued to the settee.

NICK HORNBY:

I was working out near Heathrow. I had this weird afternoon job and I was living in Finsbury Park and I walked down to the Tube to go to work and there was a load of coaches ready to go to the game. I was like, 'Go on, you're welcome to it', as I saw all these people getting on the coach. They're going, 'Come on! 2–0 no problem!' And I thought, it's very sweet but there's no way. The sheer agony of those games against Derby and Wimbledon lingered. I couldn't see how we were going to win the league. It was a reminder yet again that football teams will always let you down and the players are all useless. I got on the Tube. After work it's a long Tube ride back and I remember panicking a little bit about not getting home in time. I was watching with friends just around the corner from the stadium. I got home about 7 and sat down to watch.

DERMOT O'LEARY:

I was in a band with a guy called Simon Wild. That was our band – just me and Simon. He had a guitar and we both tried to harmonise and we did Springsteen and Prince covers and we were awful. He used to come round and practise every Friday after school and this particular day was two days after my birthday and I remember I said to him, listen, we can't do band practice. But I really want you to come over and watch Arsenal versus Liverpool because if we win by two goals we win the league. He just didn't like football at all but he was a lovely guy, a good buddy, so he sat down with me not really getting it. We watched it in my sister's room because she had a bigger room and the portable television.

MARTIN FROW:

Me and my mates had booked our annual lager-fuelled summer holiday to Magaluf (I know, I know) earlier in the year for late May. Of course we didn't know the season would be extended past the FA

Cup. A day or two before the game we noticed the Everton players were in Magaluf too on their post-season holiday. On the night of the game we'd found a bar showing the game and the Everton lot were in there too. Whilst at the bar getting a few San Miguels in, one of the Everton lot was also getting some in. I asked him what he thought Arsenal's chances were. His reply . . . 'No fookin' chance, mate, no fookin' chance at all.'

Alan Davies:
I couldn't get a ticket for the game. It was a Friday, which was a bit unusual. It was my brother's birthday. He's a Tottenham fan. Great. I was down in Whitstable, which is where I'd been to university and I still had lots of friends down there and I was with my good friends Damian Harris and Tom Connolly. Tom was a student with me. Damian was from Whitstable and I used to play pool in the pub with his older brother when I should have been studying. We went to Damian's house and we watched it there with his dad, who was a big Arsenal fan, and I thought I was going to be late. I remember we've got to get some cans in. We've got to get some cans from the 10 o'clock shop. And cigarettes obviously. Because it's the 80s, everyone's got to smoke. We got some cigarettes and the game started late. So now we're even more wound up. We're really tense sat on the sofa.

Ian Childs:
I was 13 at the time of the game. Growing up just outside High Wycombe the local team was non-league so everyone had a First Division team. My best mate was Andy White and he was an Arsenal fan too. We were both in the Junior Gunners. I was mascot for the first game after we lost the League Cup final to Luton. I still have the pictures of leading the team out alongside Tony Adams through a tunnel of mascots as it was the Junior Gunners' somethingth anniversary.

Andy was round for the game and we watched it in the front room, just the two of us. I can picture that room clear as day now. Green sofa, mahogany coffee table in front of it that the parents still own, big rug with a red flowery pattern and white tassels round the edge with polished dark wooden floorboards underneath. In the corner was the TV, a boxy number that was pretty big for its day but would be dwarfed by anything you have now. We were having our garage extended and redecorated and that Friday when I got home from school one of the builders asked me if I thought we would do it. I distinctly remember pausing, saying yes, and for the first time actually believing it.

Paul Bingley:
I started regularly attending Arsenal games from 1987. I lived in Billericay, Essex, and would attend with my friend Greg, whose grandparents lived in Highbury New Park. We'd drive there in the morning, eat a nice roast dinner with his grandparents, and then walk to Highbury. Greg's dad worked for the Met Police. He would go to the front of the Marble Halls on the first game of the season and get chatting to the policeman on duty. He managed to wangle free tickets to the Clock End almost every game. During the 1988–89 season, I went to every home game bar Liverpool and spent a grand total of £20. When it came down to that last game I couldn't get a ticket. I didn't hold out much hope. In fact, I didn't hold any. Liverpool were just too good. They were unbeatable at home and they'd just suffered the Hillsborough disaster. If anything, I thought we should just give up.

Jon Hossain:
In 1989 I was a junior doctor working in the accident and emergency department at the Whittington Hospital. On that Friday night I was rostered for a late shift, 3 p.m. till 10 p.m., but I managed to get a

colleague to come in early so I could get off. I was living in South London so had arranged to meet up with some friends in Victoria to watch the second half on TV. I got into my car about 15 minutes into the second half and listened to the game on Capital Gold. The roads in North London were empty, the only similar memory I have of this phenomenon was being in Italy when the World Cup was on and Italy were playing.

Andrew Norton:
That season was my first as a season ticket holder after answering an ad in the programme which called for volunteers to work at the ground during the redevelopment of the Clock End. Aged 15 and arriving at Highbury I was asked could I paint? I said no and after a week largely spent leaning on a broom I received my season ticket. Living in a family of non-football fans I watched the Anfield match alone on an old TV on my kitchen table.

Ross Adams:
I sat there in my yellow Adidas away shirt willing the boys on. I had a job as a paperboy and had made a scrapbook with cuttings of every match from the season, so felt a victory and the final reports of this would complete my scrapbook and make the effort all worthwhile.

Mike Feinberg:
August 1988 had brought me – at the time a 15-year-old American who had never left the country – over to London for what was supposed to be a one-year stay due to my father's business. I arrived as a 'sports fan' with no particular attachment to football, a curious teenager who wanted to assimilate into the culture and loved the incredible underground transport system. I decided immediately to find a football club to latch on to and, living on the Piccadilly Line, the choice was obvious – Arsenal.

I arrived at Highbury early on in the 88–89 season and immediately fell in love. The North Bank became my second home that year. Friday, 26 May 1989, I knew I'd never have the chance to go to Liverpool to support The Arsenal in person, so I made plans to join my mates at a local pub to watch the game on a fuzzy small television next to the pool table. I got in a huge argument with my then girlfriend – 16-year-old romantic dramas are the best aren't they? – and missed a good portion of the delayed kick-off and first half dealing with that insanity.

Someone whose arse I would've loved to have kicked put Gerry and the Pacemakers' 'Ferry Cross the Mersey' on the jukebox at the pub and there was a near riot. As for me, I must've walked the distance between London and Liverpool in pacing back and forth in the pub.

MARK LEE:

My best mate Tommie and I worked in Pizza Hut, Cambridge Circus at the time; I was the restaurant manager and Tommie a shift manager. Owing to staff shortages we both had to work, which meant we couldn't even watch the game. Although the restaurant was busy I dialled up the Arsenal Live phone line from the main restaurant phone and put it on speaker.

ANDY GRONNEBERG:

During the week leading up to the match at Anfield arrangements were made as to in which pub we would be watching the game. The Kings Head? Nah, too small. The Cat and Lantern? Nah, Dave's been barred after a fight the weekend before. We agreed on a 3 p.m. kick-off at the Prince of Wales. A good-sized boozer which was often frequented by a good bunch of Spurs fans too.

On the Thursday afternoon my boss dropped the bombshell that I'd be required to work overtime on the Friday – *that* Friday. Talk about deflated. He apologised profusely, saying that he had no other options due to the workload and that he'd make it worth my while. I had considered phoning in sick on the Friday but you can't do enough for a good boss. I made my way into work that day wearing the now famous yellow shirt defiantly. On the journey from Cockfosters into London that morning I copped a few 'You haven't got a chance, Gooner,' from people. Fortunately I had a Sony Walkman with a built-in radio, so at least I'd have some coverage of the match. I arrived at work to find my boss waiting by his office door. He explained again how sorry he was for asking me to work and informed me that he'd brought in a portable TV for me to watch the game on and that he would afford me a two-hour break when the game was on. He set it up in the conference room to afford me some privacy. Privacy? My arse! Every few minutes someone would pop their head in: 'Any score yet, Andy?', 'How's your lot getting on, Gooner?' 'You ain't got a chance aaaaaaaahhhh!' to mention but a few.

Gilbert McInnes:
So here in Australia the game was being shown live on SBS TV. I was up very early in the morning to watch the game, hoping against hope. Unfortunately my one-year-old son was also awake. 'It's OK, I will take care of him,' I tell my partner. 'You can go back to sleep.' What a good father I am!

Peter Norton:
As it was a Friday night my girlfriend at the time was expecting to see me. I watched the game with her dad. We sat engrossed and tense, with my girlfriend completely marginalised.

Christopher Stone:
I was 11 in 89. I was allowed to stay up late to watch the game. I remember my parents (who weren't particularly enamoured with football) were interested because of what had happened to the

Liverpool fans at Hillsborough. They also were quite keen on Liverpool winning for the same reason. It was the first time I had *really* wanted a team to win a match. I had been to nearly every FA Cup final since Man Utd beat Everton 1985 as my grandfather ran the line in a League Cup final in the 60s and got two free tickets until he died in the 90s.

STEVE KELL:

I had been to every game that season. I was able to make the original fixture but had something organised for 26 May that I could not get out of. I offered my ticket to a friend who was obviously delighted to go. The day before the match the planned thing I had was cancelled and so I could go to Anfield but my mate quite rightly told me to bugger off; he wasn't handing the ticket back. I ended up in my local pub that night, and met my future wife. Destiny or what?

RICHARD STUBBS:

Reg Lewis, who scored both Arsenal goals in the 1950 FA Cup final against Liverpool, was my stepdad. By 1989 I was a teacher at Thomas Tallis School in south-east London and was also working at the youth centre every Friday evening. In those days it really was 'in loco parentis'. Nothing much was on my mind that day except the game that night, and I had arranged with everyone that I would leave the youth centre at 7.30 p.m. so as to get home easily for the 8 p.m. start. At 7.30 a mother rang me up at the centre regarding her daughter Natalie, who very worryingly had not gone home that night. Natalie's mum was in a terrible state. She begged for my help. Did I have any idea where she might be? I said, 'Leave it with me and I will do what I can.' I felt the most important game for years disappearing from me and felt awful. Amazingly I remembered something that I thought I heard briefly, in one ear, earlier in the day about 'tonight', 'my house', a boy's name. Yes, Natalie was there! Her mum phoned me back full of relief and thanks. I got home in time to see the Gooners going to all corners of Anfield handing out wreaths respecting the loss and horrors of Hillsborough – what a genius, wonderful thought of Ken Friar to organise. Reg was his favourite player and I am sure that it is also down to Mr Friar that Reg is one of the legends at the stadium, with Patrick Vieira's arm around him.

GRAEME HART:
In 1989 I was living back in Melbourne, Australia and received the Arsenal matchday programmes by mail subscription. The match was broadcast live on TV here early Saturday morning our time. I was watching by myself as the wife and kids were still sleeping. I looked through the programmes to see whether we recorded league runners-up in our list of honours as I thought that would be an achievement in itself.

TEN

A Night of Chilling Simplicity

Brian Moore:[*]
So a night of chilling simplicity about it really. Arsenal must win by two goals to take the title. Anything less and it stays on Merseyside with Liverpool. And Arsenal, in their change strip of yellow, get the game under way, attacking the goal to our right. Just think, ten months of struggle in all conditions since last August and it's all on the last 90 minutes now. And for the first time a huge TV audience will actually see a title decided in the Football League. I just hope you are going to be comfortable there on the very edge of your seats for the next hour and a half or so.

George Graham:
Nothing surprises me at Liverpool because I'd been a player. I knew what it was like to go up there and usually lose. Most teams did lose there because they were so dominant. They had some fantastic players. But I had the little game plan. It had to be well organised. It had to be a disciplined performance. The first thing was the change of system to a three at the back. Then it was selling the idea to the players, trying to explain it to them and trying to build them up. Although some of it was probably a little bit of bullshit. 'Listen, guys, we've got to go out there nice and solid. We've got to keep it 0–0. We mustn't go out there thinking we've got to attack.'

* Brian Moore's commentary from ITV's broadcast of *The Match*, 26 May 1989.

The funny thing about it was, Liverpool never came at us. The first 20 minutes and we're thinking, what's happening here? They don't want to come forward. We didn't want to go forward. So it was stalemate. To be honest I thought, well, this is going nicely. This is fine.

ALAN SMITH:
There was always a great atmosphere at Anfield. It was doubly so that night. It was just charged. The emotion and passion of those first 20 minutes, 100 miles per hour, was frenetic. I remember getting fouled by Steve McMahon. I just got my toe there and he clipped me. Mickey Thomas was rampaging around like a mad man and Rocky was certainly fired up.

MICHAEL THOMAS:
I think it's always a responsibility when you play for Arsenal, a George Graham team, to get involved from the off. You try and put teams to the sword straight away if you can. We always wanted to start fast. I might be built like it but I'm not really a physical person. I like to nick balls and try and win balls but not that way. I used to like watching Rocky smash into people. Ha ha ha. It was good to see him and Tony and Bouldy. Oh, they were immense.

STEVE BOULD:
I think they had quite a big dislike of us. I think we'd been touted all season in the press as being the new guys in town.

ALAN SMITH:
As players we could sense, I could certainly sense, that they were just caught between two stools a little bit. I mean, to think that you could go out and lose a match 1–0. It's not an easy psychological thing for any footballer. So they didn't quite know how to approach the task. Do we push on? Play our normal game? Try and get a goal? Might

leave ourselves open. Or do we just sit back a little bit? I think they did sit back a bit and that helped us.

DAVE HUTCHINSON:
I hoped that my reputation was as a referee that let it flow. It wasn't over-fussy. Having said that, I'm just conscious that I blew the whistle an awful lot in the first half but the players responded well to me. As a referee my instinct told me that I'd got two teams there who despite what was at stake shared great respect between the clubs and between the two groups of players.

MICHAEL THOMAS:
That first ten minutes we could have scored. From my cross Bouldy headed it and I thought it was in and someone hit it off the line. We knew we were in the game. We knew it was going to be a long game. If we started on the back foot then it would be all about Liverpool coming on to us. We thought it best to take the game to them.

STEVE BOULD:
Was it from a corner? It couldn't have been from open play because George would have shot me if I had been that high up the pitch in open play. Steve Nicol cleared it off the line. Thank God really, because I think had we gone in at half-time 1–0 up, I think it probably would have changed the course of history. I think we might have had a little bit of a panic up, and I think they probably would have changed their shape and their system a little bit. Nil-nil helped us all round.

ALAN SMITH:
Apart from Bouldy's header there wasn't much at all. Ian Rush came off, did his thigh. We thought, ooh, that's good news, but then of course Peter Beardsley trots on. He wasn't a bad player. Ha ha.

89

Perry Groves:
As a sub I was watching on the bench, talking to Hayesey. It was packed. Usually it would just be the subs but we had everyone and his aunty in there. Normally first half, whether it's home or away, George would be in the directors' box. He liked to get an aerial view of how the team was set up and the team shape and if he ever came down halfway through the first half you knew someone was going to get a rollicking. But he was in the dugout for the whole game. There were no technical areas then. You could go basically where you like. If he wanted to run down the touchline and have a word with Nigel Winterburn he could have gone and done it but he stayed in his dugout, sometimes leaning over to shout and scream and point a bit, otherwise passing a message through Theo. I wouldn't say that we were really comfortable but it wasn't as if we were being bombarded. There was no panic.

Steve Bould:
They weren't the Liverpool that we all expected. I think they were nervous, all the ground was nervous, and also I think the Hillsborough factor might have affected them too. It was a difficult time for football but I think it was part of the deal too.

Tony Adams:
I can't remember a single thing really about the first half. It was uneventful. You set your stall out. Boring, boring Arsenal. You're not going to score in the first 45 minutes. We were bloody good at that.

Brian Moore:
The mood of the game is still very much intact. There's still everything to play for. Remember Arsenal need to win by two but we've come to an interval where it's Liverpool nil Arsenal nil.

GEORGE GRAHAM:
Half-time. I said to the boys, that's OK, now we'll try and grow into the game. We'll start going forward a bit more and a bit more and hopefully we'll get one. Then they're nervous and we'll get another one and we'll finish up with three. I actually thought we'd win three-nothing! Whether they believed that or not is another story.

DAVID O'LEARY:
George Graham gave as good a half-time speech as any manager ever could. George believed chances will come. Whether you'll take them is another thing but the chances will come. George is a great script-writer. He really is.

PAUL MERSON:
I remember sitting there like, what? I was thinking, he's on what I'm on, isn't he? Apart from Bouldy's header we never ever looked like scoring in a month of Sundays. At half-time George was like: 'Brilliant. Outstanding.' And I was thinking, we ain't touched the ball yet. We've got to win the game 2–0. What's brilliant about this?

MICHAEL THOMAS:
George knows how to keep you calm. Come on, boys. Don't worry about it. Come on. Sit down. Relax. Take your drink. Be quiet. It's all sorted. The plan's going well. Nil-nil. Don't worry. We got them. Just keep doing what you're doing.

ALAN SMITH:
At half-time I think a few of us felt a bit disappointed. Gaffer says brilliant, lads. That's what I wanted. I wanted you to keep a clean sheet. It's all going according to plan. All I want you to do now is push on a bit. Lee, Nigel, I want you to push up the pitch. Get some crosses into the box to Smudge and Merse and just let's be a bit more

adventurous. But again we went out thinking, OK, the gaffer thinks everything is going well. Going according to plan. Let's do it.

NIGEL WINTERBURN:

George thought they might panic and the mood would change if we got a goal, and another would follow. It was as if he'd already seen the game. It was absolutely incredible. How a manager can stand there at half-time and tell you what's going to happen and make you believe it, it's absolutely sensational. You've just got to go with it, haven't you? You've just got to go with it and give everything and hope it's going to happen.

BRIAN MOORE:

And welcome back to Anfield. In the next 45 minutes the championship of the First Division of the Barclays Football League will be decided. Ian Rush saying at half-time the first 15 minutes of this second half could well be crucial. Arsenal, you can be sure now, will be searching even more diligently for that crucial opening goal . . .

NIALL QUINN:

We were right near the front in row 1 behind the goal we were shooting into in the second half. The most vivid memory I have is Bruce Grobbelaar spotted us and he kept coming around and joking with us. He was known as a clown and he was laughing at us and pulling funny faces at us. It was all a bit unusual.

TONY ADAMS:

Rocky wins the free-kick and gets up with his gritted teeth and fist pumping. Oh my God. Shiver down my spine. We might have been young but we weren't boys. You know, we were men. We stood up and fought and they were brave guys and Rocky was like that. I love him and we were kids together and grew up together and you mess about together and get a bond and you're on the pitch together and you get close, don't you? He was a fighter. Maybe too much at times. Had to calm him down on a few occasions.

ALAN SMITH:
That was him. It was those gleaming eyes. Those pearly white teeth. Come on, lads. Come on.

DAVE HUTCHINSON:
It was an indirect free-kick I gave and that's critical. I gave a free-kick for an obstruction as we called it in those days.

GEORGE GRAHAM:
I don't think there was any other team in the country at that time that worked more on set-pieces than we did. It always amazes me that some of the top clubs do not work a lot on set-pieces even nowadays. But we did it. Adams, Bould on the near post for corner kicks. Magnificent. Even when the opposition knew what we were doing we would add a little bit more to it. It worked superbly. It was a lovely inswinging delivery, where the goalkeeper can't come for it because it's too wide and at the last moment maybe he should have come.

ALAN SMITH:
We'd practised that free-kick so much in training and it had never worked in a match. Nigel swings it in with his left foot. Then me, Bouldy and Tony are lined up. Tony's supposed to peel round the back. We had practised it so much in training and you think, oh, gaffer, this never works. Are you sure? Tony just ignored what he was supposed to do and just flung himself at the ball, created a distraction, but Nigel delivered a great one in with that trusty left foot.

89

Brian Moore:

Winterburn and Richardson behind it . . . Adams has made a darting little run in there . . . And Smith! And Arsenal have scored!

Tony Adams:

My decoy run let Alan touch it. I think I touched it as well. I was convinced. I said to Alan, I think I touched it. He said, no you didn't. I said I did. That's my goal but I'll let you have it. I was so full of shit in those days. As if it mattered but I'm sure I touched it. It was a good run. I wanted to take some credit. It was my decoy run that let you in, Alan. That was it. He's one of the best headers of the ball in the game, Alan, and he won two Golden Boots. Really underestimated and it's embarrassing to say that because he's definitely not underestimated by me. A fantastic centre-forward.

Alan Smith:

I snuck in. I was supposed to make that little dart and I lost my man and got my head to the ball. I just remember it coming in and me just helping it on and not changing the direction of the ball but getting a really solid touch. Grobbelaar had no chance because I managed to get it right in the corner. I followed through, bumped into Steve Staunton and swivelled round to go to the crowd. Ah! Our section going absolutely ballistic. Oh my God.

Penny Smith:

I knew straight away it was a goal because Alan was right in front of me, that side of the goal. I saw it clearly come off the side of his head. People were all going mad. I felt very sick, and actually it turned out a week later I was actually pregnant with Jess. I thought that was just nerves at the time.

JOHN LUKIC:
When he scored I've got 20,000 Scousers behind me and I wasn't one to celebrate goals anyway because I was too transfixed in the game but I could've heard a pin drop in the Kop when the goal went in.

DAVE HUTCHINSON:
The ball went into the goalmouth and finished up in the net. I thought Alan Smith had touched it. A direct free-kick means the side who are taking the free-kick can score by kicking the ball directly into the goal. If it's an indirect free-kick then the ball has to be played or touched by another player before it enters the net and that's why it was critical that Smithy's nose was big enough just to touch the ball. I couldn't see any reason why it should be disallowed but about seven or eight Liverpool players did.

ALAN SMITH:
They were all gathered round the ref. They were appealing. What's going on? We're thinking, oh no. Offside? I knew I wasn't offside. Did I get a touch? I had quite a lot of mud there, which looked good because it made people think that was from the contact. But it was a two-pronged appeal.

DAVE HUTCHINSON:
I looked at my linesman, Geoff Banwell, and he followed my instructions. Right to the very letter. I said if a goal is scored and you're happy I want you to go back as quickly as you can and hit that centre line and if you've got players chasing you go beyond the centre line and my reasoning for that is that if a player goes beyond the centre line he's had half a pitch to calm down and he deserves to be introduced to my yellow card then. Geoff was on his way as soon as that ball was in the net.

Alan Smith:
The ref has got this huddle surrounding him, all the vocal boys: Ronnie Whelan, Steve McMahon. Alan Hansen getting in the ref's ear. Dave O'Leary was our sole spokesperson. Senior man. Go on, Paddy. Go on. Tell them it was a goal. But you're thinking, no, 90 per cent chance he's going to disallow this for whatever reason.

Steve Bould:
It was just a strange atmosphere. I don't think anybody in the ground really knew if we'd scored or not.

David O'Leary:
I kept saying to the referee and the linesman, don't you get talked out of it. That's a goal. It was only seconds but seemed to be ages. I was thinking, don't you change your mind.

Dave Hutchinson:
The Liverpool players were surrounding me. It wasn't a nasty vitriolic sort of protest. There was frustration and the theme that was heard from one voice and then two voices then three voices – go and talk to your linesman – and I had no need to in my book. I was convinced Smith had nudged it in but how do you manage a situation like that? You've got everybody in the country looking at it. I don't want to start booking players unnecessarily so I said, OK, I'll go and talk to him. I was so confident in what I was going to be told that I thought, if it gets the players off my back . . . I said, leave me alone while I go and talk to him and I went across to Geoff and I said, Geoff, I've given a goal, some questions. Did I put my arm up for an indirect free-kick? He said yes, you did. I said was there an offside? No. Was there a foul or any other reason why I shouldn't allow the goal? He said no, none at all.

NIGEL WINTERBURN:

To be quite honest I had no idea what was going on. You are just waiting and waiting as if you're going to explode.

PAUL MERSON:

I'm sure it came off Alan's nose. Phil Thompson tells a good story. He was on the Liverpool bench that night. Kenny Dalglish said, 'Thommo, go down and see if he's touched that. Have a look.' Thommo said he watched it in the tunnel about three or four times and he came back and said he touched it. Fair play, though, as the linesman could have melted.

JIM ROSENTHAL:

I'm watching the monitor and I think the Liverpool players protested because they felt they should. I don't think they actually knew what they were protesting about. As far as I could see it was a legitimate goal and it was underlined on the replay.

DAVE HUTCHINSON:

So, I turned. It's a goal, lads. I went back to the centre and thankfully the Liverpool lads just moved away and got on with the game and for the rest of the game I can't recall a single Liverpool player having a crack at me about the goal. They got on with it.

ALAN SMITH:

When he pointed to the centre spot we were thinking, wow. He's been strong there. What a decision.

GARY LEWIN:

On the bench when the ref gave it we all went mad. Game on.

89

GEORGE GRAHAM:

Afterwards we were told that both the referee and the linesman knew it was a goal but they did that just to quieten the game down. It didn't quieten me down I can assure you. Ha ha ha. At the time I was caught up in the moment really. Everything was going to plan.

ALAN SMITH:

We did practise that free-kick until we were blue in the face and it did actually work on the big day finally, after all those weeks and months of it falling flat on its face. Yeah, about time that came off, lads, wasn't it? I said something similar to the gaffer. See that free-kick? It's about time it worked.

NIGEL WINTERBURN:

When we got the goal you start to realise: wow. The manager has just stood there and said if we score they're going to panic. We knew after what George had said, getting into the lead, getting that first goal, was so, so important. As the Arsenal end just erupts you know, boy, something special could happen here. You've got that massive high but then all of a sudden, you've got to recompose yourself again because one's not enough. You've got to get another one.

JOHN LUKIC:

When Alan scores the goal, that's when it all changed for me. At that moment, the whole thing turned on its head because at that point you're at a tipping point in a game. You've now got half a chance of winning the league so you know now above all else you can't concede. Had we conceded I think that would have been a long road back. So my concentration levels as soon as Alan scored have gone through the roof.

BRIAN MOORE:
Merson . . . Richardson . . . A chance here, Thomas . . . and Grobbelaar was able to grab it! Suddenly Thomas totally unmarked deep inside the Liverpool penalty area, and what a golden opportunity that was . . .

PAUL MERSON:
Mickey missed an unbelievable chance to score. I thought that was it.

ALAN SMITH:
It was a bit of a stabby toe poke.

NIGEL WINTERBURN:
I wanted to throttle him. Ha ha.

MICHAEL THOMAS:
Oh, stop it, will you? Stop it. God, I'll always get that. Oh no! That chance. I don't know. When the ball came to me on the edge of the box and I turned I just thought I had no time. I had two players right beside me so I tried to toe punt it in and . . . pfft. When you see it now on telly you think, oh, bloody look at the chance you had. But at the time I felt I had no time to do what I wanted to do and so I just basically rushed it. I hate looking at that and getting told about that.

NIGEL WINTERBURN:
If I was bigger and stronger and brave enough – oh, what did I want to do to him at that moment! It was the best chance of the game. He's pretty much around the penalty spot, maybe a little bit further back. It's a scuffer, hits it straight along the ground and Grobbelaar said, thank you very much, that's it, the league title is ours. It was an unbelievable chance. Oh, Mickey was so calm as well. Nothing gets under his skin. Nothing.

LEE DIXON:

I went: that's it. I remember thinking, typical Mickey, with his languid finishing style.

MICHAEL THOMAS:

At the time I thought, I've missed that chance but I know I'll get another one. I believed I'd get another chance.

JOHN LUKIC:

It would have been nice if it had gone in but had it gone in you think you've got a long 15 to 20 minutes to hang on. Which would've been quite interesting.

BRIAN MOORE:

Quarter of an hour left. Remember Arsenal need two goals. At the moment they have one. If it stays this way Liverpool will be champions for the 19th time. But will it stay this way . . . ?

JEFF FOULSER:

The longer it went on the more you thought there could be something on here. I listened to Brian Moore's magical commentary – and he was in my view the best in the business. He was the master of making the viewer feel that something special was just about to happen and he created that sense in our OB truck that maybe, maybe, there is something going on here. As the game went on and on and we got down to the last few minutes we had a little clock, a little graphic, running. There were no running scores or times on the screen in those days, which is impossible to believe now. Every single sport has got a running scoreline. We didn't have that because the technology wasn't up to it. But we had this little digital clock that was counting up towards the 90 minutes and I said to the director, 'Let's put that on the screen.' It had never been done. There had never been a running clock on a football match before and he said, 'No, no, it'll look shit.' I said, 'It doesn't matter. The story is more important than how it looks!' He went, 'All right then.' So, he put it up there.

Jim Rosenthal:
As the clock ticks towards 90 I'm getting ready to talk to Kenny, who was not the greatest if I'm honest in front of a camera. He didn't like doing it but I am preparing to talk to him about the year they've had, about being a Double winner.

David Pleat:
One of the things that comes out of the game, which was made famous through Nick Hornby and *Fever Pitch*, concerns one thought I was trying to make on the night and the phrase didn't come out quite right. Somebody reminded me of the exact words recently: 'I think in a way if Arsenal are to lose the championship having had such a lead at one time it is somewhat poetic justice that they have got a result on the last day.' Brian Moore nudged me and said, 'They would see that as small consolation I would think, David.' Whenever I did a commentary the first thing I thought about afterwards was have I made any faux pas? Usually I hope to have done OK. The amazing thing was whenever I commentated on Arsenal I almost went out of my way to make sure there was not a hint of bias in any shape or form.

Tony Adams:
It did change gear and we were running out of time. I did sense that and decided to run around like a lunatic. I don't know, I think I lost my head a little bit. Luckily those around me kept calm, in particular Kevin Richardson, good pros that just steadied the ship. But I was getting anxious. Sometimes you get so carried away and so vain you

think you can win the game on your own or you try too hard, stupid hard, and I remember chasing Barnesy and chasing someone else and being out of position and just running around.

ALAN SMITH:
There's not a clock in the stadium like there is today so you look across to the bench or ask the ref. How long? You're hearing the high-pitched whistles coming from the Kop particularly begging the ref to blow the final whistle.

GEORGE GRAHAM:
With a minute or two minutes to go I thought, we've given it our best shot. We've been absolutely superb. The way we'd planned it, the way the lads carried it out on the pitch, it was superb. I was a bit down because we've given it everything and it's not happened. I was thinking, what do you say to the fans and the press? You know, we've just lost by winning one-nothing. We've done our best. I felt really low.

NIGEL WINTERBURN:
I knew it was getting pretty late in the game. I had no idea about the time. You're so wrapped up in what's going on and what you're trying to achieve. You're so focused and I suppose you are dreaming, if I'm honest, that you're going to get another chance.

BRIAN MOORE:
Richardson is down with a leg injury . . . and he's still down but Arsenal want to go on. 41,783 is the crowd here at Anfield and not a soul has left before the final whistle, you can be sure. Treatment for Kevin Richardson, the referee will have to add on time. Unless there is an amazing and dramatic twist now it looks like Liverpool, David.

GARY LEWIN:

I ran on to Kevin. I remember having a conversation with him while I was stretching his leg out. 'You've got to carry on, mate. You've got to carry on.' He said, gimme a sec. I was stretching his hamstring and then relaxing it and I pulled him up and ran off as he carried on. I was just worried we were going to run out of time. Theo said, there can't be long left, but I knew there was another two minutes of stoppage time as Kevin had been down for ages.

BRIAN MOORE:

One minute to go. McMahon has got the word from the Kop obviously. But nobody knows exactly how much time the referee will add on . . . The faces of the players are something to behold at the moment.

LEE DIXON:

Obviously, we didn't see that happen on the night. Steve McMahon and the one-minute signal has become an iconic thing. I always say it to my friends, you know. Instead of one minute, 'Oh, I'll be there in a Steve McMahon.' I didn't see him do it on the pitch. I just remember at the time I presumed it wasn't long to go. Just after that moment I actually asked the referee. How long to go? He just went, 'It's done.' It's over.

JOHN LUKIC:

I roughly knew that it was all over. You can tell by looking at the opposition.

STEVE BOULD:

The whole night was a really strange, surreal atmosphere. I felt we'd done a gallant job but not quite good enough.

Brian Moore:
Just a few seconds more now for Kenny Dalglish unless Arsenal can mount something absolutely spectacular in the minutes that remain.

Michael Thomas:
After Kevin Richardson went down injured I said to Richo that I'm just going to break forward now. You'd best hold the fort. I'm just going to look for another goal somewhere and he was like, OK, no problem.

Nigel Winterburn:
John Barnes went behind me down the right-hand side. So there's little that I can do. I can't affect the game. I'm thinking as everybody else is thinking: why is John Barnes not going to the corner flag and flicking it up and booting it out the stand? Everyone would do that, wouldn't they? But you're talking about John Barnes. Skilful winger. Unbelievable player. Liverpool Football Club have been brought up and built up on playing and passing and scoring goals. Of course, he's not going to go to the corner flag. He's going to go and try and score. Well I'm so pleased he did try and go and score. Because history has been changed by him doing that and Richo comes in and tackles him.

Paul Merson:
He was one of the best players in England and not far off the top 10 or 20 in the world. He could have done anything that day. He could have literally flicked it up and booted it 30 miles into the stand and everybody just jog back.

Tony Adams:
I remember Kevin Richardson knocking the ball down and just calmly giving it back to the goalie. I was still in the 'boot it' phase. Get it up there. Just fucking boot it. Excuse my French.

JIM ROSENTHAL:
I never interviewed Kevin Richardson. I don't think I ever spoke to him because he was not the most approachable of human beings and he wasn't one of the stars. But that night for me he was man of the match for Arsenal. He got cramp and the subs were already on and then right at the end he gets the ball away from one of the greatest players in the world, John Barnes. Passes it back – another thing you could do in those days – and then the move starts. I think for that night Kevin Richardson is the unsung hero really.

NIALL QUINN:
Very near the end it was getting really tense and we realised we wanted to get round to the dugout.

PAUL DAVIS:
We were asking a steward if we could go round the perimeter of the pitch but he wasn't sure. The fans around us were shouting at him to let us through. 'Look at their blazers! They are the players!'

NIALL QUINN:
We were whisked around. As we were walking down the sideline to the dugout the whole thing suddenly developed. We were running down the side of the pitch. It was mad stuff.

BRIAN MOORE:
Arsenal come streaming forward now in surely what will be their last attack . . .

JOHN LUKIC:
It was one of those moments in life. Theo says he's got me to thank for a scar that he's got on his head. Because when I threw the ball out

that night rather than kicked it he went to stand up to give me a round of vitriol and he banged his head on the dugout.

GEORGE GRAHAM:
I thought it was gone anyway. I thought it was all over. You know, whether he kicked it or threw it you think, there's not enough time. It's finished.

JOHN LUKIC:
I was absolutely mentally shot at that time, which is probably hard to believe but as a goalie I was always intense and that second half, from Alan's goal going in, my concentration levels had gone through the roof so I thought to myself, it's not going out the box here. That's as far as I'm going to get it. About five minutes previously I had a kick which I duffed out to the left-hand side. I looked up and I saw Dicko and to me it seemed like he was in oceans of space and it just seemed the natural thing to do at the time and so I bowled it out to Dicko.

NIGEL WINTERBURN:
What are you doing? Dicko? Why are you throwing it out to Dicko?

LEE DIXON:
I was looking at him picking the ball up and he sort of looked at me and I was running up the pitch. Because I know it's over so just kick it. There's no point throwing it to me because all I'm going to do is do what you're doing and you can kick it farther than me so just get the ball and kick it up the pitch.

JOHN LUKIC:
I don't think he wanted it – he was running away at the time – but he got it because I didn't want it.

LEE DIXON:
I remember him shouting 'Dicko!' and pulling his arm back. I literally didn't want it. I was like, 'No. Don't do that.' So now I've got one thing on my mind. I'm just going to launch it as far down the pitch as I can. I've taken a touch and looked up and Smudge is coming towards me and I'm like, what are you doing? Run the other way! This is all happening in slow motion. Smudge is coming towards me. I only had that one ball. So I just thought, for once don't shank it off the pitch. Try and find your man.

GEORGE GRAHAM:
Lee used to like overlapping and he used to hit the ball at Highbury into the crowd. He used to find this guy in the crowd all the time. Ha ha ha. Anyway this time he whacked it.

LEE DIXON:
I didn't whack it. It was a cultured right foot!

BRIAN MOORE:
A good ball by Dixon . . . finding Smith . . .

ALAN SMITH:
When Lee gets the ball I know where I've got to be because we've done it so often that season and Lee knows where I'm going to be. You've normally got one or two or even three options but I knew he was going to play it up to me and he really did ping it up with some force. As it was coming I thought, I've got to turn first time here. I can't afford to just take a touch and have the centre-half behind me and lay it back.

LEE DIXON:
Smudge did what Smudge does best and took a velvet touch. He has looked inside and Mickey's set off on this run.

89

ALAN SMITH:
There's seconds to go. I've got to take a chance – and it was taking a chance that I'd swivel as I took the touch – but it came off perfectly.

BOB WILSON:
Throughout the season Alan Smith was being hit with these missiles. Pragmatic was the term that was given to the Arsenal side at that time and you would hit Smudger with these balls and it would be like a magnet. On that last game of the season even everybody at Liverpool said you could have hit him with anything on that night and it never moved off him. It obviously was crucial.

ALAN SMITH:
The touch was spot on and it bounced just in front of me as I've turned and I see a flash of the yellow shirt in my peripheral vision. I don't really know it's Mickey but I just help it on in that direction. A little poke forward and there he is running.

BRIAN MOORE:
For Thomas charging through the midfield . . .

MICHAEL THOMAS:
I just remember the ball hitting Smudger. As usual Smudger chests it and he turns inside and all I see is a gaping space and I'm going to go for a run. I'm going to go for a run. Smudger sees me. He's going to put me in and that was it. When I tried to hit the ball over Steve Nicol's shoulder and it hit his shoulder, it hit me and bounced into the path where I wanted to go. Meant to be.

NIGEL WINTERBURN:
Mickey's on to it. I'm on his outside about five yards wide of him, slightly behind him and I'm watching him. You cannot miss this time. I know what you are like. You are super cool.

ALAN SMITH:
I could see the whole picture unfolding as I was running behind him. The little break of the ball. Those red shirts closing in on the right. Ray Houghton being the closest. I just remember being convinced that he was going to leave it too late because Mickey being Mickey, he always did everything in his own time. Never ever rushed. Stubborn as you like.

LEE DIXON:
I'm now 30 to 40 yards away looking at the back of Mickey's shirt and it looks like he's through on goal. He can't be. Surely not. Talk about time standing still. When you're looking that far down the pitch you can't tell where the lines are, whether he's in the box or he's outside the box. I just saw players converging on him, thinking, he's going to get tackled right now.

PAUL MERSON:
If there's one player in the whole of the team that you would want that to happen to, to go through one on one with the keeper with a minute to go when he's just missed a sitter ten minutes before, I would say Mickey Thomas. Because if he did miss he wouldn't give a shit. He wouldn't. That's how laid-back he was. If he did miss it wouldn't have affected him. I think I'd still be in a mental home now if I'd have missed. I don't know how I'd get it out of my head.

89

George Graham:

Mickey was really a cool dude. A talented boy, he just wanted to play football and go forward.

David O'Leary:

I'm looking straight down the pitch and I see him get through and it's completely still behind the goal. I'm going, you put that ball in the net, Mickey Thomas. It's just going on and on and on for ever it seems and I was thinking, get over that line.

Paul Davis:

In those situations he did seem to just relax more than anybody else. He has this way about him, when the pressure's there he'll just extra relax.

Michael Thomas:

I'm thinking, I'm right on goal here. All I've got to do is put it over Steve Nicol's head and I'm in. I didn't get enough on it. It hits his shoulder. It hits me and then bounces beyond Steve Nicol towards their goal. Towards Bruce Grobbelaar. And I'm thinking now, this is my time. I'm going to score this. Ray Houghton was so close. I had no idea he was that close. It is scary. My heart beats even now with the tension every time I see it.

Everybody knows how great a goalkeeper Bruce Grobbelaar was. Very flexible. I'm waiting for him to make the first move. It's like a poker game. Me and Bruce have a little stand-off with each other. Who's going to show his cards first? I'm there waiting for him. Waiting and it seems ages before he made the move. Bruce was taking so long to dive and I'm thinking, come on, please. I want to get this over. Just as he showed his hand I knew what I was going to do.

Perry Groves:
All the great sportsmen say all their great moments go in slow motion. They say their body slows down and their mind slows down and it seemed like it was slow motion to me. I'm facing that way and Thommo's running through. Basically I go to being a fan. I'm on the pitch but in that moment I am a fan with kit on because I can see it happening and there's nothing I can do to influence it because I'm too far away. I can remember just thinking, for fuck's sake, Thommo, shoot!

Alan Smith:
It was a cat-and-mouse situation. Under those circumstances, he's incredible. So many players would have just panicked and just got the shot off quickly, especially as he missed that earlier one. But he didn't. Cool as a cucumber. He was determined to wait for Grobbelaar to make a move and wait for him to go down before he was going to flick it and that's exactly what he did in the nick of time before the challenge came in. It's not even about points at this stage and it's not even about goal difference. It's about goals scored. So to score one goal more than them over 38 games brings us the spoils. But that's the beauty of football. That's how things can condense. After all that blood, sweat and tears it can come down to that. Just five seconds. You flunk it and it's all gone to waste and you keep your cool and you're a hero.

Paul Merson:
Ray Houghton was saying not too long ago he could have brought him down that day. I talk to Bruce Grobbelaar and he thought he had it.

Michael Thomas:
The pressure probably would have crushed me if I knew what time it was. Because there was no clock I didn't know how long it was to go

so that's why I just thought: no pressure. Once Bruce showed his hand all I needed to do was a little clip and that was it.

Brian Moore:
Thomas . . . It's up for grabs nooooowwww!

Michael Thomas:
Once it hits the net I'm just thinking ecstasy really. It's just incredible. I've done what I wanted to do. That's that feeling. I've done it.

Nigel Winterburn:
I'm off. It hasn't even gone in the net. Whoomph. Straight across the goal. I'm already celebrating.

Alan Smith:
We all just peeled off and went to the corner to take the acclaim of the fans. The scenes. Absolute bedlam.

Lee Dixon:
As it hit the back of the net I remember just bursting out crying on the pitch. It sounds melodramatic but that's what it was.

Tony Adams:
I pretty much lost my head. It was probably the only time in my career I had been knocked off my feet. When Mickey scored I was actually emotionally knocked off my feet. It's a weird sensation but the legs had gone and I was down on my knees. You know, just phew. It must have been the build-up of the occasion and the enormity of what's happened because that doesn't normally happen. I don't think I've ever been knocked off my feet since. So that was pretty powerful stuff.

PAUL DAVIS:
Myself, Brian and Quinny just celebrated as a three together at the side of the pitch. We were jumping up and down amongst ourselves. It was indescribable.

NIALL QUINN:
I wanted to have played, to add a jersey on the night, but it was the next best. We were right beside it all.

STEVE BOULD:
I saw the goal from the bench as I had been subbed. I remember there was a police officer in front of us with a big stick and as we jumped up he started to knock us back with it. I think he realised it was going to be mayhem on the pitch.

GARY LEWIN:
That police commissionaire with his cane was trying to get us to all sit down again on the bench. He wasn't happy at all.

JOHN LUKIC:
From my end of the pitch I saw the goal go in and it was like somebody had just turned a switch. The place went absolutely silent apart from the 4,000 Arsenal fans up in the top corner. It was almost surreal.

TONY ADAMS:
I couldn't run up the other end and congratulate him because I was on my knees. In real time it's very quick and all I remember is Nigel wheeling off to the crowd. The game wasn't over yet and if I'd run up that end and done a Nigel I don't think I'd have got back.

Jim Rosenthal:
For a moment, the whole place went quiet. Because I don't think Arsenal could believe what they'd seen and the Liverpool fans were just dumbfounded. Then Mickey Thomas did this celebration and I've never seen a celebration like it. He's like a corkscrew trying to screw himself into the Anfield turf.

Michael Thomas:
People always remind me that I nearly broke my neck in that celebration. Why didn't I just run into the Arsenal supporters? I didn't know what I was thinking.

George Graham:
I was shocked. I didn't really embrace the second goal as much as I would have liked to have done. I should have been on the pitch, jumping and hugging everybody, but I was so taken aback because I had been thinking: we've given it our best shot and we've come up short.

Jeff Foulser:
I was on the phone to ITN because following us was *News at Ten*, and I had been talking to their programme editor and they were going to come to us right at the top of *News at Ten* if Arsenal managed to win by two clear goals. As he's saying that I can hear Brian Moore's commentary building up and him saying it's up for grabs now and I sort of look up with the phone to my ear and oh my God Mickey Thomas scores and all hell broke loose. I said I'll have to ring you back.

Andy Cowie:
As a photographer towards the end of a game that's poised the thing you had to worry about was your film was only 36 frames and you

wondered, have I got enough film in the camera? All of a sudden sometimes when you press nothing happens and you think, oh, I've run out of film. That's it. Because Thomas kept coming and coming and coming, I was still firing and thinking, how many frames have I got in the camera? Have I got enough if he does score? I'm still clicking away. I don't normally shoot more than two or three frames but I shot 18 frames. I was panicking so I kept going and kept going and going.

MARK LEECH:
I was the opposite side of the goal from Andy and took a frame that never saw the light of day because Nicol's arm is across Michael Thomas. But the point missed there is the fact that Ray Houghton's toe of his boot is on that ball. It's just a whisker away. Just before Thomas pulls the trigger and puts the goal in the net. Houghton is unbelievably close.

JIM ROSENTHAL:
As a piece of sporting drama you'd struggle to find anything to compare with it. How it can just change like that. At that moment in time. With that prize. With millions watching at home. You couldn't script it. But of course there's still time to play and Brian Moore is saying, hold on a moment.

MICHAEL THOMAS:
I don't know how long we've got left, ten minutes or whatever, before this game finishes. Just sit it out.

LEE DIXON:
I've managed to stop myself crying on the halfway line. I got back to my position and then thought, come on, ref, you just said it's over. Then they kick off and they have another attack. Mickey is

there at the edge of the box, cool as you like, and rolls it back to Lukey with the outside of his foot when he should've just launched it in the stands.

Michael Thomas:
I remember Rocky and the lads saying afterwards, what the hell were you doing? Why didn't you put it over his head or whatever? I was facing our own goal at the Kop and then someone was coming towards me and I did a side-step and passed it back to John Lukic. I can't believe I did that. We were 2–0 up and if they scored a goal we've lost the league and I didn't really think about it. But for me to do that was normal.

Lee Dixon:
But that was him. Like the goal was him. Take as much time as you can. Don't hurry or anything. It's just fine.

Alan Smith:
I don't know what was going on inside his head but from the outside it looked like water off a duck's back. He was the most laid-back man going and he seemed to just revel in it. I suppose, why wouldn't you?

Michael Thomas:
A lot of players would say it couldn't fall to a better person in the team than me because everybody else would have stressed out about that situation. Whereas I was thinking that I've missed one before, I've got to bury this one and that was it. To put it in was just amazing. Being a London boy. Scoring that goal. To bring the trophy back to London for the first time since 1971. It was fantastic. Just see our travelling supporters, that was it for me.

LEE DIXON:
The ball is launched up and I think Smudge hears the final whistle. He does his little double skip thing. Then the realisation that it's over and then mayhem. Everyone's just running.

MICHAEL THOMAS:
It was nice to be a part of history in the making. Especially for Dave O'Leary because I've watched Dave O'Leary throughout my whole life as a kid. Seeing him in cup finals. The next minute I'm being an apprentice to these guys and I'm in awe of them. He's been through everything and not won the league. He was part of the family. Graham Rix was there, which was great. Kenny Sansom was there, which was fantastic. They had both left but to celebrate with them, see them there, seeing Arsenal win the league, was fantastic for me. It doesn't matter if you leave. We're still family.

There are pictures of me with David Rocastle, Tony Adams, Paul Merson. Paul Davis, Kevin Campbell, Niall Quinn and Martin Hayes were there. Just seeing us. What we came through. We've come through the ranks as a group and the only person that was missing was Martin Keown. It meant so much to us all. We fought together, cried together and this one was obviously a big one – to win it and to feel we were all part of it. It's a brotherhood. We never had many arguments in that squad. We all got on very well. It's weird to have a squad with no squabbling, no in-house fighting about anybody. It was just great to be a part of that. Nothing ever better for me.

DAVID O'LEARY:
I had my brother and my dad behind that goal and I remember going down at the end to see them. Both of them were saying at the time the same thing. They didn't think that ball was going to make it over the line for Mickey's goal.

Paul Davis:
We just rushed on to the pitch after the game and just celebrated with the players and everybody was on there. To be fair to the Liverpool supporters they stayed behind and they were complimentary. I remember them just clapping us as we went around with the trophy.

George Graham:
I was in a state of shock. Honestly. I could not believe it. I thought it was an unreal situation, a fairy tale.

John Lukic:
As a sportsman you don't pick the moment, the moment picks you. And it was one of those nights where that certainly happened. You know it was our moment and it was meant to be. Just the euphoria of it all. It's a monumental thing to win the league.

Alan Smith:
I remember by the bench at the final whistle the gaffer going, 'Let's calm down.' Everyone was jumping on top of each other and he obviously had Hillsborough in mind and to maintain some respect.

George Graham:
I didn't know what to think. I honestly couldn't believe it. Because I'd been through it in my mind. We're going out of here with our best shot and it's not worked and then when Mickey scored what do you do? What do you do? It was wonderful but I couldn't have got up and started running because I was not a runner anyway, you know. I wasn't much of a hugger either. Look at all the coaches nowadays, the way that they're behaving and acting. I think it's great. It's fantastic the way that they're so emotional. Emotion in a game, that's what football is about surely. The fans get emotional, the players on the pitch. At times I wish I'd become more emotional.

ALAN SMITH:

When George came on the pitch and hugged everyone it was obviously out of the ordinary. He would never hug the players. I remember all the Liverpool stewards were saying well done, and the police, and the fantastic reception of those Liverpool fans who stayed and applauded. That meant a lot to us.

PAUL MERSON:

The one thing I always remember is the Kop clapping us off. That's some going. To lose the league in the last minute on the last day and do that.

DAVID DEIN:

Directors' decorum is that you don't celebrate when you score a goal. You try to be a bit low-key. Well I must say that when Mickey scored with the last kick of the season, the directors' decorum for me went out the window. I just catapulted myself about six foot in the air, punched the air and when I came back into my seat there was Peter Hill-Wood and he took out his cigar. He calmly turned around to me and he said, 'Never in any doubt.' Ha ha.

Of course you feel so ecstatic and proud. This is the team that you love. That you worship. Where you go to pray every weekend. That's the team that has just won the league in sensational style and it was memorable and I always say this: no matter how often football is spoken about, written about, filmed, broadcast, that moment, the Mickey Thomas goal, the last kick of the season, will always be remembered.

BOB WILSON:

Although I was the goalkeeping coach in 89 I watched from afar. The fact that I'd been in the side in 71 with George and Pat in such similar circumstances I felt I was really out there with them at

Anfield. I was out of control at the end of the game. I think I went unconscious.

Paddy Barclay (*Independent* football correspondent in 1989):
For every journalist the 'runner' – the running match report which is written during the match – is probably the most terrifying experience. Every night match I did in the early days I would go home with a bad tension headache. The last section you send has to be in on the whistle, dictated down the phone to a sub-editor in the office for reasons of speed. When you are in big, big trouble is when you get something like events at Anfield. Everything you have written up to stoppage time shows that brave Arsenal fell short. It puts you under enormous pressure. Michael Thomas turned a routine drama into one of the greatest, most unpredictable and most shocking dramas ever seen on an English football field. My word it was difficult, though, rewriting it in the space of 30 seconds. Once I had telephoned in my initial report I remember looking up at the Kop, which was to the right of the tight little press box at Anfield. It looked like a lot people had sat down they were so shocked. They rose to their feet again and applauded Arsenal's achievement. Something I will never forget.

Jim Rosenthal:
After the game, look at George, he's Mr Cool. As he was throughout the night. I felt deeply for Kenny because he had that horrible glazed look that coaches get when they just don't know what's happened. I interviewed Tony Adams on the pitch. It was chaotic out there. As an aside I'd had a little bet with Tony Adams in pre-season. This was a different era when the media and players were friends because you could mix with them. There was no social media. There was no one taking pictures. On the back of a disastrous European Championships in 1988 I'd spoken to Tony and we'd talked about the title and

he said, 'We'll win it' and I said, 'No chance, Tony' and he said, 'Go on then, what do you say? £100?' I went OK. And at the end of the game the first thing Tony said to me was '100 quid!' I did pay him and I was happy to pay him as well.

GEORGE GRAHAM:
Later I caught up with my son and daughter who came to the game. There was some nice pictures with my daughter walking up the steps with the famous 'This Is Anfield' sign behind. It was a lovely little thing that Bill Shankly came up with wasn't it? This Is Anfield so everybody would be frightened. Oh my God. Let's shake.

JIM ROSENTHAL:
Back in the tunnel the referee David Hutchinson at the end of the game came up to me and his face was as white as a sheet. He said, 'Jim, Jim, did he touch it?' And I went, 'Of course he touched it, David' and the colour came back into his cheeks. He gave me a little hug and said, 'Oh thank you so much for that.'

DAVE HUTCHINSON:
It's one of the things if you have made a mistake, you've got to be big enough to live with it. But I was certain it was a goal. Geoff was certain it was a goal. The first hint of any pressure was as we came off the pitch at the end and Kenny Dalglish just shook hands and said thank you very much, are you absolutely certain that that was a goal? At that time I can remember saying well, as of yet, I have not had chance to look at it on the box but yes, I'm as certain as I can be. And then bless his heart, Jim Rosenthal suddenly put his head in between and said you're OK, Dave, on the goal. Smithy touched it. Phew! And all credit to Dalglish. Twenty minutes after the game there's a knock on the door. Dalglish is there with a bottle of champagne and he said, we were hoping to drink this but you may as well have it. I don't

think he was being sarcastic. He was being very genuine and it was appreciated.

There was a huge sigh of relief. Not audible but you know I can feel myself just starting to relax. I'm told by my colleagues that I was always ice cool in the dressing room before a game and I did that deliberately. It was my job to keep my colleagues calm and I needed that for that particular match. But after the game, I think we all relaxed a bit. Only problem was I'd still got to drive 200 miles back down to Oxfordshire after the game. This game was on the Friday but on the Sunday I was fourth official at Wembley for the final of the Sherpa Van Trophy. Torquay and Bolton. A different kettle of fish.

LEE DIXON:

I was just completely taken over by the emotion. I vaguely remember them wheeling this wallpaper pasting table out that the trophy got plonked on and then we were all standing around willy nilly, not organised at all. Some bloke from Barclays came on. There were two trophies. One was a trophy that nobody seemed to know what it was (it was from Barclays) but then the proper trophy was there. It's a beautiful, beautiful trophy as well. Absolutely stunning. I remember looking at it going, wow. The lights of Anfield shone and it all started to flood into the system. I remember holding it up and from then onwards I've no clue what was going on. You just go mad but it was quite surreal in the dressing room because it wasn't expected.

ALAN SMITH:

There's always a few extra people in there on occasions like this and then the TV cameras came in and I gave an interview with Mickey and people are chucking stuff at you, the champagne's flying. Then you get in the bath – a small bath like a lot of the places had back then – and you just can't believe it. I think what we all agreed, we thought, it's not going to get better than this. It can't get better than this. How can it?

TONY ADAMS:
We smashed in the false ceiling in the Anfield dressing room. Sorry. Apologies.

PERRY GROVES:
I was sitting with Bouldy and Merse in the dressing room. We've got a couple of beers and I said, 'Do you remember what Mystic Meg said there before the game? The gaffer predicted we go in 0–0 at half-time then if we get a goal the tension will swing and then we'll nick it?' That's folklore.

DAVID O'LEARY:
I was tearful. Tony Adams told me to shut up, you big tart. He said, 'Man up.' I just couldn't believe it! I couldn't wait to go in and see Pat Rice in the dressing room afterwards. I'd heard it all from him about how they had gone over to Tottenham and won the league. I remember him even saying beforehand 'It's about time you got a medal. It's about time you went and done the business.' I couldn't wait to get in there and shut him up because I had to listen to him for years saying that type of thing to me.

JOHN LUKIC:
The celebrations in the dressing room bring you even closer together. There is almost an invasion of people who want to be part of it. But one thing that stands out on the night is a couple of Liverpool players came in. One was Bruce Grobbelaar and the other one was Peter Beardsley, which was a very magnanimous thing to do. That's not an easy thing by any stretch of the imagination. To have it snatched out

of your hands in the final kick of a football match and to have that about you to actually be able to rise above that and congratulate the other team. That takes a lot of doing.

Michael Thomas:
That was Bruce. I got to know him afterwards. To come in to bring the champagne in and to congratulate us was class from him. He said, we're not going to drink it, give it to them. I'm so pleased that I celebrated with my team-mates and my best friend and my teacher, Brian Johncock, who looked after me as a footballer from a young age and now he was there celebrating with me in the dressing room, which was fantastic. He used to follow me everywhere like a father figure. Wherever I went to play football he used to take me. He managed me and David Rocastle at county level.

Niall Quinn:
Ronnie Moran came in, giving us a crate of champagne and saying, 'You guys deserve it.' It was really nice and he was humble in defeat, representative of a great club. Interestingly, what he didn't realise, the bottles had 'Liverpool Champions 1989' on. We should have kept them. We started spraying them all around the room, which was silly.

Alan Smith:
The medal comes in this little box and you open it up and it's made in Birmingham – they used to make all the medals back then, which I'm particularly proud of because I'm a Brummie. It's just a little coin really and then it's got a little hook on the top which you can put a lanyard or chain around but nobody does. All the lads were picking them out the box and looking at the back. League Championship winners 1988–89. Phew. That's what it's all about. It's a lovely little thing.

GARY LEWIN:
I went back out pitchside to phone my wife with a brick of a mobile phone that the club had and I remember crying on the touchline. She was crying down the other end. I remember Ronnie Moran and Roy Evans coming in, Bobby Robson popped his head in. We took forever to get changed, the lads were going mad in the dressing room.

DAVID PLEAT:
After the game George Graham was as cool as a cucumber when I saw him upstairs outside the boardroom. Although I was Tottenham orientated, I always had great respect for people I got to know at Arsenal. George I knew for years. We had played against each other as schoolboys at Wembley. I knew the family very well. I remember clearly saying hello to his daughter, Nicole. I imagine it was quite a shock when it is winner-takes-all like that. When it is the very last game and so much depends on it, to be able to relax the players to cope with the tension was impressive. The tension must have been unbearable.

LEE DIXON:
I didn't go back to London with the lads. It was probably the biggest regret in my football career. My uncle was over from Australia and I hadn't seen him since I was six months old. He came to the game and my mum had organised a party for him in Manchester the next day as he was going back to Australia. I'd promised the family I'd be there. I remember the lads getting on the coach arranging this party and I was standing in the players' entrance watching them drive off into the distance thinking I should be on that bus.

Halfway through Liverpool, because I'd had all this champagne and I hadn't eaten anything, I was a bit woozy. I said to my brother, I'm starving, I need to eat. We saw a chip shop. So he pulls in and I jump out the car and go running into this chip shop without even thinking about it. I've got my Arsenal blazer on, my tie on a bit to one side. 'Three lots of fish and chips, mate,' and I just had a sense of people in the chippy staring. Oh that's it, I'm going to die because we've just beat Liverpool. I'm in Liverpool. I'm in an Arsenal suit and tie asking for fish and chips. I looked up and this bloke's looking at me. He said, you can have extra, la' because we're all Evertonians in here. Everyone in the chip shop started jumping up and down going 'Wahey!'

George Graham:
Isn't it lovely to have moments in your life where you think, oh, nothing can beat that. Nothing. Sometimes you sit back at my age now and you think, hey, I've had a great career. I've been a goodish footballer who's won most of the trophies in English football and then I went into coaching and management and even surpassed that. You know I've won more as a manager than I did as a player. What a lucky person I've been. It was the best.

On the way back home all the boys went celebrating and all that. Early next morning my son and I drove up to Glasgow to play golf with my brother and my nephew. We had a fourball. So I could keep away from the media. I knew it would drive me mad. After the golf game this guy comes up and says 'You look just like the guy on television last night, the game between Arsenal and Liverpool. You look just like the guy on the touchline.' I said, a lot of people say that. Ha ha ha. I just got on with my cup of tea with my family.

ELEVEN

Fandom

PART I: OVER LAND AND SEA

CLIFF BROOKS:

I was on holiday in Corfu with two mates, one Spurs and the other a West Ham fan. I hunted high and low for a bar, pub, house, anywhere that would be showing the game, but these were pre-Sky days and I had little joy. Knowing what we needed to do, I'd kinda resigned myself to us not winning, so decided I'd give it a miss and we all went out on the beer. Alan the West Ham fan, seeing me later that evening, said 'Fuck this, let's find Brooksy a phone box. His nervousness is getting on my tits.' So a phone box was found in a bar and I rang my local boozer, the Railway and Bicycle in Sevenoaks, owned by Ray Brady, brother of Liam and father to my best mate, Jamie. I knew the game would be on in there.

So the phone call was made and Ray answers. 'What's the score?' I ask. 'One-nil to The Arsenal,' he replies. 'Bollocks. That's that, then. It's nearly over, ain't it?' I think that was my response, knowing I've got a bleeding Spurs fan to go back to. Only for Ray to come back with 'But the kick-off was delayed. It's not over yet.' The line goes quiet.

Ray suddenly says, 'Cliff, you still there?' 'Yes.' I then hear nothing but pandemonium. In the background Jamie grabs the phone, I don't recall anything he said apart from 'Thomas has done it, Mickey Thomas last fucking minute.' I don't remember hanging up or what happened in the next few seconds. But I do remember running down the street towards my two mates shouting something like 'We've only fucking done it!' Only to suddenly realise I'm being chased by two Greek fellas cos I've not paid for the phone call.

Neil Jacks:

At the time I was serving in the British Army as a vehicle mechanic, in the Royal Electrical and Mechanical Engineers, and had been posted to Germany in the early April. My first weekend in camp was for the FA Cup semi-finals on 15 April, and keeping tabs on the scores back home, I listened in on BFBS radio as the Hillsborough tragedy unfolded.

As those of us who were there know, the 80s didn't offer the luxury of instant communication and wall-to-wall football on TV, as enjoyed today. No mobile phones or internet obviously, but my situation, in this respect, was even more desperate. My posting was to a tiny Military Police detachment of 20-odd personnel, on what was the border between West Germany and East Germany, adjacent to the small but perfectly formed town of Helmstedt. You will have heard of Checkpoint Charlie, the border crossing between East and West Berlin. Well, we were Checkpoint Alpha, the gateway to the 200km 'corridor' road link to West Berlin through the Soviet-occupied East Germany (DDR). Checkpoint Bravo got you into West Berlin from the corridor, through the DDR. Basically, if you didn't fly, this, and a train, were your only way of getting in and out of Berlin, and all allied (British, French, US) traffic had to pass through us. We were responsible for the safe transit of all allied travellers to and from Berlin, and for keeping the corridor 'swept' and open. It was a truly fascinating place to be with many interesting personalities passing through, and a few months later, of course, in the November, quite out of the blue, the Wall fell, and the world momentously and irrevocably changed.

Although we were part of the British Army of the Rhine, we were out on a limb, 200km from our parent regiment in Berlin. Because we were so far east, we could not receive a BFBS television reception, our vital link with all things UK. This will sound ridiculous to the kids, but in order that we could keep up with events back home our daily TV coverage was recorded on to VHS cassettes in Berlin, and sent to us by train each day, meaning all of our TV was 24 hours behind (if and when we actually got it). A central VHS player then relayed the recordings to our adjacent flats/rooms, with a duty 'tape swapper-overer' rostered on to change tape every three hours. While not relevant to this particular night, there were many occasions when watching a late night movie or similar the tape ran out, only for the designated tape-changer to have fallen asleep/gone on the piss etc . . . oh how we laughed. German TV, you may be surprised to hear, opted not to broadcast the most momentous game of football the world had ever witnessed, so that particular option was not available.

So, six weeks after my arrival, the game we had all been waiting for, for ever, had finally arrived, and I had no means with which to watch it. I could think of nothing else. But what to do? I was unable to leave camp for any extended period, due to being on standby, and knew very few people nearby. Eventually, I befriended a Rangers fan who worked on camp, in a civilian admin capacity. He lived near Hanover, and said he would get his son, who could get a BFBS reception, to tape it for me.

I managed to get someone to cover for me, while I drove an hour and a half each way to collect the tape. I had avoided the result, quite easily (no other Arsenal fans for miles), and I picked up the tape with barely a word spoken between us, other than a quick *danke*. I didn't even want to look him in the eye, for fear of getting wind of the result.

So, picture the scene, there I was, in the camp communal TV

room (the only place other than the guard room that had a VHS player) completely on my own. With the time difference, I think it was now well past two in the morning, settling down to watch the game, and well, you know the rest. My celebrations were mostly silent screams – and crying. I can feel almost every emotion. Still one of my clearest and most vivid memories, which in the footballing sense, I know will never be surpassed. I couldn't sleep, and had absolutely nobody to celebrate with, and just remember walking around our tiny compound, German beer in one hand, VHS tape in the other, until daybreak.

James Baldwin:
In 1988 I got a job in Muscat, Oman. Nominally Muslim, the people were very friendly especially to the British. In those days there was no satellite television, only local, and that was in Arabic. I lived in a quiet suburb in the capital. I remember that evening as being very quiet and very hot, 38 degrees C.

In those days there was no instant contact with the UK other than phone or fax and we were three hours ahead of London. I knew what was at stake but there was no possibility of a live broadcast or radio. In fact, the only way of knowing what happened was to listen to the BBC World Service – Middle East section. As that was broadcast on long wave the only access was in my car. I knew that at 1.30 in the morning they would devote a minute to world sports and I hoped this game was important enough to get a mention. To make sure I did not miss anything and to ensure I got everything right, i.e., radio on but not the engine, I settled in at 1.15. By then I knew the game was over but I just had to sweat it out – literally. At 1.30 came the smooth tones of the BBC presenter announcing that it was time to go to the sports desk. Without any ado he went straight into 'And Arsenal . . .' I leapt out of the car and ran down the road screaming. I did not need any more from the presenter as I knew that the first club mentioned would be the winner.

'I'm going to say it was the best. I happened to be there. I get so many people even to this day who talk about it. It's iconic. It's just a moment in time.' Tony Adams

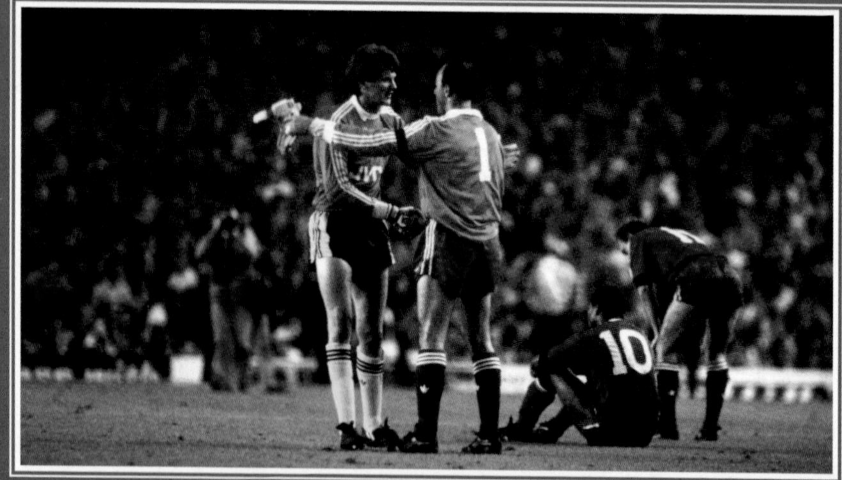

'It was our moment and it was meant to be. Just the euphoria of it all. It's a monumental thing to win the league. For Liverpool, to have it snatched out of your hands in the final kick of a football match and to have that about you to actually be able to rise above that and congratulate the other team. That takes a lot of doing.' John Lukic

'I was in a state of shock. Honestly. I could not believe it. I thought it was an unreal situation, a fairy tale.' George Graham

‘I was tearful. I couldn’t wait to go in and see Pat Rice in the dressing room afterwards. I’d heard it all from him about how they had gone over to Tottenham and won the league. I remember him even saying beforehand “It’s about time you got a medal. It’s about time you went and done the business.” David O’Leary

‘To bring the trophy back to London for the first time since 1971. It was fantastic.’ Michael Thomas

'Two of the biggest teams in the country, away from home, you're going to go and play five at the back and it was a good option. George kept us normal. It's just another game. Just perfect. As I remember it he called every shot right.' Tony Adams

'I come from Stockwell. Dave's from Bermondsey. Both true South London boys at this massive club Arsenal. What could be any better? With my daughter, who at that time was a little baby, and David Rocastle's daughter. We were family.' Michael Thomas

'It's a beautiful, beautiful trophy. Absolutely stunning. I remember looking at it going, wow. The lights of Anfield shone and it all started to flood into the system. I remember holding it up and from then onwards I've no clue what was going on. You just go mad but it was quite surreal in the dressing room because it wasn't expected.' Lee Dixon

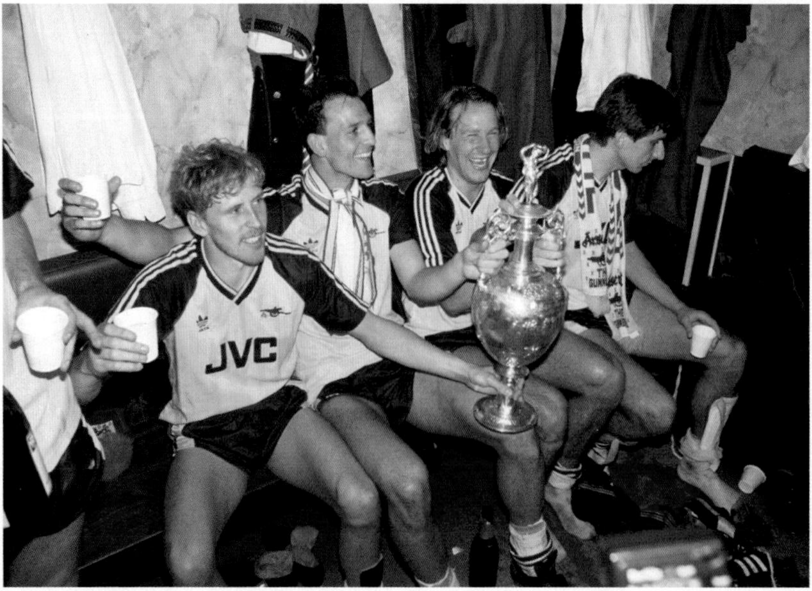

'We're all at the back of the coach singing songs and banging the window at people who were beeping their horn. "Look at this lot over here!" We'd all go over to the side of the coach, waving. People were hanging out car windows. Stood out the top of sunroofs. They'd slow down and they'd overtake again and were waving again and it was brilliant.' Alan Smith

'I didn't realise what we had actually achieved until we did the open-top bus on the Sunday and then you start to realise you are league champions. That means something pretty special.' Nigel Winterburn

'I knew the guys in Winners, a club in Southgate. I knew they would put on a decent night for us but in those days I had to run out and ring ahead from a call box to ask if they would look after us when the lads got back. By the time we got there word got around and there were huge crowds outside. It was like Hollywood movie stars trying to get into a premiere. We got in there and it was pandemonium.' Niall Quinn

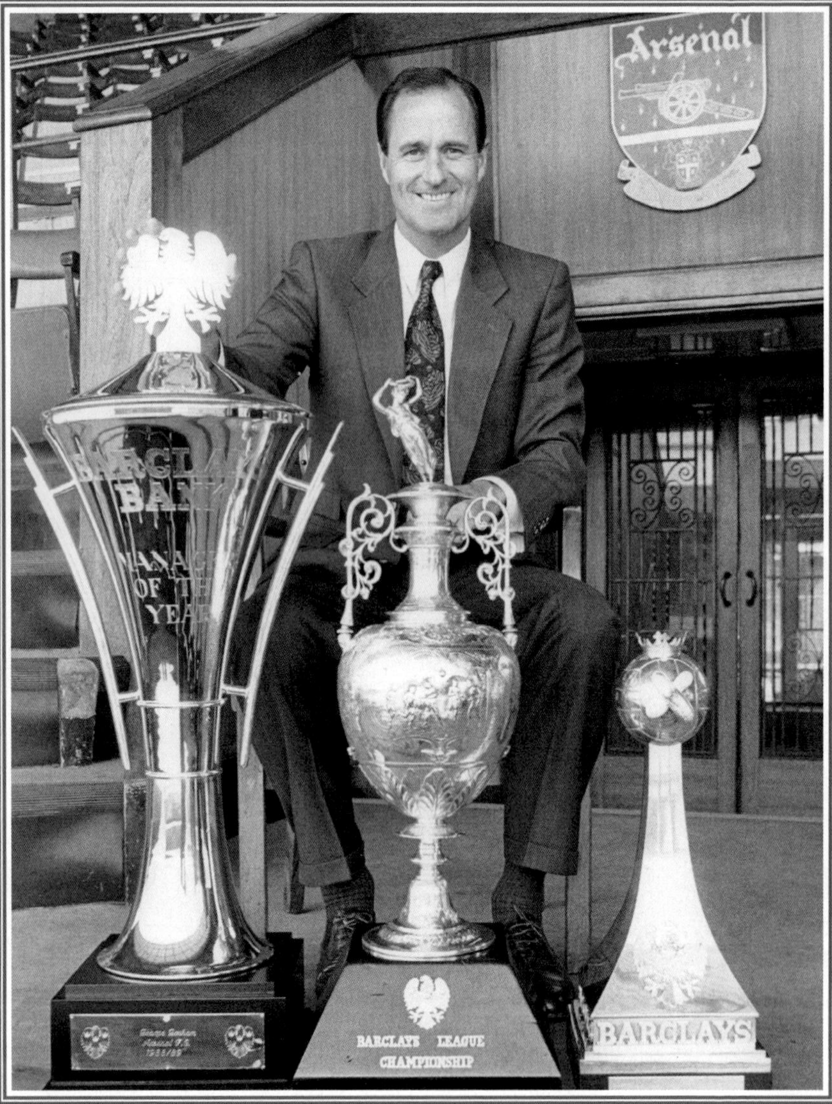

'Isn't it lovely to have moments in your life where you think, oh, nothing can beat that. Nothing.' George Graham

PHOTOGRAPH CREDITS

Page 1. Action Images. Page 2. Doug Poole/Darren Epstein. Page 3. Top: Doug Poole/Darren Epstein. Bottom: Mark Leech, Offside Sports Photography. Page 4. Top: Doug Poole/Darren Epstein. Bottom: Popperfoto via Getty Images. Page 5. Top: Mark Leech, Offside Sports Photography. Bottom: Allsport/Getty Images. Page 6. Eugene Harper. Page 7. Top image: Eugene Harper. Bottom images: Tony Paraschou. Page 8. Doug Poole/Darren Epstein.

Stephen Johnston:
I missed the goal. I was working in a pub in Dundalk, Ireland and was late for my shift (because of the game). When Richardson went down injured I gave up hope and decided to slink into work and save my job. I hopped on my bike and ten minutes later walked into a bar in chaos. I don't remember seeing the goal until the next day.

Kev Whitcher:
In the spring of 1989, my best pal, a Spurs fan, his friend and I spent the summer travelling around Europe in my Peugeot 504 estate car, picking up work where we could, and sleeping in the back with the seats folded down. We planned to depart in mid-May, starting with a drive through France to reach Barcelona in time to see if we could get into the European Cup final on Wednesday 24 May. By the time of our departure, the First Division should have been done and dusted, 13 May being the official date on which the final round of matches were scheduled. Of course, Hillsborough changed everything.

We had reached Barcelona and caught the commentary of the FA Cup final on the BBC World Service whilst sitting in a park. My friend and I had managed to pick up a pair of tickets for the European Cup final between AC Milan and Steaua Bucharest and were treated to a Nou Camp overtaken by Milan fans, and a 4–0 masterclass by a classic Milan team with Gullit and Van Basten scoring the goals. After they had finished parading the trophy and were off the pitch, we – along with a few dozen others who hadn't left the stadium – were able to get on to the pitch and have a good wander round for about five minutes before being chased off by security. It was a fantastic night.

Forty-eight hours later and we were further south along the east coast of Spain. We had settled down to sleep in the car near a dry river bed. My two compatriots were fast asleep. There was no chance

89

of me getting a signal for Radio 2 here, but I could get the good old World Service on long wave. Not that they had commentary on the game. No, I had to wait for a news bulletin to get the news. There was a dull science programme on before it which seemed to drag on for ever. Finally, the news came on and they read the headlines, concluding with 'And the league title is decided in dramatic fashion in the last minute at Anfield', except they didn't say who had actually won it. I was obviously on tenterhooks, but had to wait for the theoretically more important non-sporting stuff to be read out, before learning that Arsenal had actually won the title with Mickey Thomas scoring the late goal that sealed it.

I went nuts inside the car, waking up my two travelling companions. My Spurs-supporting best pal was not exactly enthralled by the news, and got out to relieve his bladder. Unfortunately it meant a minor invasion of mosquitoes, although we didn't realise at the time. It was only in the morning we discovered that he'd been bitten all over, but for some reason they didn't take a bite out of me or his mate.

Christian Gilbert:

I grew up in the Channel Islands and was spending a long weekend in Guernsey on a school football trip aged nine. Our match overlapped with the Liverpool v Arsenal season finale and a few of us were gutted to miss the game. Walking back to our B&B we passed someone's house and they happened to be watching the game in their living room. We crept up to the window and caught the last five minutes peering through the glass, trying to get a good view through the net curtain. It was the most surreal moment when the winning goal went in – disbelief, euphoria and wild celebrations through a window with the unsuspecting family on their sofa. They had been unaware of the three little boys who had unwittingly shared with them one of the greatest ends to a footballing season.

John Walsh:
I was on a fishing holiday in Ireland with my dad, who hated football. We'd booked a room above a pub in a dreary town in County Cavan for the night. The bar was full of local Liverpool fans, flags, champions posters, shirts etc, getting ready to watch the match so I went upstairs with the old man to watch the game in our room. All through the second half Dad was moaning about wanting to go downstairs for a pint. Finally, as Steve McMahon made his 'one minute' gesture, I cracked and decided to face the Liverpool fans. Got down the stairs. Telly was off, people quietly leaving, flags coming down. I asked the barman what was going on. 'The cockney bastards scored in the last minute.' Me: 'YEEEEESS! Turn the telly on, mate.' Not a chance! Didn't see the goal for ages.

Karl Taylor-Robinson:
I still haven't watched the whole match. Friday, 26 May 1989 I was in Tasmania, Australia near Wineglass Bay, nowhere near anywhere I could get any live info on a football game in England let alone commentary. Sharing remote shoreline hostel accommodation with a New Yorker and a rugby fan, neither of them interested in football, I went on to the beach, looked up at the starry night sky and prayed to the gods of football for Arsenal to please do it. And went to bed. No access to news next day either. At an Aussie party on Saturday evening this diver dude reckoned he'd seen something about a team in red winning the 'England cup'. Bollocks, must've been Liverpool.

Trekking/hitching my way on to Hobart on Sunday I arrived somewhere I could buy a newspaper. Columns on Aussie Rules and other sports, no football news. But then low down on an inside page I saw a black and white picture of John Barnes. Bollocks, must've been Liverpool. And then I read the 40 to 50 words that told me that favourites Liverpool had lost and Arsenal had won the league at Anfield. I read it again. And again. I couldn't believe it. I'll never forget it.

Martin Frow:
When that goal went in most of the bar in Magaluf was in uproar. It was amazing, I don't remember feeling that happy before or after in my life. I cannot remember much else about that holiday.

Aaron Bates:
I was actually in my mother's womb at the time. My dad got the news of my not-too-distant arrival while on holiday in Italy, the same week that Arsenal had to do the unthinkable and win by two clear goals away to Liverpool. In those times, it was really difficult to even find out the score, let alone sit and enjoy a live match in a very small suburb in Italy, so when my dad found a bar only half a mile from the apartment he was over the moon. He watched the game with another Englishman on holiday until the seventieth minute. Then he put his family first, even on such a big football occasion. With my expectant mum watching my restless two-year-old brother, who was kicking and screaming for attention, she decided to take Ritchie back to the hotel. Feeling guilty and worried for his young family he left too, thinking they wouldn't do it anyway, and headed back to the apartment. He had no clue how the game unfolded until he bumped into that English bloke from the bar the next day.

Chris Collins:
I was in a pub in the middle of Merthyr Tydfil, not exactly known for its hospitality to the 'English' let alone a Londoner. It was better known for its loud music, drunkenness and a clientele with a tendency for violence and mayhem. The girl next to me was glad the game was coming to a close as she was ready for the nightclub. She was what you would call a 'Barbie doll': petite, good figure, perm,

make-up, manicured nails, tight white trousers with matching blouse; you know the sort. As Thomas ran through on goal Barbie had a full half pint of lager about an inch from her lips. As the ball hit the net, I shot to my feet, arms in the air, knocking Barbie's elbow on the way up. I think she wanted to join in the celebrations as she tipped the full contents of her drink over the top of her head. With perm soaked and lager running down her blouse and trousers, she screamed, 'Look what you've done!'

David Webster:

I was living in Amsterdam at the time and listening to the game at home on an intermittent BBC commentary. The commentary kept dipping in and out so it wasn't always clear what was happening. Once Thomas scored it was almost surreal to realise that Arsenal had won so dramatically but everywhere around was so quiet. My wife, not being a football fan, came into the room to see what the noise was about and promptly left with a 'that's good'.

Tony Winyard:

January 89 I headed to the far north of Norway to a town called Bodø just inside the Arctic Circle where I was contracted to DJ in a club called Joe's Garage for a few months. I decided I wanted to drive back to London with the forlorn hope of possibly getting a ticket to see the game. On Monday 22 May we set off from Bodø to drive the almost 900-mile journey to Bergen in the south of Norway. Although it was May, high up in some of the mountains that we drove through there was still a bit of snow. Once we made it to Bergen we took the ferry over to Newcastle and then drove down to London.

My best mate was a bloke called Bob, but Bob wasn't into football at all and knew nothing about it. He'd arranged for us and a few of the lads to go to a club called Hollywood's in Romford. Five minutes to go and Bob understood that a 1–0 win wasn't enough and he said 'Tone, come on, mate, let's put an end to your misery and head over to Romford and have a laugh at Hollywood's. Let's go now.' I told him in no uncertain terms that I was watching until the end. Within a minute of Adams lifting up the trophy we were back in my trusty GTi and flying over to Romford. Before I drove back to Norway I had decorated my car in yellow Arsenal flags and scarves and was wearing the yellow away shirt. I stopped at a service station in the Midlands and lost count of the number of blokes who approached me telling me they supported Forest, Leicester, Birmingham etc but wished me well and said they'd never seen a game like it. The same thing happened in Newcastle and in Scandinavian places I stopped on the way back to Bodø.

MARTIN:
Here in Australia it was the middle of the night and when Thomas scored I threw my little bundle of joy into the air, he brushed the ceiling, and in true Bob Wilson style I managed to catch him before he hit the floor.

EUGENE ABRAHAMS:
On that Friday night in Cape Town, South Africa, my girlfriend at the time, knowing what was going on, decided to go out for the evening, leaving me alone to watch the game on TV. My only company that night was the cat, Teddy Bear. After Michael Thomas scored, I jumped up, shouting. Teddy Bear, startled by this, also leapt up but dug her claws into my leg. But what's a scratch or two, or blood rivulets – it was the best night ever.

EIRIK HELLEVE:
I was in Norway and had promised to pick up my dad at home and take him to the train station, where he was catching a train at midnight. As he left the car, the news at midnight came on. I screamed,

ran up to my dad, screaming '2–0! They did it! 2–0! 2–0!' My dad, of course, had absolutely no idea what I was talking about, and judging by the looks from the rest of the waiting room, no one else understood it either.

JACK LANCER:
I was in Tenerife for a week with my wife and one-year-old daughter. Managed to find a phone and ring a mate. He said it was 2–0. Then I said, 'Oh well, at least we tried.' He said, 'No, Arsenal won!' Well, I couldn't believe it. Lots of hugs and kisses for my daughter (and wife).

JEFF BOORER:
I was in a bar in Malta on holiday, the game was being shown live and a Gunners fan said, 'If we win this I will buy champagne for everyone in this bar.' He was true to his word.

NICK C'S MATE:
Three days before the Hillsborough tragedy I'd booked a week's holiday in Italy, leaving on 26 May. I don't even want to recall what I put myself through trying to sort this out – I agonisingly explored every alternative, spent hours on the phone to travel agents, but it all came down to this: go to Italy and miss the game, or go to the game and forfeit the cost of the holiday (which was considerable in relation to my wage) and leave my travel companion in the lurch. In the end I chose what I thought was the 'mature' option (I was 23).

Friends made it perfectly clear to me that I was making the biggest mistake of my life, implored me to think differently, to chuck the holiday and forget about the money because we were going to win the league at Anfield and I would never, ever forgive myself. I can still picture my closest Arsenal mate at the time, now sadly gone, putting his hands on my shoulders and looking me straight in the eyes and telling me, 'Do. Not. Do. This.' And I knew he was right.

89

It was Sicily. Taormina. We arrived in the afternoon. As soon as we'd got to the hotel, I went out on the prowl to find where I'd watch the game. Some likely-looking bars. Nothing. I'd bought a radio with me, with short and long wave, as a back-up. Nothing. Couldn't find any broadcast of the game. So I went to bed, completely self-absorbed, miserable and agitated. By now my travel companion was wishing we'd cancelled after all, or they'd come on their own. I remember continually checking the time – oh yeah, so it's kicked off now . . . half-time now . . . trying to imagine what was happening whilst at the same time trying not to think about it any more, read something, watch meaningless Italian TV.

And I remember thinking, that's it, full-time now, it's over. And feeling nothing, absolutely nothing. A world away my Arsenal family were . . . experiencing something, but I couldn't know what. I half drifted off into an unhappy sleep.

So I could end there, but there is one more thing to say about that night. It's embarrassing and I've told very few people. But it's true so it belongs here. Somewhere in that space between sleep and wakefulness, I was suddenly wide awake, sitting up. I'd felt a surge of energy shoot through my body, a jolt – no, more like a colossal wave – right through my body, an incredible physical rush like nothing I'd experienced before, and I sat bolt upright and noticed – with surprise and confusion – tears prickling my eyes and there's this one thought, this one thought in my mind clear as a bell, utter, utter clarity: we've fucking done it. Ecstatic joy running through my veins, desperately needing release and expression, sitting in this stupid fucking hotel room trying not to appear utterly unhinged.

I am crying as I write this.

I looked at the clock. It's about ten minutes after the game should have finished if it had kicked off on time.

PART II: I WAS THERE

CHRIS LITTLE:
Us four started a 'Georgie Graham's red and white army' chant right at the beginning of half-time, the entire seating section responded and then the standing lot joined in and it went back and forth for a bit and then all of us in metronomic unison for pretty much the entirety of the interval. I have two children but I am pretty sure that was the proudest moment of my life.

Seeing that net bulge and realising what that meant sent me into an almost indescribable delirium. Total disbelief, informed by never having seen Arsenal achieve something like this and also supporting a club since 1976 that had won things but had always been the butt of even our own jokes. I'd seen Lee Chapman, John Hawley, Colin Hill, George Wood, etc, some truly average, often terrible players who never indicated we would ever scale the heights we did in 1989. We writhed around for what seemed like a lifetime, crying, shouting, shrieking. And then the whistle blew and we just carried on. I can't remember how long after the final whistle it was but my friend Nick and I both slumped down, our backs against the barrier between the standing and seating sections and just wept.

MARK PEARCE:
The biggest thing that stays with me is that it was the first time I had seen an older man cry. I haven't a clue who he was and he must have been 65 if not a day. I just remember looking around at everyone celebrating and looking towards the white wall and seeing him standing there.

PETE BEAUMONT:
It was my stag weekend. I sat with my brother Bob, my best man, and a Liverpool fan. At the final whistle he gave me his camera and I

walked down to the front of the stand until I reached the tunnel. As I got there a lot of Arsenal staff were just rushing out and on to the pitch, so I took my opportunity and blended in. I suddenly realised I was in amongst the players and on the hallowed Anfield turf. I managed to hug most of the players and George Graham, and then I took my chances and made my way with the official photographers to the centre circle for the trophy giving. At this point I was challenged for the first time by a steward (he probably realised an official photographer was unlikely to be wearing an Arsenal shirt). After asking who the fuck I was, I just said I'm a fan, please can I just get some photos. Amazingly he just said 'Five minutes', and that was enough. I ran off to the away end and saw my mates looking down, gobsmacked.

PETER HARVEY:
My friend had got tickets from a tout up in London – about ten rows behind George Graham and Kenny Dalglish on the halfway line. If I had a bad heart it would have gone that day. The thing is we were totally unaware of the time. It was just going so slow and yet so fast, it was a real spooky feeling. When Michael Thomas scored we knew it was near the end but we didn't know how close it was. We just went mental. But the Liverpool fans around us were all right – they were shaking hands and saying well done. The best thing about it for me is that I actually managed to get on to the pitch. There was one security guy. He understood that it was an amazing night and he let me on and I shook hands with O'Leary and I actually kissed the man who scored that goal. My sons, by the way, are called Thomas and Michael.

MIKE BIRCH:
I'd driven up to Anfield with my seven-year-old son Greg. I made my way to the front so my son could see, whereupon a police officer lifted him over the wall and sat him there in safety. Upon the final

whistle he beckoned me over as well. When the players came over they handed him the trophy and held him up to the crowd.

BRENDAN BOYLE:
After the players had left the pitch I witnessed one of the most moving things I had ever seen. We had been speaking to an old Arsenal fan in a wheelchair in the disabled section earlier, and he had since been wheeled on to the pitch. George Graham was the last to leave the pitch with the trophy, and on his way he walked past the wheelchair guy. He then stopped, turned around and walked back, and placed the trophy in this guy's lap.

SPIRITMAN:
At the final whistle, the atmosphere in our section was indescribable, way beyond anything I had experienced. The police held us in, as that used to be necessary for safe crowd dispersion, but we were in no hurry anyway. I think we sang our 'Are you watching, Tottenham?' chant about 200 times.

SARAH TURNER:
We just go mad. I'm aware of bare-chested grown men, on this warm, balmy night, hugging each other and crying. We finally leave the ground and on our way back to the car we walk past an old Liverpool programme seller. 'Well done,' he says, 'Well done to The Arsenal.'

MICK WINNETT:
After the game some Liverpool fans came down the pitch and stood in front of us, and all the Arsenal fans sang 'You'll Never Walk Alone' all the way through with all the proper words, out of respect for the Hillsborough fans. About half the Liverpool fans stayed behind and (bitterly disappointed though they were) applauded the Arsenal team on their lap of honour. I've never forgotten their conduct that

night. When I left the stadium I got grabbed and kissed by two rather attractive Scouse girls.

RUSSELL JONES:
That must be the only time 'you'll never get a job' was not sung. We really felt for them at that moment and it was moving that they all hung around at the end. Anfield was very emotional and we all sensed a feeling of togetherness.

I remember the first services on the motorway. What a party. People were just jumping around, dancing, singing and hugging everyone. Eventually back home to my mum's and up at 7 a.m. to start the Saturday shift at Asda.

PAUL AUSTIN:
When Mickey scored it was really hard to describe the joy. I remember trying to grab a copper's helmet, no idea why. We got home at 5.15 a.m., ecstatic. I then went to work on the adrenaline. I was a carpenter/joiner, had a job booked in for Saturday morning at 8.30. I was on a high, the bathroom went well.

RICHARD ROBERTS:
At 1–0 we saw the police ring the ground, so we knew time was getting short. An unforgettably emotional version of 'You'll Never Walk Alone' was being sung by all sides of the ground, including some of us. I remember looking up to the sky, which still retained some light, saying to my uncle, who had died that year, 'It's just one more goal, please.' Then it happened. Tears of joy, disbelief and sadness for all those that weren't there. The Liverpool fans continued their serenade and were generous in their applause. We left the ground in silence as a mark of respect. I recall a massive skinhead breaking through the police lines and approaching me . . . only to put his hand out and say, 'Well played, mate, only one team tried to win tonight.'

STEVE KING:
After the match, as we poured out of the ground, there were a number of Liverpool supporters waiting to shake our hands and offer congratulations, young and old. Really classy and not something I could imagine I'd have done had the positions been reversed.

JEREMY MCREDDIE:
We were in the Main Stand at Anfield and very near the Kop so had to stay as under cover as we could. I had my shirt buttoned up over my Arsenal shirt. The people around us soon clocked we were Londoners but were generally quite good. At the final whistle the men around us were shaking our hands to say well done and it was a woman who gave me the choice line of 'lucky cockney bastards'. On the final whistle, readying for the presentation of the trophy, we jumped down into the paddock alongside the pitch and stood on top of the old dugouts and shook the players' hands as they went down the tunnel. We then walked around the pitch to join the away fans in the corner for the escort to the coaches. On the way out of Liverpool we were flagged down by two Arsenal fans whose car had been nicked due to leaving a scarf on the parcel shelf.

MICK COPPOCK:
One incident stands out in my mind, as it will always do. As John Lukic got the ball and played it out to Lee Dixon, my brother Steve nudged me and simply said: 'Now would be a good time to score . . .' Simple as that. After the game we went back to our hotel (where the Liverpool players were staying!) and we just stood at the bar with our friend Mike, who we also went with, and looked at each other in total disbelief.

KELVIN MEADOWS:
When Mickey went through the first time and virtually back-passed it to Grobbelaar the crowd pushed forward and my glasses were

knocked off. I managed to catch them, the lens and the little screw. How? Who knows? Who cares? I asked this copper next to me if he had a small penknife and showed what needed to be done. He fixed 'em. Nice one, officer. Every time we went forward, the crowd swayed and I held on to my glasses. We had no idea how long was left as Mickey went charging through the middle. I grabbed my glasses to save them being knocked off . . . and didn't see the ball hit the back of the net. Didn't care.

Neil Lach-Szyrma:
I was in the Kop. After the goal my only physical action was to drop my head and close my eyes. Heaven. I glanced round at my mate a few feet back – he gave me a funny half-smile – then back to the pitch and carried on celebrating in my head.

Mel O'Reilly:
The trophy bit was a bit of a haze but I do remember Rocastle, his face lit up and his eyes dancing. You see, he was our bloke on the pitch despite Mickey Thomas getting the goal. Rocky's medal was ours as well and when he smiled, we smiled.

Gary Franklin:
Mayhem is an understatement. The hairs on my body felt like cold nails, never-ending noise, it was quite unimaginable. Hugging, kissing, jumping up and down, grown men crying. I thought I had experienced everything emotionally but this blew my mind. I got up on a barrier – standing with arms held wide, head tilted back thanking God, eyes closed, just soaking it all in. We, as one, singing 'Boring, Boring, Arsenal' over and over again. David O'Leary was in tears. We sang all the way home.

MICHAEL COHEN:

I honestly don't remember the goal but I do remember collapsing on the floor with Pierce O'Leary as the seats collapsed and everyone just lost their minds. I found my uncle and cousin who were sitting a few rows away at the final whistle. The next thing I remember is us making our way to the players' entrance and into the inner sanctum of the stadium. Martin's jibbing skills led the way, but as I remember the Liverpool staff were so shell-shocked we just waltzed past. Next thing we're in the dressing room and I'm standing next to Nigel, Lee and the boys as they celebrate. Surreal doesn't come into it. My cousin Dean and myself then grabbed a ball and walked out on to the Anfield pitch, ran up to the Kop end and had a kick-around until someone shouted for us to get off the pitch.

DEAN WENGROW:

We found ourselves living out our wildest fantasies on the Anfield turf after the game. As we ran out of the tunnel, I recall looking towards an empty Kop end and seeing some of the bouquets of flowers that the teams had both brought out before kick-off laying forlorn on the terraces. In our elation, Hillsborough had for those wondrous moments lost its significance. I ran down to the away end to re-enact Mickey's goal, and I recall how the section where the Arsenal fans were sat was a total wreck. I found my seat, yanked it off and took it home with me, where it remains to this day, a filthy piece of cream-coloured plastic in a cupboard above the washing machine.

STEVE TARR:

It must have been about ten minutes after the final whistle and we were all finally catching our breath. As they were preparing for the trophy presentation, a guy in his sixties asked me how old I was. I told him I was 20 and while smiling he shook his head and said he felt sorry for me. When I asked why he said that even if I was still following Arsenal when his age I would never have a moment better than we'd just experienced. He was right of course.

Simon Rich:
I just remember being lifted off my feet and into orbit. I chose to go to Anfield that day instead of doing my GCSE history exam. It was well worth the U grade I got, trust me.

Dave Daniels:
When we scored I had jumped up on to my seat and my leg went through the plastic backing leaving a permanent scar on my leg that I show to anyone given half a chance to say I WAS THERE! After the game I can remember that the Arsenal supporters ransacked a petrol station for drinks and food (apologies).

Mark Leech:
Even though I was working that night as a photographer I was able to feel this sense of pride as an Arsenal fan. On the way home we stopped at a service station. I thought I had seen it all that night. I heard this guy first of all, he had his back to me, with a very loud cockney voice screaming down a payphone. I passed him and noticed his blood-stained shirt was ripped open, his nose wasn't looking too good and he was singing 'We won the league on Merseyside' at the top of his voice. Today he would have been surrounded by people on mobiles taking a video. As a photographer it's an image I never got to take but it's an impression I have never forgotten.

Amy Lawrence:
In hindsight, given what had happened a few weeks before at Hillsborough, it is a painful paradox to reflect on how many of us around that time loved the motion and energy of a football terrace much more than being in seats. My memory of Michael Thomas's goal and

its aftermath is mashed up with how it felt to be within this sprawling mass of emotion. The best analogy I could ever come up with was like being in the sea. It was like going under a sudden wave – that slightly surreal world where things get muffled and dizzying – and then coming up for air and into the light and noise. Sensory overload. A whirlwind of happiness. I found I had travelled to a different part of the terrace, away from my friends, and grabbed the nearest people to hug. One was straight out of the skinhead, tattooed hooligan school of the times, sobbing like a baby. The next was an Irish guy in a trance mumbling 'It's my birthday' again and again. Those seconds were like an out of body experience.

All these people who I never saw before or since – we overlapped in each other's lives for a minute or two at most – but I remember them so clearly. Two Liverpool fans who hopped on to the pitch and ran down to the away fans before opening up their home-made flag in honour of those lost at Hillsborough. A tall skinny Scouser with trademark tracksuit and moustache had been part of the group who waited outside for the Arsenal fans to emerge and clasped my hand to shake while saying well done. We swapped mementos. I offered my yellow and blue bar scarf, he offered his red silk flag adorned with the liver bird. Still have it of course.

PART III: THE NIGHT CONTINUES

MATT LOWMAN:

I remember sitting back on the coach and a young Liverpool fan getting on board before emotionally congratulating us. Heading back to London and the one thing I remember vividly is how incredibly thirsty we were – we stopped to get petrol and one of our group tried to run in and buy some drinks, only to be ushered back on to the coach by the police empty-handed.

Trevor Moore:
Once in the car one of the lads says he's hungry so we decide to stop at a chip shop. We get our chips and I go out to the car to find . . . no car. Here I am, bag of chips in hand, standing all alone in Liverpool wearing an Arsenal shirt. Couple of minutes pass and I hear my mates giggling. They'd moved the car round the corner.

Amanda Schiavi:
Outside the car park my dad kissed an Everton fan, who happened to be a policewoman. We hit the M25 at some unearthly hour and we were alongside the coach with the team in it. What a feeling. All I remember is seeing Winterburn going mad. They waved, we waved. An incredible feeling.

Janet Cohen:
Passing the players' coach on the way back I remember the ecstatic honking of the coach horn. Later we watched the video and found ourselves in the crowd with our hats on, something we love to this day.

Emerita Gomez Sanchez:
We ended up coming back in a coach a bit worse for wear but still remember everyone drinking and on the TV was *Crocodile Dundee.*

Amy Lawrence:
We had something sounding like psychedelic Greek music on the coach home, which added to the surreal nature of it all. I remember getting off back at Highbury and being calf deep in the detritus of a party – cans, bottles, you name it. Then a lift back to Anna's house to pick up the video to watch immediately and finding her mum had decorated the front door: 'Arsenal Champions 1989'. Seeing it written out was like another big emotional wave. Jesus, this really happened.

Alan Pickrell:
We drove back to Burger King, Leicester Square, as in those days there wasn't many places open at 4–5 a.m.

Mark Brindle:
In the car adrenaline pumping. We were all singing until suddenly I realised it had gone a bit quiet. It might have had something to do with the fact I was driving at 120mph and the car was about to shake apart. The party lasted all weekend until I finally ran out of adrenaline and was woken lying in the sun on London Bridge station by a concerned British Rail man who packed me on a train to Woolwich. I have no recollection of how I got there.

Mark Schmid:
Journey home flew by and when we pulled up outside Highbury the crowd cheered us as returning heroes – we hadn't even kicked a ball! Handshakes and hugs all round as we got off the coach. On to Trafalgar Square, dancing in the fountains with new-found Gooner friends.

Simon Posner:
When we got home at around 3 a.m., our father was sitting on the roof of his car, drinking champagne.

Peter Norton:
I had an Arsenal bedspread with the crest on it. Hadn't used it for a while (I was 20) and my folks had found it. When I got home after watching the game it was hanging from the front of our house and specifically my bedroom window. It stayed there all weekend.

James Corbett:
We headed back to London in a daze. Stopping at the services we saw several familiar away day supporters and everyone was so happy,

hugging; the petrol station was like being at a party. Onwards we went and then we found ourselves behind the team coach and the objective was to follow it to see where it was heading. Into Southgate it went and then I got caught at traffic lights, we lost it and the decision was to head to Highbury, where we found no coach but still a lot of supporters. The coach had headed to the Winners club. We were gutted as we knew Niall Quinn (he was dating a good friend of our family) and felt confident we would have got in.

Simon Cutner:
I lived in Southgate at that time and heading in – not a car or person in sight at that early hour – I noticed a coach approaching us. On closer inspection it was the Arsenal team coach. And it had just stopped outside a local nightclub. So, naturally, I span the car around and greeted our Division One champions off the coach. Us dressed in our full Arsenal colours. The players hugged us and cheered with us. We tried our best to enter the club but that was not permitted.

Dan Piler:
The guy who organised the coach I travelled up on had welcomed us earlier that day by stating, 'If we win tonight all the players are coming back to my club, and you're all welcome to join us.' As we had never met him we were slightly sceptical that this would actually happen (the players at the club, and the bit about us winning). As the coach pulled away from Anfield he pulled a crate of bubbly out and we happily toasted our way back down the motorway.

Tony Paraschou:
I had organised the coach to Anfield. There were 19 of us, and I invited everyone back to the club. My brother and I ran Winners, a private members' club – a luxury bar with 24 snooker tables and a gym underneath. A lot of the Arsenal boys would come and relax in

the afternoon with a few drinks and play a little bit of snooker and stuff like that and they were left alone. I wouldn't say they were fixtures of the club but they were there a lot and one day we were just having a chat and I said to the boys, 'It's here if you want it.' We would lay on food, platters of steaks. Quinny turned round and said, whatever happens we'll come – not that we believed they would. When we got off the coach one of the staff came running up to me. He's like, 'They're coming! They're coming!' And I said, 'Who's coming?' 'The boys are on their way. We've just had a phone call. The team coach is coming down. They're about an hour behind you.'

NICK CALLOW:
One of my schoolfriends, Theo, knew Tony and that was how we ended up on his coach and then suddenly part of the group invited to the salubrious, exclusive membership bar Winners, which on the outside didn't look as good as it did on the inside. They had to clear out the people in there and we had to all go down the side toilet and hide in this little gym. We were hiding under tables all going, 'Shhh! Shhh! Shhh! The police are coming. Someone's coming.' I was thinking, why are we going through all this just to have a drink? We could have a drink anywhere. The players aren't going to come. Then all of a sudden they started coming in. One by one. Paul Merson, Alan Smith, Rocky, Michael Thomas. Brian Marwood was mental. The trophy.

TIM BATES:
They did a guard of honour for David O'Leary. He walked in through the crowd of players with everyone clapping him.

DAN PILER:
It's difficult to recount just how monumentally mental that night was. The sight of the newly crowned English Football League champions trooping in with their Aquascutum blazers suggests some

formality, but their ties at half mast hinted at the party that had already been in full swing on the team coach. Our jaws hit the floor with each player that appeared through the doorway but we eventually regained our composure and settled in for the night.

We were just one of the boys for the rest of the night, playing pool, singing songs and drinking long into the early hours. I've lost count of how many times I stepped back, looked at where I was, who I was with and what had happened with these football gods just a few hours earlier . . . and said to myself, 'Fuuuuuuuuuck!' I didn't want the night to end and we finally staggered out into the bright May sunshine in the morning. I had Perry Groves' tie, my match ticket and programme signed by the two goal-scorers and a head full of memories like no others.

Saul Lerhfreund:
The players wanted to play pool and we challenged them to the odd game. We thought it would be fun if we played for clothes. I don't think we had much to give them though. Smudger beat me and he just gave me his tie after. There you go.

Nick Callow:
Believe it or not I actually beat Gus Caesar at pool that night. He said, 'I suppose you want my tie or something.' I said, 'No, you're all right.' We all thought he was a Tottenham fan. Someone nicked Tony Adams' blazer. This lovely navy blazer with the yellow cannon on the crest. It was enormous on him. We ganged up on him and made him take the blazer back to Highbury. Even we were scared of George Graham as fans.

Tony Paraschou:
Tony Adams locked up the club with me. It was daylight. The last three people out of there were myself, my wife and Tony Adams.

THEO DEMETRIOU:
At one point I remember looking around and thinking, just four hours ago I was watching these boys score the most unbelievable goal in the history of our club and now we're sitting here. It was what we were living for. We were living for that day to win the league for Arsenal. We'd gone to every single game that season because we thought there was something special about this team. I left with Mickey Thomas and we picked up the first delivery of newspapers. We walked around the corner from the club. There was a sweet shop as you used to call them in those days. It was about 6.30 in the morning. The papers were piled outside in their bundles. He went and picked the bundles up. I helped him. Then we sat there on the floor reading the newspapers. We were splattered all over them obviously. Just amazing.

PART IV: MEANWHILE BACK IN LIVERPOOL

MICHAEL DIGBY:
In the pub in Liverpool before the game we'd bumped into a random bloke with his girlfriend and got chatting. He gave us his number and we thought nothing of it. Anyway after the game we called this bloke and he invited us round to his flat. We got there and there was wall-to-wall photos of him and his brothers with celebs – turns out it was the brother of the boxer John Conteh. We stayed up all night drinking.

BARRY HUGHES:
I remember leaving the stadium and wanting to go on the buses back to London, but I walked back to the city centre and went to my regular indie club night at JD's on Hanover Street, which I went to being a student in Liverpool that year. The next morning I got up and

bought all the papers from a shop on Penny Lane. Unfortunately a lot of them were northern editions and had headlines like 'Robbed'. I still have them.

SI TALBOT:

I was in my final year of teacher training at Chester College in 1989. A good friend of mine was a big Liverpool fan whose uncle was chief scout. I stood on the Kop with him. After the game my mate took me back to his dad's working men's club where I was bought drinks all night.

MARK DAVIES:

I am a Middlesbrough supporter so was one of the few people there that night that was neutral. I was editor of the student magazine at Liverpool Poly and we'd gone down to Anfield on the Monday after the tragedy to leave flowers on the pitch. The atmosphere on the Kop at the game was buoyant, a sense of expectation of a Double which might ease the pain a little. So the sense of disbelief, anger even, was palpable when Thomas scored and the league title disappeared into the scrum of yellow at the other end of the pitch. I stayed on to congratulate the Arsenal players on an emptying Kop. The game continued to play a role in my life. On 13 April 1997 I went to see *Fever Pitch* for a first date with the woman who is now my wife of 18 years.

CHRIS WIGGINS:

We had parked in the street a few minutes' walk from the ground before the game and as we got out of the car the person whose house we parked outside said he would keep an eye on the car for us. After the game, when we got back to the car there was some shouting from up the road. He opened the door and asked us if we wanted to come in till the shouting was over. In conversation with him and his wife it turned out they were Everton fans, but their son was a Liverpool fan who had died at Hillsborough. They made us sandwiches and poured beers. Their hospitality was amazing, especially as football had taken their son from them a few weeks previously. Of course, for us it was 'one of those nights' but for them it was something different entirely.

PART V: I WASN'T THERE

JASON WOODS:
As a Spurs supporter, I was working as an 18-year-old behind the bar at The Compasses in Abbots Langley, Watford on the night of this match. The only TV in the pub was a tiny set perched on a ledge very high behind the bar above the optics. The landlord, Ron Vodden, was an Arsenal fan and most of the pub had Gooners obviously drinking in it that night. As a Spurs fan, I had to watch and serve all these people all night. When Mickey Thomas went on that run and scored the whole pub erupted! The final whistle blew and Ron went down to the cellar to get two crates of champagne and then ordered a lock-in. He asked me if I could serve on for a bit and he would make it worth my while. The party got started with all these Gooners standing on chairs singing their hearts out. After 1.30 a.m. with everyone eventually gone Ron thanked me and gave me an extra 20 quid. I said thanks, Ron, and can I say something? Yes, he replied. I said, you can stick your job right up your effing Arsenal, and then left.

JANET ROCASTLE:
I was at my mum's house on the border of Brixton and Clapham in what was my childhood bedroom because David was away and, with a new baby, it was nice to be around my family. I had just had Melissa in February. I had just fed her, she was lying on my lap, I was patting her to sleep when the second goal went in. I nearly leaped up and dropped her. But I didn't. I managed to remember I had a baby on my lap.

89

James Lukic:

It is all so vivid. When Arsenal scored early in the second half I can remember that my mum was cleaning the downstairs toilet and obviously heard the commentary. She came running through with her rubber gloves on and said 'Who's scored? Who's scored?' The move for the second goal still feels like it was yesterday as it started with my uncle John in goal. My dad recorded the match on VHS and I remember for weeks afterwards watching it back on video and rewinding the second goal and watching it over and over again. The final thing I remember was the camera showing the Arsenal fans celebrating after the final whistle and just thinking of my dad and grandparents being in the away end. It looked absolutely joyous.

Nick Hornby:

After Alan Smith's goal I remember thinking, oh, there's no point scoring again now because they're only going to go and let one in. So don't do it yet. That would be a disaster. Winning 2–0 now would be a disaster. When Michael Thomas missed that chance I remember the thought going through my head that we'd be talking about this for years, when Michael Thomas could have won us the league . . . and then we entered this parallel universe where my team who I'd been watching for all those years could win the league and there was an ecstatic pile of bodies on the floor in this living room in Highbury. And then everyone got up and went 'How long's left? How long's left?' Those last two minutes were terrifying.

Then it was just shouting and hugging. I ran to the corner shop and bought a bottle of champagne. It was a make of champagne I'd never heard of before. I don't know what the bloke said to me. 'That's £30 please' or something like that – in 1989 – and I was like 'Oh whatever' and went back in and drank this bottle of champagne. People just started pouring out and then arriving and so we went back out having drunk the champagne and I stayed there for quite a while. It felt like you were living in Greece or somewhere. It was really extraordinary. People in their cars hooting their horns. It wasn't like English behaviour in fact. I mean, perhaps it is. Perhaps people do that in Liverpool every year, it's just that we never got to see. But it was very exotic and carnival-like.

ALAN DAVIES:
We love Mickey. We used to go 'Oh Mickey, Mickey, Mickey, Mickey, Mickey, Mickey, Mickey, Mickey, Mickey, Mickey, Mickey, Mickey, Mickey, Mickey, Mickey, Mickey . . .' Mickey was one of ours. Mickey played left-back in the youth team. He was a monster. He was so fast. So fit. So strong. So fearless. Quiet. Never spoke. Just patrolled the field, winning the ball, giving it to good players. But he had a lung-busting fitness. He could get forward and he got in the box at the end and he took his moment. He didn't snatch it, like he had the first chance. He had a look at Bruce Grobbelaar. One of the best goalkeepers in the world. He had a look at the net. He took his time and we're like, HIT IT! We just want him to lamp it. Just blast it through his face into the net. Why is he waiting?! Then pandemonium. That's the only word to describe it. Pandemonium. Just all over each other. Tom swears he took my virginity in that moment. Cigarette down the back of the sofa. Damian's dad trying to stop the sofa burning, which was a big fear in the 70s and 80s – the smouldering flame.

We were very excitable. We watched the post-match interviews such as they were. The whole thing was being steered by Brian Moore in the most exemplary way, and we can all recite his commentary. We went down to the Neptune pub, which was on the beach in Whitstable, and there were loads of students in there who didn't like football. We found one other Arsenal fan who was going around Whitstable looking for Arsenal fans to be with and then someone had a house party. They played quite a lot of Motown songs and

Damian and I turned the lyrics of every song into some song about Arsenal to the point people were pouring drinks on us to shut us up. It was one of the greatest days of our lives.

DAVID MILES:
A few of us staff were watching it together inside Highbury on a rented TV. The way the goal built up it was like suspended animation. Everyone was just rising from their seats as they do at the games. The son of our current chairman Sir Chips Keswick, Toby, was actually working in the box office and was one of the guests on the night. When Mickey started his run he stood up and he started walking towards the TV, and it was as though it was sucking him in, saying: this is it. We were shouting: 'Get out the way!'

When Mickey scored the goal the whole thing went to mayhem and then a few minutes later we were aware of people in the street and we opened the windows. We were about three floors up and looked down and there were people congregating – 50 turned to a hundred and in the end it was like that scene out of *Fever Pitch* with over a thousand people. That went on for quite a few hours.

IAIN COOK:
They were renovating the front of the East Stand and it looked like a scene out of one of those old movies where everyone's hanging from the rigging. Everyone was out there celebrating. When we went to go the only way out was out the back of the West Stand and at the time the pitch was having the under-soil heating done so it was like a ploughed field.

LYNNE CHANEY:
I remember leaving at 7.30 in the morning and walking across the pitch in the mud.

DERMOT O'LEARY:
I'm in this quiet village called Great Horkesley just outside Colchester and it's killing me. I was on the floor. I remember looking up and seeing my legs kicking. I was so elated and excited and all I wanted to do was to go to Highbury so I could just celebrate with other people. The only person I could celebrate with is my buddy who doesn't really know anything about football and is just round my house for band practice. Nothing compares to watching that on the television and the effect it had on me at the time.

MATTHEW CYZER:
I covered for my sister, Amy, who went. Had a row with my girlfriend when I said I wasn't going round. Watched it alone on TV. Put the phone receiver against the TV with two minutes to go so Dad, who was abroad, could hear the end. Writhed around on the floor when we scored. Went out to the Bull and Bush where Arsenal fans had started gathering to get pissed. Ran down the road at 5 a.m. to welcome Amy home from Anfield.

PAUL CARTER:
I joined the *Daily Star* in November 1988 as a sub-editor on sport. It was my first job on a national. My early memories of the day was that shortly after getting in at around 4 p.m., the death of Don Revie was announced, but, despite this, the night was going very smoothly until kick-off time.

Off-stone timings, the point at which no more changes can be made, were always tight for us on match nights. But the plan was to fill the paper during the evening and leave the back page and the inside two pages clear for the game. The deputy sports editor, a legend called Ian Stirrup, was running the desk. Stirro was a massive Liverpool fan and had the air of someone who thought the night would be smooth as you like and he could start celebrating as soon as the paper was done.

Ian drew up two back pages, one for an Arsenal win, one for a Liverpool win and we would have copy for both. The inside spread was drawn up to allow for a couple of big pictures and a slot for the match. It was just another night in the office. The closer we came to the final whistle the more straightforward things looked. Our man covering the game would file on 80 minutes and it would be a case of subbing it up and waiting for an intro and four pars on the whistle, and getting it away as fast as we could because the presses were holding for us. I remember seeing a spread headline along the lines of: KENNY'S CROWNING GLORY.

When Mickey scored I jumped about three foot in the air and hugged a messenger I didn't know. Then somehow I got a grip because we had a job to do. The Kenny headline was changed in a flash to: BY GEORGE THEY'VE DONE IT.

Richard Greene:

When we scored the winner our very possessive poodle thought I was attacking the wife so he bit my leg. I have kept that tracksuit with the hole in them all these years and I've still got the scar.

James Barker:

It was very tense in our living room. I admitted defeat with five minutes to go and actually turned the VCR off. I was gutted. David Pleat said maybe poetic justice had been done with Arsenal winning on the night but Liverpool taking the title. My dad always said he was full of piss and wind. Then came the goal and we both lost it.

Phil Gibbs:

I only just made it home in time for kick-off. Sensational commentary from legendary Brian Moore (I had been at UEA with his son

Simon). The blessed goal. My girlfriend (non football fan) was in the bath upstairs. I leapt in the air punching upwards and thereby smashing the lounge chandelier and fusing all the lights in the house, but thankfully not the TV. My girlfriend shouted from the darkness 'what the hell is going on?'

JOE JAGGER:
My mum just went ballistic, which was totally out of character. She jumped up and down like a mad lady.

JAMES BRENNAN:
I recall my mum's sister called round just before the game and I honestly couldn't believe she had called in for a casual chat as the game was about to kick off. The scenes when Mickey Thomas scored will never be forgotten. I have never seen my dad move so quick. Although he was a season ticket holder he rarely showed much emotion. On the final whistle our house phone rang and it was my uncle David from Dublin ringing to congratulate us. He fondly refers to us as the Arsenal Brennans. After the TV coverage finished we played darts in the garage and my older brother Tom and his mates were allowed a can of beer. To this day on the ply around the dartboard the Scousebusters graffiti remains.

STEPHEN GOURD:
I was 18 and although a massive fan, decided to work on the night as I just couldn't take the stress. I was working at a hotel in Bar Hill, Cambridge, in the leisure centre, on my own that night. I had to man the swimming pool. I closed the centre at half-time and watched the second half on a 14-inch colour TV by the pool. The winner, well I had no choice but to jump fully clothed into the pool of course. My dad picked me up just after the finish in his new Audi 80 and was really upset I was so wet until he smiled and said, 'I have waited for

this for a long time.' He was born in Islington – went to Arsenal during the war, where he was passed down to the front to sit on the side of the pitch.

Steve Rusbridge:
When Mickey scored, my sister's boyfriend Bernie, cigarette still in hand, launched himself towards the TV screen. We were still picking up fag ash days later. Thirty years on, and Bernie, who would later marry my sister, is sadly no longer with us but I will never forget our celebrations that night. And now, whenever we're playing a big match, I raise a glass to him.

Jon Hossain:
Whilst driving near Old Street, Smudger scored. I pulled my car up and leant on my horn. Across the road the only other car on the road, a black cab, did the same. We both got out of the car, ran to each other, did a jig, linked arms and then got back to our vehicles. I made it to Victoria for the second half, my brother was there and there were about six other medic friends who had absolutely no interest in the game. We were told to turn the volume down and stop making a noise on a number of occasions. They were surprised at me being a football fan who went to games. In the 1980s you didn't admit to that; going to gigs sure, but football was full of hooligans.

Mike Feinberg:
I did not see the celebration, didn't see Thomas's fish-out-of-water dance, didn't see Winterburn storm across the goal, didn't see the rabid away supporters having out-of-body experiences. At the time, I was lying face down, on the filthy floor of a London pub, on the bottom of a pile of men and boys that must've totalled 15 people. I'm not a clean freak, but I was lucky to get away from that experience

without life-changing infections and illnesses. But it was, to that point, the single greatest moment of my life.

FRANK STUBBS:

When Mickey scored me and my dad were rolling around on the lounge floor in floods of tears and my mum was knitting. That night all I remember is running down Maidstone High Street in my Spandau Ballet-style suit wearing my yellow and blue bobble hat and jumping up and down uncontrollably with anyone who wanted to join in.

RICHARD KATZ:

I had a terrible bout of food poisoning and hadn't been able to keep a thing down for a day or so . . . except apple juice. I bought myself a little juice box – it was going to be my celebration tipple – and tuned in for the game. I reckon I must have peeled off the little straw just as Thomas went 'charging through the midfield'. I never drank it. Kept that apple juice carton for *years.*

MIKE GRAY:

On my way home from work with my fiancée I told her I had put £100 on Arsenal to win 2–0 that evening at 16/1. We watched the game on TV and when Michael Thomas scored she was dancing round the room thinking of £1,600 whilst I dropped to my knees punching the air and announced, this is the best thing to happen in my life. She turned and looked sadly at me as we were getting married that July. To make matters worse, I didn't have the nerve to put £100 on a bet so she missed out on the £1,600.

CHRISTOPHER STONE:

I was 11. I ran out on to the street and just ran, arms stretched and screaming. I didn't see the end of the game and there was a moment outside that I realised that Liverpool might score and we could lose, so I ran back inside to see the celebrations on the pitch. The TV was turned off, my parents sent me off to bed and I didn't sleep for hours. I was reading my *Junior Gunners* magazines over and over again, imagining I was Rocky.

David Greenall:
I wasn't there. Had to go to an 18th birthday that night in a cricket club. I went confident they would have a TV and was distraught to arrive and find that wasn't the case. So intermittently I sneaked out to my Mark II Escort to listen on the radio. With 15 minutes to go I returned to the car. A Spurs fan soon joined me and laughed as Thomas missed a chance. Tension rose and then the famous goal. I started to headbutt the steering wheel in joy and the Spurs fan swore and got out of the car.

Patrick Rochford:
I was an 11-year-old kid. My abiding memory is jumping up on the coffee table (hand-made by my father) when Michael Thomas netted, breaking said table and waking my baby brother who was asleep in a bassinet beside us.

Stuart Roberts:
I will always remember the night of 26 May 1989. There was something magical about that day and summer, the sun always shone, everything was brilliant, life was perfect. I had a lovely girlfriend who hated football, but it was Michael Thomas who I was really in love with.

Tim Salter:
I was 17 and at a party in Croydon. It was the days before mobile phones, so I had to find a payphone so I could call my parents. I had

to keep phoning for updates from this crappy little room in Croydon Arena, and totally missing the party. Eventually, after I got the news, cue the best party for one.

Steven Oakley:
My dad, who used to live on Avenell Road, had a thing where he could never watch a match live because it was too stressful so he used to tape them and watch them back after, if we'd won. That night I persuaded him to watch it with me but as it moved closer to full-time, in true *Fever Pitch* style, he started to insist on turning the TV off. Noooo, I begged and pleaded. All the while he was getting more and more stressed. So what happened . . . did my dad win, the TV was turned off and neither of us got to see Mickey Thomas score the most famous goal in Arsenal history, or did the 13-year-old prevail and we shared the best footballing memory I have to this day? Of course, I won.

Mike Murphy:
I was babysitting two young kids, both also Arsenal fans. As kick-off was fast approaching, both kids poked their heads around the living room door pleading to be allowed to stay up and watch the big match. Being the big softie I, of course, let them stay up. What a great atmosphere we created in our little corner of north-west Kent. I'm glad I let them watch the greatest ever ending to a season in real time.

Elda Fouch:
I was five months pregnant and jumping up and down in my living room! On and off the sofa . . . not to be recommended.

Richard Mays:
Absolutely the best day of my life! For two reasons: the first being obvious, but the second was because my wife told me she was

pregnant that day. On 5 February 1990 my wife gave birth to a boy called Thomas.

DANNY RHODES:

I was a teenager living in Grantham and a huge Nottingham Forest fan. A group of us travelled all around the country every single week to watch them play. 89 was obviously Hillsborough. Then there was the peculiar rematch of the semi-final at Old Trafford, which Liverpool won before going on to win the FA Cup. There was some bad feeling after that game between Forest and Liverpool due to the behaviour of John Aldridge, who ruffled the hair of Brian Laws after Laws scored an own goal.

I recall the Liverpool v Arsenal game. We were all supporting Arsenal simply because the game was against Liverpool. When we arrived at the works social club there were loads of lads in the car park and all mayhem was breaking loose. The rest of the evening involved several scuffles, fights and numerous expulsions (I think the police arrived at one point) as trouble broke out between Liverpool fans (lots in those days), Arsenal fans (a scattering) but mostly fans of other sides.

ALAN MYERS:

At the time I was driving a taxi in Liverpool. I picked up a fare who was desperately trying to get into the local pub for the last few minutes of the game. 'Quick, quick,' he said. He threw a £10 note at me for the £1.40 fare and ran into the pub, which at this point was absolutely pounding out Liverpool songs and great delirium. As he disappeared into the pub and I put away my money, all of sudden a deathly silence came over the pub, you could hear a pin drop. I realised what had happened and I drove away quickly.

JOHN GERRARD:
I remember ringing my dad from the pub after the final whistle. No words were spoken, we just laughed for a few minutes (bitter Evertonians).

GARY TURNER:
I was 19 and watched on a giant old wooden TV in my bedroom with a few mates. It was the only game we'd ever watched together at that time. When Thomas scored the room erupted and one of my friends snapped my bed by jumping on it. It was all very poignant as my mum had terminal cancer and she was watching downstairs. It was her dad who told me all about The Arsenal and made me the fan I have always been. I celebrated with her afterwards and it was the last football match she ever watched, passing in the September. My mates and I then headed off to a college band night and proceeded to drink the place dry. No one knew the score and I had great pleasure drunkenly announcing it over the PA.

JOHN HILDITCH:
I was 13 and got to watch the game alone on the big TV at home, that's how big a deal it was, trying not to wake up my mother sleeping next door. Imagine hopping around a tiny front room celebrating Michael Thomas scoring in silence so as not to wake my mother. It ended with me waving a flag out of my bedroom window using my dad's pool cue as a flagpole. I still have the flag. Oh yeah, I lived in South Tottenham, not really Arsenal territory.

JOHN POWELL:
My wife and I had a flat on Upper Street, Islington in May 1989. We were expecting our first child and it was therefore not exactly the kind of calm and relaxing evening we maybe should have had. When Michael Thomas scored, I instinctively ran to the back of the flat and

kicked open the doors leading out on to a terrace, from where I let out a guttural, primeval scream of pure joy.

Given it was a warm and still evening, my clear memory was of sporadic whoops and then a gradual groundswell of cheering, laughing and excitement crackling through the Islington night air. Looking back, it was probably the absence of mobile phones that made such a difference. News and excitement filtered around groups of people engaging, smiling and singing. We spontaneously headed down to the off-licence and then joined others on what felt like a rather noisy pilgrimage. Highbury was the only and obvious place to be. Just sheer joy and a feeling of togetherness. And for my wife (new to football's madness) she says it was the first time she 'got it'.

Scott White:
I went to Highbury where I joined thousands of Arsenal fans celebrating outside the stadium. It was like I had to go and be around Arsenal supporters to share the best moment of my life at the place where I had grown up dreaming of this day. There was scaffolding up around the stadium as they were doing refurbishments and fans were climbing it and dancing on the platforms. I remember seeing people on the roofs of buildings singing songs and strangers hugging each other. I never wanted it to end.

Jon Hossain:
The next day I was on a 9 a.m.–9 p.m. shift in A&E. It was one of the quietest I've ever done. I swear the whole of Archway was still drunk. Most folk who came in with minor ailments were so happy. Many had red shirts on and they were delighted to see my red tie emblazoned with a cannon. I spent more time talking to patients about the game than their illness.

Peter Antonioni:

89 still leaves me deliriously happy and very remorseful at the same time. I was 22, had just started my dream job, the game got switched to Friday night and I didn't have the balls to ask my new (football atheist) boss for the day off. I had and still have a ticket, a reminder of the day that never was for me. To make things even worse my mates not only went to the game without me but they also got in to the after-party with the team. So I am constantly reminded of what could have been.

Neale Coules-Miller:

Having been a home and away Gooner most of my adult life (including a run of 500-plus games) I was then offered a match ticket by a work colleague on the morning of the match, only to decline on the grounds it was my wife's birthday. Now ex-wife, but there you go. Never had any trouble remembering her birthday though . . .

Matthew Robinson:

I was seven and back in the days when top-flight football was on terrestrial TV, I watched the game. My first ever Arsenal game. I remember thinking, wow, is every game like this?

John Foster:

I was eight years old. When Mickey scored I sprinted upstairs to the bathroom, flung open the door and screamed at my startled mum 'WE'VE DONE IT! WE'VE DONE IT!!' I still remember her in her shower cap leaning forward from her prone relaxation in the tub and looking at me saying 'We've done it?' She was as disbelieving as the whole nation. The final whistle and my dad grabs me, his beard bristles against my cheek. My mum comes down in her robe. Then my grandmother, born in Essex Road, Islington, comes round, celebrating. My aunt drives straight over. Our next-door neighbour

Clive – a Spurs fan – rings the doorbell and graciously gives my dad a bottle of wine. The landline phone does not stop ringing. All night. Friends long out of contact picking out my dad's name from their phone book to congratulate him. Family far away doing the same. At that moment, that night, my dad was the centre of the universe, and it is all thanks to Mickey Thomas.

John Fairclough:
The next day, hungover but still elated, I was at home relaxing and planning to go back out celebrating again when the phone rang. It was my wife phoning from Ireland. I thought she might have been phoning about the result, but unfortunately no. She just blurted out, 'Mammy's dead.'

I then had to try and find her two young nephews, also Arsenal supporters, who had only recently arrived in London looking for work. Back down in my local looking for my wife's nephews, the celebrations were still continuing and while I was there someone connected with the club brought the trophy in. I have a photo somewhere of me holding it. Talk about a weekend of mixed emotions. Anyway, to finish, I eventually found the two nephews and needless to say they were both completely broken and cashless. The governor of the pub, Tom, who had met my mother-in-law a couple of times, actually paid both their flights back to Ireland.

Nick Capara:
I was studying in Cheltenham in my halls of residence and a load of us had a TV set up in the hallway with beers ready to watch Liverpool's inevitable win. I was the only Arsenal fan and was sat next to a friend of mine who was a Liverpool fan who was fortunate enough to turn down a ticket to Hillsborough where his friend was one of the unfortunate 96 not to make it away. As a result there was an odd atmosphere in the group. With the clock ticking down and our feat

of leading 1–0 looking like an honourable effort I turned to Matt and congratulated him on the title. The rest is history.

TONY FISHER:
I had obtained two tickets the day before the game to pick up in Liverpool. I didn't tell my son and on Friday I waited for him to arrive at work with the exciting news that we were going. I waited and waited. No mobile phones then so I was at a loss to know what was happening. It was now the afternoon and reports were coming in about the terrible traffic jams on the motorway. Result was that I decided it was now too late to go and had to make the call for the tickets to be released elsewhere. I next saw him on the Monday and he had no good reason for not coming in on the Friday. We had a massive row and I didn't speak to him for weeks. He never did tell me what had happened. We obviously made it up later and he was a crowd extra in the Highbury celebration scene in *Fever Pitch*. I tragically lost him in 1999 and every 26 May I watch *Fever Pitch* as a memory of my personal events of that day and for my son.

JOHN POWELL:
After some dark days in the 70s and 80s, and particularly the Hillsborough tragedy, the evening felt like a new dawn. A cathartic re-fresh, and 1989 became a very poignant year for us; along with the backdrop of the Berlin Wall coming down later that year, with our daughter born on the day it came down, and also with a new job and a new house, the league win seemed to be the catalyst for an exciting change and a new era of hope.

ANTONY SUTTON:
The next morning there was a knock on my front door. 'Sorry, mister, my dad's a Liverpool fan and he says can you take down your flag?'

I would like to apologise to that lad for my reply. It was unseemly and impolite.

PART VI: AT THE OTHER END

Chris Tranter:

I remember watching this match on TV in my bedroom as a 16-year-old. I often watched with a friend but this match was too important to be somewhere else. When it finished I turned the TV off and sat in the dark for about an hour. Just a feeling of emptiness I've never felt in any other game. I didn't want to go to school or do anything, didn't want to talk to anyone. I still can't quite believe it happened. I'm sure it's related to Hillsborough and the feelings are probably linked. I hope I never have to feel that low again for any sport.

Tom Brown:

When Michael Thomas got the goal at the end I remember just stunned disbelief, and I sank to the ground and just sat on the terrace with my head in my hands. We left quickly after the final whistle and the atmosphere on the 27 bus home was one of silence and shock – I remember saying to Andy as I got off 'at least we won the FA Cup' and immediately regretted it as it just sounded so hollow. In retrospect it was a devastating day for us, but, while we all felt the pain, the bigger picture meant that we really couldn't feel too sorry for ourselves in light of the wider context – we had lost a championship in the worst possible way, but our friends had lost their lives, and the press and establishment were busy spewing their lies and hatred on all of us.

Lloyd Blackler:
The game was played on our final day of school before we left for study leave and sat our A levels. My best friend had never drank beer before and decided that this day would be a good time to start . . . The four pints of Kronenbourg at lunchtime and a couple of Newcastle Brown Ales for good measure ended up being deposited in my lap by 'Boy Chunder' as we watched Michael Thomas score the winner for Arsenal. We are both Liverpool fans so . . . NOT. A. GOOD. DAY. PS: He then ended up snogging the best-looking girl in school.

Dean Griffiths:
I was ten years old and followed Liverpool the best I could from South Wales. My father, a Liverpool fan, had been promising to take me to a match for a while. I had very little contact with my dad as he'd separated from my mother when I was three and it was a bit sour. Anyway on this occasion he followed through with his promise and got us on to a supporters' bus trip from a nearby town. He was a regular on this bus which didn't normally take children. The trip up to Anfield is around four hours and I loved every second of it. I was in awe of all the men around me drinking and singing songs that I only knew from the TV. But honestly, the best thing for me was spending time with my father.

When we arrived at Anfield I don't think I blinked for a good hour. I'm not sure I took many breaths either. It was everything I expected and more. The smells, the noises and the crowds. It was also a bit of a reality check for me seeing all the scarves and flowers still laid out, outside Anfield in the aftermath of Hillsborough.

We were sat three rows from the front of the paddock right in the corner by the Kop. The noise was incredible. I do remember the Arsenal fans singing too, it was a different noise though, obviously fewer supporters but still very loud. We all know how the game ended. I vividly remember some of the Arsenal players coming around the pitch towards us with the trophy and getting the applause they deserved but I was numb. I remember thinking, maybe I'm not into football as much as I thought, because this feels shit.

The journey home was horrible, almost four hours of silence, a bad copy of a film playing on the coach video player (*RoboCop* I think). That would be the one and only game my father ever took me to. I didn't return to Anfield for a few years, until I was old enough to go on the coach with friends. My second game was against Blackburn at Anfield, the year they won the league. So my record was two games, two league titles. Unfortunately none for Liverpool.

Jon Friend:
I have always felt, given the utterly incredible context of the game, that I was honoured and privileged to have been at it. The way in which it played out just enhances the sense of witnessing football history and the uniqueness of the match. The personal reason for this match holding a place in my heart is it invokes such melancholy for my dad. He passed away many years ago now. It was my dad, wholly unfamiliar with the world of football and culture around tickets and touting, who somehow, miraculously, produced my oh so precious ticket for the Kop that night.

Simply *the* hugest game in Football League history (certainly of the modern era), he had gone outside of his normal world and comfort zones to get a ticket for his youngest, knowing how much it would mean to this child to get one. I will now never know exactly what this meant or how much money he handed over. I don't think I made my gratitude and love clear to him at the time. My other memories include it being packed on the Kop that night, that the bouquets of flowers from Arsenal players went down very well amongst us, and the strange mixture of crushing disappointment and relief that the season was over. Just about all the Kop waited not just to see our own players but also the trophy presentation. My personal belief is this was one of the Kop's best moments, one I am very proud to have taken part in.

CRAIG BALMER:
I stood on the Kop as a season ticket holder. Plan for the night was simple: win the league, go to Planet X (a nightclub in town) and blow off school (I was 17). It had been my second season as a season ticket holder. Spirits were high, few bevvies on the train on the way in. I watched in horror as Thomas ran the length of the pitch unchallenged to score the second. I'd never before seen grown men crying, 21,000 of them in the heaving Kop. I'd never felt so bad about a football result. Upon trudging out we saw bus stops being smashed, road signs ripped down. We walked the 20-plus miles home in near silence; sober, cold and fed up.

JAY RAY:
It was almost silent coming out of the ground. No blaming the officials, or players, or Kenny. Just a numbness running through every fan. The events of the previous six weeks caused that. Even if we'd have won the league that night, it wouldn't have been celebratory, like other title wins. If the fans were exhausted, then imagine what the players were like. Attending funerals, trying to train, matches every few days at the end of the season. They were on their knees at the end. They had nothing left. I would imagine the dressing room was like the streets outside Anfield at the end. Completely silent. In retrospect, it was all about winning the cup that year. The league was something of a side issue. The team and fans had to honour the 96 and we'd done that at Wembley.

KIERAN DAVIS:
I was at Anfield that night with my brother Michael, Kemlyn Road, Kop end. I don't recall an overwhelming sense of excitement given

what had happened at Hillsborough, just wanted the season over. But I also had a sense that we would never be beaten by two clear goals, which is what they needed. When the second went in there was silence from the Liverpool supporters but there was also anger I recall. 'This can't be happening.' I glanced over at the away end, complete fervour. Then on the pitch, Liverpool players on their knees, each on their own in the positions they were at the final whistle. It mattered so much more than I thought it would. Hillsborough had put everything into perspective. Of course we wanted to win but the players as well as the fans had endured a terrible five weeks. Is it any wonder that there was vulnerability. It wasn't a sense of disappointment, it was a sense of injustice. As we walked to the car I witnessed a fight between two frustrated Liverpool fans. I got home and went to bed. In the morning my mum came in and said, we'll win it next year. We did, though the injustice of that season, what happened to us, what happened on that night, has never been resolved. Still gets me.

Chris Smith:
I was down south hosting a party with my now deceased wife, Jacqui. I keep one eye on the video recorder whilst explaining things about the weekend to our guests, as I was the organiser. But I checked my watch and said 'excuse me, I just have to make sure that I have recorded this special game!' . . . and turned on the TV . . . *exactly* as Thomas stuck the second goal in the net. I turned the TV off, and the tape off. I think I pulled the plug out from the wall.

Jacqui looked at me with a stare, expecting me to say something. I just stared at the black TV screen, I don't know for how long. I don't know if I made any sense. I felt empty. That night will always stay with me, as will the other event that season that changed LFC, and me, for ever.

IAN GOLDER:
I had met a girl in late 1988 and we had started dating. We split up a week before Hillsborough. I went to Hillsborough and there was obvious concern from herself and her family as for my well-being in the aftermath. Hillsborough brought us back together.

From 15 April until that night at Anfield seemed to last a lifetime. The city was in mourning. There was a cloud. A horrible feeling yet football was still keeping us going. That game was going to be on the Friday night at Anfield due to the rescheduling of games. Normally, of course, the league programme would be completed before the FA Cup final. We were going for the Double, as we had in 1986. I had a season ticket for the Kop and managed to get my girlfriend a ticket too. I said to her that she would see nothing like it. We win the league and the celebrations afterwards would be immense. We were totally confident of wrapping it up. The game also had an air of inevitability about it, like we were entitled to win it because of what had happened.

It didn't work out that way of course. Arsenal were superb that night and I think we were maybe overconfident and also very tired. Our legs were gone. Drained physically and emotionally. The ball broke to Michael Thomas and I swear time stood still. It certainly did on the Kop. Silence. I still can't get my head around why Stevie Nicol didn't just take Thomas out. It was an obvious choice to make.

I was heartbroken. This wasn't supposed to happen. We walked back to my girlfriend's house five miles from Anfield. I felt so low as the emotions of the previous six weeks took hold. We got back to her house and I decided I had to be on my own so walked back home to my mum and dad's another six miles away.

That is the lowest I have ever felt after watching my team lose a game. It meant everything to win the league that particular year and we fell short in the cruellest way possible. It was a long summer but I had a rethink and got my girlfriend a season ticket for the 89–90 season. A year later she witnessed us win that league title back. A year after that our son was born and in 1994 we were married, having our daughter in 1996.

We have split up since but are still on good terms. Highs and lows of football and fate. If it wasn't for what happened in those six weeks I honestly think my life would have been different. No girlfriend, no son, no marriage, no daughter.

I was lucky as I got out of Hillsborough but I still see so many people in pain due to what happened. RIP 96.

TWELVE

The Goal that Changed Everything

George Graham:
It sunk in when I was on my way back to London. I thought: done the business. Thank you very much. Let's get back home. The famous Desmond Morris idea. Get in there, hit them hard and get the hell out of there. I was so proud of the players. I've got nothing but admiration for them. You work at it during the week and make sure it can happen and they were fantastic and they did it.

Michael Thomas:
I always remember George Graham coming to the back of the coach. He never came to the back to have a drink with the boys. Never ever. So when he came to sit at the back and to drink with us, obviously you know it's a big moment. It was a fantastic journey back. Cars beeping. Everybody out of the cars. Flags flying all the way down the M1, M6. It was incredible. I do remember the start of the bus journey back. But I don't remember getting home.

Gary Lewin:
We were supposed to be having food but that went out the window. Food wasn't my problem, but beer was. That was my job. It was a party atmosphere with everyone on the bus singing and celebrating.

Alan Smith:
We're all at the back of the coach singing songs and banging the window at people who were beeping their horn. 'Look at this lot over here!' We'd all go over to the side of the coach, waving. People were hanging out car windows. Stood out the top of sunroofs. They'd slow down and they'd overtake again and were waving again and it was brilliant.

David O'Leary:
I didn't want the coach journey to end. I wish we could have kept going, got delayed on the motorway for six or seven hours. I don't think we'd have even known. A convoy of cars beeping all the way. When we got back North London was alive. It was a fairy-tale night.

Steve Bould:
The police met us at the end of the motorway to give us an escort to the club, which was kept open for us.

Niall Quinn:
I knew the guys in Winners, a club in Southgate. At that time it was predominantly a snooker hall that all the pros practised in – Cliff Thorburn and Kirk Stevens would be there each day practising ahead of tournaments and Alex Higgins would come the odd time. Snooker was huge then. It was a fun place to be with a lovely bar. I knew they would put on a decent night for us but in those days I had to run out and ring ahead from a call box to ask if they would look after us when the lads got back. By the time we got there word got around and there were huge crowds outside. It was like Hollywood movie stars trying to get into a premiere. We got in there and it was pandemonium. So happy, so giddy. We had a fabulous night, which went on and on and on.

TONY ADAMS:
Snooker all night. I lost my blazer, gave it to a supporter. I got it back many years afterwards.

ALAN SMITH:
I was in a restaurant the other day and a chap came up to me and said: 'I was in Winners that night and you gave me your tie and I've still got it.'

JANET ROCASTLE:
It was really early hours that they came home. A couple of years ago when I was having a clear-out in the garage I found David's and Mickey Thomas's jackets from that day and one of their ties. I got them dry cleaned and sent Mickey's one on to him.

GARY LEWIN:
Once we dropped the lads off in Southgate we went to Colney to drop off a few of the staff and Tony Donnelly and I stayed in the bus to go back to Highbury with the kit. We went down Highbury Hill about 4 o'clock in the morning and there was a street party going on. Once the crowd saw the team bus they went mad. We unloaded the kit, I bought all the newspapers on the way home. It was a long day. I used to take the trophies. Nobody at the club was there to take the trophy so I took it home for safety. I had it at home and brought it back on the Sunday. I've got pictures with the kids. I didn't tell anyone it was there though; I was so nervous about having it.

NIALL QUINN:
When we came out the club it was bright. Paul and Tony stayed with me and then everyone went home. I had to get ready to go to the airport. I went by taxi and collected Dave O'Leary and we were gone by lunchtime.

89

David O'Leary:

Looking back, my wife and son had missed the whole thing. It had been his birthday the day we won the league. He was tired, he was young. My wife took him to bed and they both fell asleep. The phone started exploding in the house about half past ten at night. She was thinking, what's gone on here? People from everywhere were ringing. Have you heard? Have you seen? The next day I went to give my son my medal but he was more interested in his Thomas the Tank Engine. I had to go to Dublin that day to go and join the Irish squad. I got on a plane that morning and everybody started clapping. A person at the ticket desk told me he was an Arsenal fan and said if I wanted to drive the plane I could. I got off the plane in Dublin and Man United fans – they weren't even Arsenal fans – were patting my back saying, Dave, we're so delighted for you. There was a few happy people but also there was a couple of very unhappy people in the camp. Seeing Ray Houghton and John Aldridge, I don't think they were over the shock.

Penny Smith:

We got back really late. I was back at work Saturday morning; I left more or less as Alan came in. My friend Martin stayed at our house, and when I got back from work he said, 'Oh, I've been run off my feet!' Alan was a bit worse for wear and Martin was answering the phone, everyone had been calling and ringing the bell. He was fending people off.

Roy Dixon:

I was so excited to see Lee when he came home but more relieved than anything after all that worry. My wife had been at the golf club watching it on television there and when they won she bought drinks all round and it cost me £500. There you go. That was my experience of Lee winning the league. After all the years going to the park, watching him play as a boy, putting the nets up, taking the nets down, it was wonderful.

Alan Smith:
The next day we went to Lee's with our friends Martin and Clare, who had driven to the game with my wife Penny. Lee had got the old VHS. He'd got the match. We watched the game again. Lee kept stopping on his good bits! Come the evening we decided to have a barbecue at my house and invited all the lads.

Paul Merson:
Alan's face was a picture. Honestly, when he opened the door to see us all there he thought, for God's sake. He didn't think we'd come!

Penny Smith:
God knows where I got food from because in those days I don't think supermarkets opened all the time. I did feed everyone but Alan wasn't feeling very well and he said, 'Off I go to bed.' He went off and left me with all these people. Perry Groves went into my bathroom and put bottles of bubble bath down the toilet and flushed the chain and there were bubbles coming out the toilet.

Alan Smith:
Grovesy was rearranging things and being annoying like he could. He was obviously drunk but I was also quite ill that night. I'd got a bit of the shakes. Obviously too much alcohol and I went up and lay on my bed and eventually the lads went.

Nigel Winterburn:
I didn't realise what we had actually achieved until we did the open-top bus on the Sunday and then you start to realise you are league champions. That means something pretty special. The other day my

wife said to me, 'Do you remember the phone calls I got when the game was going on?' I had completely forgotten. During the game my wife's sister-in-law called up and said, I've had a funny feeling something's going to happen in this game. Then we get a free-kick. I take the free-kick and Smudger scores. Later on in the evening as the game is still going on she calls again and says, 'I've had that same feeling.' I mean, people are going to say that's so made up it's absolutely ridiculous. It was incredible. I didn't know that those feelings were going to produce those two goals. Maybe it was fate. I don't know. I'm going to believe it. I couldn't care less what anybody else thinks if I'm honest. It's fantasy stuff, isn't it? It was our destiny. As time goes by you start to realise what Arsenal Football Club is really all about and by the time you finish and retire it sits in the heart. It's always there.

ALAN SMITH:
When we came in for the open-top bus ride on the Sunday morning Tony Adams was sat on the steps of the Marble Halls because he'd been out all night. He'd lost track of time. I think he'd got here about 7 in the morning. He just came in from a night out; he was a state.

LYNNE CHANEY:
I was on my way in to Highbury and there was Mickey driving up Drayton Park and he pulled over and said 'hop in'. He was the last one to arrive. I jumped in and got a lift. Everyone recognised him. I remember as he came in the car park at the Clock End he clipped the gate. I was like, how did you score that goal? Ha ha.

DAVID MILES:
At Highbury we were doing some annual renovation on the front of the stadium and we had the whole front of the East Stand scaffolded.

Scaffolding is designed probably to hold half a dozen guys and two pots of paint. On the Sunday morning, the parade left from the stadium to Islington Town Hall and I was on the front steps with the chief of police coordinating which players were going to go on the bus and which players' wives. Then all of a sudden, the chief of police said to me, we're going to have to move quickly. I said, why? He said, turn round and have a look on the scaffolding. There were hundreds of people trying to get a vantage point to see the team leave and we looked up and the scaffolding was actually moving and swaying and whipping away from the stand because of the sheer weight of people. The policeman said to me, 'Go and tell George Graham now. Unless we move in two minutes the buses will go, players or not.' We got everyone on and luckily everyone came down the scaffolding to follow the buses without any incident.

Jo Harney:
I was up on someone's shoulders and I've not got a clue who they were. This guy was just walking me round. He had a bulldog on a lead with an Arsenal shirt on. There were people everywhere. Hanging off lamp-posts. Four or five people like sardines sitting on a window ledge.

Michael Thomas:
I came back to life then. That was the best. I don't know how many people were there at that parade. It was incredible to see everybody there and us with the league trophy. I had a hat on someone gave me: 'Mickey did it'. It only took a minute and Mickey went and did it. I've still got that little baseball cap. It was crazy.

Steve Bould:
They said there were 250,000 people lining the streets. I actually realised that day what a huge club it was.

Perry Groves:
I remember someone was hanging off a tree and they jumped on to the top of the bus. Everybody was laughing and joking. Normally you'd go and get him out of there but it was: all right, mate, how are you doing? We said, look, you'd better get off at the next stop and he was having photographs and a laugh with the lads. Things like that really hit home.

Lee Dixon:
That was another big, big high. I've never seen as many people around Highbury and Islington in my life and I think it was a shock to everybody. I love the scenes in *Fever Pitch* when the goal goes in on the night, of all the people flooding round Highbury and they filmed that bloke on the taxi. It really hits home to me how much it meant to the people of that area. It was mad. There were people hanging by one arm out of windows. I remember they just kept throwing cans of beer up on to the bus. At the town hall they'd constructed a couple of planks hanging out the window and we were sort of climbing out this window on to some sort of platform. Health and safety would have had a nightmare. We were just leaning over with thousands and thousands of people below us and how anyone didn't fall off I'll never know.

Perry Groves:
I remember saying to the lads, I'm going to sing a song. I remember the gaffer going, 'Get him off that balcony.' He said, 'Grovesy, you're tone deaf. You can't sing.' I went pfft. Frank Sinatra hasn't had 250,000 fans. I just had them in the palm of my hand. It was pretty surreal to be honest.

John Lukic:
As a player you're almost cocooned in your little world but suddenly you see the pleasure that it gives to so many people around

the place. That's what brings home the enormity of what you've actually achieved.

NIALL QUINN:
All those lovely shots of the boys on the bus with the crowds. David O'Leary and I watched them in a hotel in Dublin on the news. I didn't get a medal because in those days you had to get 14 matches under your belt to qualify. I got a silver tray from the chairman. But I still felt part of it because we had shared all those years together. Besides, the title was decided on goals scored and I got one against Everton that season.

PENNY SMITH:
I'd had shorts on at Anfield because it was a hot day and when we went on the open-top bus my legs were black and blue, because after the goals and after we'd won we were all diving around the plastic seats. After the open-top bus we all went to TGI Friday's in Covent Garden for something to eat. I was still feeling a bit queasy at this point, not knowing I was pregnant. The next day Alan met up with England, and the England doctor, who was also the Arsenal doctor, had to give him an injection in his bum because I think he'd got a bit of alcoholic poisoning. It was a mad few days.

LEE DIXON:
I had the biggest emotional crash you've ever seen. I'd never been that high before as far as football emotion is concerned. It was just a peak. It was incredible. It was overwhelming. So coming down over the next couple of days it was just dreadful. So low. So depressed. I couldn't understand it because I'd never experienced it before like that. I've since spoken to John Lukic about it and he said the same. You learn as you go through your career that when you're up there there's only one place to go and it's just a matter of time before you

start to come down to reality. So there was a definite learning curve of how to deal with the ups and downs of sport emotion.

I've got the game in its entirety on VHS. When I'm a bit down or I need a bit of a lift for whatever reason I'll shove it in there and wind it on to 88 minutes and then press play. I sometimes put *Fever Pitch* on and watch that film because you get a supporter's viewpoint. As players we're very privileged to be on the playing side of it but you miss out on some of the supporting side of it, which I think is the most important. Because when I talk to people who went to the game I want to hear their stories.

John Lukic:
I went off a cliff. You have the build-up and the momentum of trying to achieve something and when you've actually achieved it and you've got it in your hands you're sort of going over the edge. And that's where I found myself. What's the next thing? I don't know how to describe that. Now the memories are always there whether you watch it on TV or whether you replay it in your head. I don't watch my old games – that's for my children and, God willing, the grandchildren in future if they want to get a few tapes out and have a look at what the old bloke did. To win the ultimate in British football, I'll take that.

David O'Leary:
The best team over the whole season wins the league. If you have ever won a cup final that's the most memorable day. I thought we had a bit of both there. It was a shoot-out for the biggest prize out there. I just don't think there's anything to top it so far in football.

Paul Davis:
Even now I'm not sure if Mickey knows how big it is. I don't think he knows how to deal with it. I'm not sure. It's almost like he hasn't

come to terms with the whole thing, what's happened to him. Or to us. It is just the impression I get.

MICHAEL THOMAS:
It is quite strange. I'm a private person. I don't like the fame side of the football world. It's even hard talking about it sometimes. But it was a bit weird when you've got people looking at you wherever you are in the country. I thought: wow. I don't think I can get used to this. That was tough. I don't think I've ever got used to it. I wouldn't say it's a burden because it's never a burden to score a winning goal and to see your team win the championship. But fame and me, I don't think we mix. I just like the quiet life really to be honest. Just as long as I'm appreciated that's all that matters to me, more than anything.

TONY ADAMS:
You might laugh at this but having won a lot of youth team trophies, winning felt pretty normal. When I started to speak to people like Dave O'Leary he was like, what are you on? This might never happen in your career again. Don't you realise what you've just done? What we've just done? I'm going to say it was the best. I happened to be there. I get so many people even to this day who talk about it. It's iconic. It's just a moment in time. With Hillsborough you had something else in the equation and it was powerful. I just was enormously grateful that I was there on the day to lift the trophy up after 18 years of hurt.

There's a certain place that you've been to together. I don't want to get too deep but I've been to hell a couple of times in my life already. Other people have been to the same hell that I've been to so once you've been to the same hell you can identify and you can enjoy and laugh about those kind of things. Only people that were at Anfield that day and in that dressing room can laugh and joke and appreciate the story that we wrote. I'll always be grateful for that. It was a magical moment in my career and I'm really grateful that I shared it with some great pals and some great winners. Great stuff.

Alan Smith:

A lot of us were mid-twenties. We had a long time to go in our careers – those back four lads did especially – but I think we sensed something, which is quite unusual, because at the time you are enveloped by the occasion and by the passion and you're not able to take a step back. But I think we realised that it can't possibly get any better than this. How can we trump this moment? And I don't think anything did. Even for those boys that went on to win the Double under Arsène Wenger, in terms of one-off matches, that was it. The Sergio Agüero goal for Man City against QPR is the most famous in Premier League times. It was an amazing moment for City to clinch the league in the last seconds. But of course what makes ours stand out was it was a standalone game. It was the two teams vying for the title at the end of the league campaign. Everybody else had packed up. Gone home. Gone to the beach. It would never be allowed to happen now but that's how it panned out so you've got a huge audience watching this shoot-out. With all due respect, the City game can't compare.

Paul Merson:

I was lucky enough on Sky to cover the Man City game when Agüero scored the goal. That's nothing like it. It was a great finish. But these were the two top teams playing. The season is finished for everyone else. This is the last game. You've got to go to the best team in the country for the last how many years and win by two clear goals to win the league. Honestly, if it was a book and I was sitting round the pool on holiday and I read it and that was the end I'd throw it in the pool. Someone would say 'What are you doing?' And I'd say 'I've just read the biggest load of shit I've ever read.' It couldn't happen again ever. It's impossible.

PERRY GROVES:
When we do meet each other nowadays there's a warmth there and a happy feeling because you've shared that one huge moment. It is a bit of a zeitgeist – right place, right time. You could have rose-tinted spectacles if you like with nostalgia but I think the fans look back and go, 'Wow.' Because we were working-class boys, predominantly English and Irish, just local lads who'd been the best players in their school team, best players in their district team, best players in the county team and then obviously worked their way through different avenues. We came together at that moment in time. You have to be lucky in your career and I feel lucky I was there the same time as George Graham. I don't care what anybody says, he made our careers. He turned us from players with a little bit of ability and desire into a top-quality group who won titles and won cups for Arsenal Football Club. That era was all down to him without any shadow of a doubt.

STEVE BOULD:
George changed Arsenal Football Club, for sure. We hadn't won the league for 18 years. The club really wasn't one of those that was included amongst those with a chance to win the league, and George changed that. He changed the mindset. He changed players who were hungry and he got us believing. He got everybody behaving with class. He moved the club forward massively. Everybody who comes to the club develops an affection that lasts a lifetime.

JOHN LUKIC:
We were one of the last British-based teams to win the league. So that in itself tells a story. Football from there has evolved to a very cosmopolitan sport, people from all nations. Back then the only foreigner on the team sheet from outside Britain and Ireland was Bruce Grobbelaar. The core of that game itself was a British game. From then on football seemed to develop, to gain more attention, to where we are

today with the Premier League watched across the world. You'd like to think that we had a part to play in that.

Nigel Winterburn:
Maybe we've changed the way that people look at football.

Paul Merson:
I really think it put football back where it belongs. Football just lifted and I don't think it's ever looked back. I go up and down the country and you talk to people and everybody knows where they were that night. They'll say, oh, I was sitting in a bar in Spain with a lorry-load of Everton fans. They were going mad when you won. Or, I was in a pub with a load of Man United fans. If you live in Exeter or Accrington or Rochdale, if you're old enough you remember that game. We talk about it as the goal that changed everything. It's the game that changed football, believe me. This changed football and I'll tell you the reasons why. This was on a Friday night. Football was going nowhere. We'd just had the biggest disaster in football. There was fighting on the terraces. Football was leaving a bad taste in people's mouths. People weren't liking football. People were scared to go to football matches. You wouldn't take your kids to football matches. Then this game comes on a Friday night. When was there ever a game on a Friday night live? Millions of people are watching. I think it changed football. I really do. Then after that, the following year, England go to the World Cup, they have a massive success and football starts flying again.

Michael Thomas:
A lot of people when they meet me always remember that goal. They remember what they were doing at that time. They still tell me now. You've got the Evertonians who love me because of that. You've got Mancs saying the same thing. I even got some Spurs supporters who say it. So it is unique in that case.

JANET ROCASTLE:
I come from a family of five boys and all of them supported different teams – one was Chelsea, one Tottenham, Man United – but since I met David everybody followed Arsenal after that. The whole family was so proud. We quite often watch *Fever Pitch* here. Ryan has the DVD. It really sparks a lot of memories of David and of that time. For the kids and I, we look at everyone from then as part of our family.

ALAN SMITH:
When you watch the coverage again from the game there is hardly anything after the match. Jim Rosenthal did the interview with Tony down on the pitch. Then back up to the studio, Elton Welsby with Bobby Robson, his one and only guest in a little poky studio. 'Well, Bobby, what do you make of that?' 'Oh, fantastic performance from Arsenal. Absolutely wonderful.' 'Oh, thanks, Bobby. Goodnight.' It was one of those. Time for *News at Ten*. The treatment we'd give it on Sky now. We'd be on air still dissecting every single minute of it!

At the time the only change you were envisaging was the all-seater stadia coming in. You could never forecast how the game itself would change. Italia 90 was a watershed. Obviously with the onset of the Premier League, names on the back of the shirts, players arriving from all over the world, you sensed something was happening. It was all getting a bit more glitzy. Gradually you could see different innovations coming in, but that's when it all began.

I was glowing in the aftermath that summer. Just thinking about the season. Playing the game over in your head. Looking at the video. It was a brilliant summer. We went to Las Vegas and did the old California road trip. At the Grand Canyon I came across some Arsenal fans who were obviously on a high still. 'Oh, hi, Smudge!' No selfies back then you know.

89

DAVID DEIN:

Football and television became very important to each other. Before that season it was a cartel. It was BBC and ITV and, between the two of them, football didn't get anything for their product. They thought they were doing us a favour by promoting us. Football needed and wanted television and it was ITV who decided they were going to break the cartel. We finally completed a four-year deal in 1988. It was £44 million – £11 million per year for the 92 professional clubs. So they got the whole of the old Football League. Of course, the very first season of that television contract they hit the jackpot because who would ever think that it would be the final game between Liverpool against Arsenal and the league would be determined by the last kick of the season? They had around 14 million viewers. Of course, we did have to expand and it was only when all of a sudden you had the foreign players coming in that everybody suddenly said it's the dawn of a new era. The average wage around the late 1980s would have been £200–£300 a week. They're getting that a minute now I think. Ha ha.

Our guest that night at Anfield was Greg Dyke, who worked in television. It was Greg and I who were really at the sharp end of putting the television deal together. At the end of the game I said, Greg, you've got to come down to the dressing room and, of course, as soon as we went down to the dressing room the champagne was flowing and we both got drenched. Our suits were drenched and I put my arm round Greg and said, you see this, you got it cheaply. It really was the launching pad in many respects and, of course, nobody was to know at the time that in 1992 Rupert Murdoch would come along and launch Sky television and then, in Alan Sugar's famous words, blow everybody out the water. That game in a way probably brought home the value and the relationship of football and television.

PADDY BARCLAY:
I do remember being numb with shock and excitement and the sense of privilege of actually being there. We all said once we had got our job done and our reports filed that we will never experience anything like this again. We could not conceive of football providing such a finish as that ever again. It was ten years to the day when Manchester United won the treble in Barcelona with a finish of comparable drama. All of our minds then went back to Anfield. What is it about this game that produces finishes like this? We now know that game was the beginning of football as ridiculous excitement. I don't know why but football since 1989 has produced an awful lot more of those I-cannot-believe-this moments than it ever did before. If you look back at the iconic games like the Stanley Matthews Cup Final of 1953, it was just a football match, seven goals were scored, and good old Stanley Matthews won a trophy at the end. It wasn't a match like Barcelona overturning a 4–0 deficit to beat Paris Saint-Germain 6–5 with a dramatic turnaround. That game at Anfield was the beginning of pinch-yourself drama in football.

AMY LAWRENCE:
If you are a person who is generally moved by sport then it doesn't need to be your team for the thrill of a startling spectacle to make your spine tingle. Sport matters because it makes you feel things. It makes you care. Famous upsets, heart-warming comebacks, tales of the unexpected – it's all part of what has gone on to make football so ubiquitous in our modern social landscape, so magnetic that billions are spent and foreign investors home in on this manically lucrative industry. But they were simpler times back then. It sounds silly and melodramatic but I felt I even learned a life lesson that night at Anfield that always stayed with me. People tell you things are never going to happen, that odds are weighted so strongly there is no point

in even hoping, that outlandish dreams are impossible. But that's not always true, is it?

Nick Hornby:
I don't think there will ever be another game like it. First against second and winner wins the league basically and that hasn't happened in my memory. For me, the feeling of 26 May 1989 was so intense that I didn't really notice the next season. I was still thinking about the last season. I just had this glow from that moment on.

I didn't really want them to start winning again until 1991, which was good as that's when they did start winning again, when winning became more of a part of the club's culture. I think your relationship with leagues and trophies changes a little bit. Which is as it should be for a club the size of Arsenal. You should be expecting them to win things. I'd gone from being 14 in 1971 and I was 32 in 1989. It's a big chunk of your life and you're a different person but the one thing that's stayed the same in that thread is the football. It was the one thing that connected my 32-year-old self to my 14-year-old self. There was nothing else really.

The reason *Fever Pitch* started in my head was I thought about how many games I had stories about. Some of them seemed to me to say something about Britain at certain points in its history. Some of them had something to say about being a certain kind of kid or teenage boy or young man. Some of them had something to say about football and none of them were just the scores, so I thought, maybe I can try and write it as if it were a match report but each match report is about actually about something else. The point was the feelings and the context. Writing about the Anfield game for *Fever Pitch* I knew that I had to bring out everything I had in terms of the writing for that piece. Because it was one of the emotional sensors of the book.

I've often been told about *Fever Pitch* being part of the shift in perceptions in English football. It's hard for me to see. I think that the big thing was Sky, and Rupert Murdoch had much more influence on the game than my book. Italia 90 was important. Not least because it had been quite a while since any tournament had been played during the evenings in the UK. 86 was in Mexico. You had to stay up. You had to be a proper football fan to watch England play at midnight or whatever. 82 was horrible anyway and you know we hadn't been there in 74 and 78 so 1990 was very important for the rebirth and the relaunching of football. The way it was shot as well. Do you remember all those slow-motion shots of the agony on people's faces in the crowd when Italy went out on penalties? The game entered a new era media-wise with Italia 90. It's interesting that Sky came in so shortly after 89 because it's often struck me that sport is one of the few things that's any use to cable broadcasters because we've got enough rubbish films and enough rubbish television programmes. What we need is something where we literally don't know what's going to happen next. We have to watch it at the time. It's no good watching it on catch-up. It's like a battering ram into people's homes. That drama is so intense that it cannot really be repeated in any other art form.

When I wrote *Fever Pitch* I knew there were lots of people who read books and went to football matches. There is a sort of accusational myth since that I wrote *Fever Pitch* and then a load of middle-class people came to football. But in fact I was a middle-class kid who became interested when England won the World Cup in 66. I think that's when the game's roots changed because suddenly George Best and all of the mavericks became popular culture superstars. Anyone who was 10 or 11 then grew up with the game in a way that maybe their parents wouldn't have done. My book was probably an expression of that partly. I wanted to represent fans who felt very, very connected to their team and who lived their lives in this way. Consumed by caring about something that they couldn't control.

89

When Arsène Wenger came and Arsenal reached a different peak all the players lived in North London, in Hampstead and Regent's Park, and after the game they would eat in a local restaurant and it was very hard to get a table there because the players went there. But there felt like a lot of connection between fans and players in ways that were not the same as the 1980s team but were certainly an adequate replacement. Arsène seemed to have signed players who wanted to play for the club and wanted to stay there for a reasonable period of time. I think now it feels like it has accelerated off into future football where you're not sure whether any player will be there next season and how much would I care if all 11 of them left? Not that much. The club will find 11 good new footballers. There are a couple who you could base a team around but the idea of having first of all the home-grown players like David Rocastle and Michael Thomas and so on, but also the other players – the back four, Alan Smith – is something else. You got the sense that they were fantastic but you weren't going to lose them to Juventus or Barcelona. I never felt like Alan Smith was going to go to Barcelona. I didn't think that Steve Bould was going to go to Juventus. It felt like they were playing at the best place for them and that this was the top of their game and there was a sort of happy merging of the needs of players and the needs of fans.

For anyone who was old enough to live through some of the very dismal years preceding 1989 the shock and pleasure of the win is something that always locates you back in the time. We've had lots of pleasures since but they're much more diffuse. If you think about the Invincibles season I don't think there was even quite a moment like that in the entire season. You just think, well this is a good team. They've won again. They've won again. They've won again. Even in the good times it's very hard to find that pinpoint intensity of Anfield. I don't think many fans have ever experienced it.

George Graham:
When I joined Arsenal as manager we did so much travelling that I began buying books and magazines on the club's history. That's how I started with my memorabilia and I used to go to programme and book fairs at a hotel in Russell Square on a Sunday to pick up rare things. I have quite a lot from the 30s and even before then. It's quite fascinating how the club came over the borders into North London. How they built Highbury. Who the first chairman was. Some of the great managers. The philosophy. Herbert Chapman didn't do any coaching. He just picked a team and it was down to the trainer and the physio. There was probably three staff and Chapman would just sit in his lovely oak-panelled office upstairs. Luckily I had that for a few years. To have those magical moments makes you feel nice but in time you're forgotten about and then the world has got a new hero. But, of course, you enjoy the memories. You love it.

AFTERWORD

Oh Rocky Rocky

ALAN SMITH:
Rocky meant a lot to everybody really. He was my mate. The first time my wife Penny and I met him was at a dinner down in London at the Hilton. We were sat there with some other people and Rocky came across and he was only probably a teenager then and he said, 'Oh hi, I'm David. Nice to meet you. Lovely to see you and lovely to have you here and if there's anything you need just ask.' He walked away and I turned to Penny and said, what a nice lad. What a lovely lad. That's exactly what he was. We grew very close as families and we are still close to his wife Janet and the kids. And what a player, as well as being a big personality in the dressing room. He was as strong as an ox but with the skills of a Brazilian. Lightning quick foot-overs, so hard to knock off the ball. He was a wonderful player to have on my right. He had some great tussles with Stuart Pearce. I remember Pearcey used to try and intimidate him. Crash into him. Give him a bit of verbals but Rocky just thrived off it. There weren't many about like him. I still miss him. It's hard to talk about him.

He was one of those players that everybody loved. He could get on with anybody. Nobody had a bad word. I know we always say that about people who have passed away but it was true. We were family friends and we always kept in touch. I'll never forget the day that George explained to him why he had to sell him, and he was sat in that BMW for about an hour and we all thought, God, what are they talking about? It was hard for the gaffer too because he loved Rocky.

He didn't feel he was up to the standard any more because of his knee and he didn't have the mobility. He sold him to Leeds and it was a tough day to leave the club and I remember Ian Wright had only just joined and he said, 'I've only joined the club to be with you, Rocky, and now they're selling you.' He couldn't believe it. Rocky went to Man City and Chelsea and then went across to Malaysia and that's when he fell ill and came back. Non-Hodgkin's lymphoma. The survival rate is supposed to be about 80 per cent of people of that age. I remember Janet ringing us at 3 o'clock in the morning. When the phone goes at 3 o'clock in the morning you know it's bad news. We played Spurs that day. I was in bits. We had a minute's silence and I just went.

George Graham:
David was a very talented player, not only in the Arsenal set-up but the England set-up. He picked up an injury and we tried to play him twice a week. He kept breaking down. We couldn't train him too hard during the week because he swelled up. If we didn't train him he started putting on weight. His knee was the major problem. He was an outstanding player and an outstanding person. But we got an offer from Leeds which was just acceptable. It was very sad.

Nick Hornby:
He epitomised that team for a lot of us. Because he was so gifted we always had a joke with the people I watched with that he was going to score the greatest goal ever seen in football. He scored some cracking goals. But we always had this fantasy Rocastle goal where he picked the ball up where Lee Dixon had picked the ball up in 1989 but he'd run all around the pitch and then smash it in the corner and then everyone would agree afterwards that it is officially the greatest goal of all time. We all thought he was capable of scoring it and he had some fire about him and he was a London boy. I was terribly sad

when he was sold because that really felt like something had gone from the team with him no longer there. It was terribly sad that somebody who had symbolised the resurgence and re-emergence of Arsenal was now no longer playing for them and then . . . Young players like that don't die. A beautiful man, beautiful player. I love it that that chant has become part of the club now. It's usually when there's some kind of celebratory mood in the stadium, then people begin to sing his name and there doesn't seem to be any reason why that will stop. My kids sing it.

DAVID DEIN:
When I joined the board in 83 I would always go and see the youth team play in the morning at London Colney and then double back to Highbury to see the first team play. I remember coming back and telling the family, do you know we've got a player who could be a Brazilian player playing for us and he comes from South London. He's got so much talent. Such wonderful skill. Such balance. Such technique. That was David Rocastle. He was something that every manager would crave for because he was very loyal, quite apart from his technique and his skill. Above all that he was just a natural winner. If he was your son you'd be proud of him because he was just a very genuine boy.

DAVID MILES:
We grew up with him. He joined Arsenal as a 16-year-old and at the time, as all the apprentices did in those days, he actually used to spend one afternoon a week working in one of the offices and they trained a lot more at Highbury than the teams do now. So we all became friends. I remember one day I had a knock on my office door and he poked his head round and asked to use the club phone. They weren't allowed to use club phones. When I was assistant secretary, I had a small office. 'Don't tell George but can I use your club phone?'

Yeah, come on quick. He was phoning one of the footwear manufacturers because he'd just broken into the England under-16 team and they'd offered him a pair of boots. He was just so grateful that this football manufacturer had offered him a free pair of boots. That was the mark of the man. He was very humble.

LYNNE CHANEY:
It is still raw. I still feel sad. He was so lovely, and his family are just amazing. You can see their personality comes from him.

IAIN COOK:
His daughter Melissa has been working at the club. The other day one of the lads I work with asked who she was. I said 'Oh, that's Melissa. She's just started working with us. I used to work with her dad a few years ago at Highbury.' He said, 'What did he do then?' I said, 'Well, he wore the number 7 shirt for a few years . . .'

DAVID O'LEARY:
The memory of him is ultimately one of the loveliest people you'd ever meet. We shared the same birthday. We used to go out a few times on our birthday. His family have turned out to be what he was – fantastic. His son rang me up to do something for the Arsenal magazine and I was thinking, Ryan Rocastle, how proud his dad would be of him. You lose the good people too early in life and we certainly lost him too early. I remember him as David the great fella really.

MICHAEL THOMAS:
I come from Stockwell. Dave's from Bermondsey. Both true South London boys at this massive club Arsenal. What could be any better? With my daughter, who at that time was a little baby, and David Rocastle's daughter. We were family.

89

KEVIN CAMPBELL:

I get emotional because my day at Anfield started and finished with Rocky. Myself and Dave Rocastle were South London boys. Rocky said, 'I'm going to be at Janet's. I'll pick you up at 5 a.m. at Brixton Town Hall.' This is the Friday morning of that game. So there I am at 4.55 a.m. outside Brixton Town Hall, Rocky picks me up and we get up to Highbury. Rocky and I are doing the skips [containers full of all the kit and the team's equipment] with Tony Donnelly; we are loading up the coach.

Many hours later when we left Winners we got back on the coach to get back to Highbury. It was the driver Frank, Tony Donnelly, Rocky and myself. We were the only ones going to the ground. We park up, we are doing the skips again, bringing all the kit and rubbish into the ground. There's a lad asleep on the stairs and Rocky says, 'Shall we wake him up and see what his night was like?' I said yeah, let's do that! We nudge him and say, 'Are you alright do you want a beer?' And he screams, 'ROCKY! I can't believe it!'

This is why Rocky means so much to people. He took the time to sit down with this guy on the stairs and ask what his night was like. He was in the Arsenal Tavern up to this and that and he hadn't been home yet. He wasn't going home all weekend. We took him into the Marble Halls and had a chat. Then after he left, Rocky and I got a taxi back to Brixton.

That's why Rocky meant so much to the Arsenal fans. He was like the glue. Such a fantastic man.

IAN WRIGHT:

I grew up on the Honor Oak estate with David Rocastle and everyone watched out for him. He was our own. It was amazing. When he was 12 and we were 16 he'd get the ball, zig-zag through the whole team and then jog back. They have the David Rocastle Way there now and I am very proud of that. David was the one who blasted it out and made you realise, yes, you can come from an estate in Brockley and be a world star. From the age of 15 or 16 he was going up on the bus. It didn't happen to people where we came from, people signing for a club like that. The whole estate started to support Arsenal. I was four years older than him and once we both started playing professionally we got very close.

That game in 89 was David's favourite moment. Easily. I remember him talking about how much he loved playing at Anfield. He said it's the best place ever to play football. Even that night the Liverpool fans were so knowledgeable and so appreciative, even applauding the Arsenal players. He mentioned that. It meant a lot to him.

For drama, Agüero's goal when Man City won it late was a fantastic finish. It's what you watch football for, those moments where it all turns around. But there was something about 89. It was nighttime, Arsenal going in thinking they weren't going to win it, all these young players together with my friend being out on the pitch. It's easily the best finish I have ever seen in a football match. Ever.

Mickey finishes it with the most deft, beautiful touch, which for me is one of the most difficult finishes in that situation you could do. If I had time, through on goal, I would have thought how to finish this and I would not have done that, especially after missing the chance that came before. I'd want to make sure. The stars aligned for Arsenal in that game. His instinct took over.

It's a deep feeling how I felt after that goal. After the pandemonium, when the ball went back to the centre circle, I just remember sitting there and thinking, David is going to be a champion. A winner. When the whistle went I burst into tears because I realised, when he used to stop me on the bridge and say, you can achieve anything you want . . . When it comes to David and these kind of moments the enormity of the love we had and the time we shared is so strong. To see him in his moment of triumph after inspiring me to stop smoking weed, to stop messing around, to stop doing stupid things and focus on winning in life, to see him when they blew the whistle, I felt like I had done it. I was at Crystal Palace at the time and he was my friend. Later when I spoke to him he was beside himself. Arsenal had done it. Arsenal had broken the stranglehold that Liverpool had on the league. People talk about statues, there should be a bronze piece with all their faces cast, some recognition for that young team and what George did. For me it is the number one moment in Arsenal history. I don't care what anyone says.

The game gives you hope. What that game said to me is: you can never give up. You can achieve whatever you want.

In memory of the 96, of Rocky, and of my aunt Gill, who set the best example to always dive head first into adventures.

ACKNOWLEDGEMENTS

I have to start by thanking the squad who gave me my favourite sporting moment ever. George Graham initially wasn't sure he wanted to go back over old ground but ended up, at our first meeting over a coffee, demonstrating tactical strategies with pieces of cutlery and condiments, with that unmistakable twinkle in his eye. I hope that the retelling of this story has reminded people of his status in the Arsenal pantheon.

Thanks to all the players for the wonderful part they played then and now, and I am indebted to those who shared such wonderful memories to reignite the spirit of 89 in film and book form – John Lukic, Lee Dixon, Nigel Winterburn, Tony Adams (captain), Steve Bould, David O'Leary, Michael Thomas, Paul Davis, Alan Smith, Paul Merson, Perry Groves, Niall Quinn and Kevin Campbell.

No book is possible without behind-the-scenes advice and backing, and it has been such a pleasure to work again with Ben Brusey and the team at Century, Penguin Random House, whose commitment to this never wavered. David Luxton proved a wise head and calm shoulder to lean on when very much needed.

I have to single out Lee Dixon for going that extra mile. He has been a driving force in all of this ever since he picked up the phone to have a conversation about doing something on his favourite subject. His attitude was full throttle. What can I do to help? How involved can I be? He became the most motivated right-back-cum-executive-producer in the history of football documentaries. Thanks to Lee and the rest of the outstanding *89* crew – Davie Stewart, Paul Albert, Sam Billinge et al – and the team at Universal Pictures for helping to create the film and by extension this book. Thanks also to Adam Valasco for the first piece of the jigsaw.

It was extra special to have the wider support of the Dixons,

Rocastles, Smiths and Thomases, whose wives, parents and children enjoyed being part of this ride and proved again what a family this group was and still is.

The supporting cast was also outstanding. Eternal thanks to Ian Wright, Thierry Henry, Bob Wilson, Pat Rice, Theo Foley, Gary Lewin, Nick Hornby, Alan Davies, Dermot O'Leary, Nick Callow, Darren Epstein, Dave Hutchinson, David Dein, David Miles, Lynne Chaney, Jo Harney, Iain Cook, Paul Johnson, Jim Rosenthal, David Pleat, Jeff Foulser, Stuart Macfarlane, Mark Leech, Andy Cowie and Laura Lawrence.

I am immensely grateful to everybody interviewed – from referees to photographers behind the goal, from staff who have spent their entire working lives at Highbury to ordinary fans – for their time and their treasure trove of memories. A special hand of friendship goes out to the Liverpool supporters who felt able to recall their own feelings from a desperately difficult time.

Finally, a 30-year-old thank you to Matthew, my brother, who covered for me that night to keep the parents off the scent while he stayed at home and I disappeared to Anfield. I will forever remember being greeted by the hug we shared at the bottom of the road at whatever o'clock when I got back.

INDEX